MAULANA AZAD

**By the same author**

*Amritsar: Past and Present*

*Jallianwala Bagh* (tr. Hindi and Punjabi)

*New Light on Punjab Disturbances in 1919*, Vols. I - II

*A Nationalist Muslim and Indian Politics* (co-author)

*Madan Lal Dhingra and the Revolutionary Movement*

*Sources on National Movement*, Vol. I, 1919-1920 (co-author)

*History of Kurukshetra* (co-author)

*Biographical Dictionary of Modern World Peace Leaders (Jawaharlal Nehru)*

*Sati: A Historical, Social and Philosophical Enquiry into the Hindu Rite of Widow Burning*

Azad at the age of sixteen, in 1904

# MAULANA AZAD

V.N. DATTA

MANOHAR
2025

First published 1990
Reprinted 2021, 2023, 2024, 2025



ISBN 978-81-85054-98-8

*Published by*
Ajay Kumar Jain *for*
Manohar Publishers & Distributors
4753/23 Ansari Road, Daryaganj,
New Delhi 110 002

*Printed at*
Replika Press Pvt. Ltd.

*Nor is it always in the most distinguished achievements the men's virtues or vices may be best discerned but very often an action of small note, a short saying or a jest, still distinguish a person of real character more than the greatest sieges of the most important battles.*

Plutarch

*No man makes any certain design of his life and we deliberate of it but by parcels.*

Montaigne

*The veins of my neck are strong enough to bear anything.*

Maulana Azad

*My life has been an open book. I have no desire left with me. A greater part of my life is over and whatever little is left will soon end. What is it that made me consecrate my life to the service of my nation? When a man expels personal interest from his life, he is free and detached. Do you know what it means to be free and detached? You do not know. A free and detached person is one whom not even the sharpest sword can touch because it can pierce his body but not his body and soul . . .*

*Maulana Azad in Lok Sabha*
*in reply to Purshottamdas Tandon*
*who assailed his educational*
*policy on 20 March, 1954*

*IN MEMORY OF MY FATHER*

# CONTENTS

# PREFACE

The year 1989 being Maulana Abul Kalam Azad's centenary year, quite a number of books on his life and letters have appeared on this occasion in India and Pakistan as a mark of tribute to his memory. Some more books will undoubtedly be on show before the centenary year comes to a close. As is usual with centenary publications, the general tone of the works published so far is laudatory.[1] In Pakistan the main focus remains on Azad's religious thought and literary contributions to the utter neglect of his role in politics, while in India the purpose is to project him as a staunch secular-minded nationalist who continuously fought communalism to save the unity of his country. His name is invoked in India to rally and consolidate public opinion against the rising tide of communalism which threatens the unity of the country today.

Azad is represented in Pakistan as a devout Muslim, a distinguished authority on the interpretation of the Quran and an outstanding Urdu writer who was also a great scholar of Persian and Arabic literatures. In India he is portrayed as a symbol of Hindu-Muslim unity and 'composite culture,' a great fighter for the freedom of the country who remained loyal till the end to the Congress and Gandhi. His legacy is projected as a strong weapon to beat the monster of communalism. There is certainly some merit in both these images projected in Pakistan and India but they fall short of the reality that was Azad.

Virginia Woolf once spoke of the "fear which attacks the recorder of centenaries lest he should find himself measuring a diminishing spectre and forced to foretell its approaching dissolution." The centenary celebrations should not become an occasion for an extravagant adulation of Azad, nor should they elicit from us perfunctory compliments to a leader whose established reputation stands in no need of such a ceremonial exercise. And it would be highly unjust to this great personality of the national movement to reduce him simply to a propaganda ploy for the government. Nothing is more subtly dangerous in history than a disposition to withhold criticism. I think we should attempt to re-assess Azad by surrounding him with all that can be gathered by way of historical explanation even if such an exercise may diminish his stature in our mind or upset the conventional view we have taken of him as a scholar, religious thinker and fighter for India's freedom.

In the study of our national movement the role of ideas and their influence on the political developments have not received sufficient attention. Over the last three or four decades there seems to have occurred a disjunction between our pressing concerns and the tradition of Enlightenment which formed a vital part of our national movement and provided the motive force to many social and political developments. This is perhaps one reason why we do not take active interest in our intellectual and cultural heritage. B.G. Tilak, Aurobindo Ghosh, M.N. Roy, Abul Kalam Azad, Jawaharlal Nehru, Jayaprakash Narayan and a host of other political leaders were basically intellectuals. For any adequate study of the national movement it would be necessary to focus attention on the intellectual currents behind the evolution of these national leaders into mature personalities. However, the intellectual history of our national movement is yet to be written. It is in this context that a study of Maulana Azad as a man of ideas deserves serious consideration. It must, however, be emphasised at the outset that the history of ideas and their influence is a tricky discipline since it deals with matters which defy quantitative and statistical measurements. How can we measure beliefs, thoughts, aspirations, feelings, passions and the *Weltanschauung?*

Maulana Azad was a complex personality. Taciturn and reserved, he was a strictly private person who would not easily reveal his thoughts. He was aloof, cold and detached like his arch-rival Mohammad Ali Jinnah. It is only when he allowed himself to make comments on others that we get an opportunity to understand his thinking on social and political matters. He was always unwilling to write about himself. Whenever he did so, it was under strong inducements and pressures from others which due to his courteous nature he could not always resist. In the *Tazkira*, the only autobiography that he wrote rather reluctantly, he said very little about himself and concealed more than he revealed. A man of such reticent temper is not easy to understand and to write about him is a challenging task for any biographer.

Three passions dominated Azad's life: the freedom of India from British rule, the promotion of Hindu-Muslim unity and passion for learning. As an intellectual nothing mattered to him more than the life of the mind which he cultivated unobtrusively like Voltaire's *Candide*.

As for politics, he threw boundless energy and passionate zeal into the cause of India's freedom from British rule but he was pushed into this arena by the sheer pressure of circumstances. Both the intellectual and political spheres of his activity impinged on each other and produced a sharp conflict in his life. He made a desperate effort to reconcile these two diverse trends in his personality. He lamented that the poet Ghalib's constant worry had been to obtain favours for material gains, but his own anguish lay in many unfulfilled dreams and wishes he would perforce have to carry with him to his grave.

The task of Azad's biographer bristles with serious difficulties. Like Lord Wavell, the Viceroy, whom Azad greatly admired, he was rather a 'curious silent bird.' He would dissuade others from writing on him. Ghulam Rasul Mihr, a distinguished writer from Pakistan, who was closely associated with Azad, sought his permission to produce a biography on him. Azad replied, "The right course for this (biography) is to write it after my death. So long as my life is there, it is a hindrance to a writer and my life cannot be written. The appropriate time is when I am gone. Why not wait until then."[2]

To portary his multifaceted personality, Azad's biographers have heavily drawn from *Tazkira*, *Azad ki Kahani Khud Azad ki Zabani* and *India Wins Freedom*, which are regarded in popular mind as Azad's autobiographies.[3] *Tazkira* was published by his friend Fazluddin Ahmad without Azad's approval and contains very little information about Azad. He had no opportunity of seeing its final text and remained unhappy about its production. *Azad ki Kahani Khud Azad ki Zabani* was published by Abdur Razzaq Malihabadi after Azad's death and nobody saw its original manuscript. Today not even his son, Ahmad Sayyid Malihabadi knows anything about it and when asked whether it exists declines to confirm it. *Azad ki Kahani Khud Azad ki Zabani*, a pedestrian patchwork, does not reflect anything of the high degree of literary art of which Azad had given ample evidence even in early twenties. *India Wins Freedom* is not Azad's authentic voice as will be argued later in this work. I have relied in this study only on those portions in these three works which find their corroboration and testimony in other more reliable historical sources and documents.

Quite a number of biographical studies on Azad have appeared in India and Pakistan in Urdu. These works are, however, excessively laudatory and they focus mainly on his role as a man of letters and undervalue, if not totally ignore, the significant part he played in politics. Most of these works are written by literary critics who not being initiated into the methods of scientific investigation, fail to put him in a historical perspective. Very few works have appeared in English so far. Lack of knowledge of Urdu and Persian and Arabic languages has been a major dissuading factor for English-knowing writers in undertaking this venture. On the basis of his conversations with Azad, Mahadev Desai, Gandhi's Secretary produced Azad's biography with a terse foreword by Gandhi.[4] It was published in 1940 when Azad became the President of Indian National Congress. This tendentious and sketchy work is replete with factual inaccuracies. By projecting Azad as a nationalist Muslim leader, Desai had tried to counter the Muslim League's strident propaganda that as a political formation it alone represented the Muslims.

A biography of Azad by Ian Henderson Douglas appeared in 1988.[5] Originally it was his doctoral thesis submitted to Oxford University in 1969. Douglas died in 1971 and had no opportunity of revising it for publication. Gail Minault, the historian of Khilafat movement and Christian W. Troll, an expert on Islamic studies edited this work. The basic thesis of Douglas has been kept intact while new material has been added in the light of recent scholarship. The main focus of this study is on the interpretation of Azad's religious thought from a Christian angle. Azad's literary contributions are not seriously discussed, and his political role is dismissed in a slapdash manner in just 23 pages (pp. 282-305).

The present work is not intended as a comprehensive biography of Azad, which should present a chronicle of all significant events in his life. The primary concern here has been to describe the cultural values which sustained Azad throughout his life and gave him strength to wage the political battles despite heavy odds. A biographer's subject may imperceptibly turn into a romantic or idealized creation far removed from reality. A tendentious bias generally creeps in forcing the biographer to justify his subject even when facts and arguments being marshalled by him are not strong enough for such an apologetic defence. Being conscious of this tendency, this study makes no ambitious claims in favour of the subject or its treatment. Within the limits set by the biographer's conscious and unconscious subjective preferences, this work is a modest attempt to understand Azad and his mind, to explain his personality and his actions in the climate of his time and to reconstruct the values which provided the actual motive force in his life.

In writing this biography I have breathed and lived with Maulana

Azad and tried to understand his bent of mind as it revealed itself at crucial points in his life. What he thought and felt, what he had intended to do, actually did or failed to do, what did he do to himself and the world–these are some of the questions to which I have sought to find answers. The basic question to ask is how he came to be like what he was. To portray the richness of his personality and the vitality of his mind is beyond any biographer's power but to grapple with this challenging task is an attempt worth making.

Kurukshetra University V.N. DATTA

NOTES

1. See for example, Khaliq Anjum, *Maulana Abul Kalam Azad : Shakhsiyat aur Karnamey;* M. Imdad Sabri, *Imam ul-Hind Maulana Azad;* Dr. Malik Zada Manzur, *Abul Kalam Azad; Fiqr-o-Fun, Ajkal, Maulana Azad Number* (December, 1988), Delhi.
2. Ghulam Rasul Mihr, *Naqshi-e-Azad,* p. 162.
3. Azad, *Tazkira;* Abdur Razzaq Malihabadi, *Azad ki Kahani Khud Azad ki Zabani,* and Azad, *India Wins Freedom.*
4. Mahadev Desai, *Maulana Abul Kalam Azad.*
5. Ian Henderson Douglas, ed. Gail Minault and Christian W. Troll, *Abul Kalam Azad.*

# ACKNOWLEDGEMENTS

My first debt is to my father to whom this book is dedicated. A great admirer of Azad, he wrote a poem on him in Persian which was widely appreciated.

I should like to express my gratitude to Mr. Malik Ram, an outstanding scholar and an authority on Azad, for his valuable suggestions in the preparation of this work. He generously gave me access to his private collection of manuscripts. He had laid me under great personal obligation by sparing his precious time for my persistent querries. My special thanks are due to Mr. S.M.H. Burney, Maulana Abul Hasan Ali Nadwi, Rector, Nadwat ul-Ulama, Lucknow and Dr. Mohammad Hashim Kidwai for their advice and encouragement and to Mrs. Aruna Asaf Ali, Khwaja Hasan Sani Nizami, Mr. Prem Kirpal and Dr. P.N. Chopra for sharing with me their personal recollections of Maulana Azad. Mr. Gulzar Ahmed Naqvi and Khwaja Munir Ahmad of Azad Bhawan Library enabled me to consult Maulana Azad's correspondence and other material and I am beholden to them.

I would like to thank the following individuals and institutions for their courtesy and assistance: Mr. S.G. Mohiddin, Director, Maulana Azad Memorial Academy, Lucknow. Dr. Syed Saiyidain Hamid, Dr. T.R. Sareen, Mr. K.S. Dalal, Librarian, Kurukshetra University Library, Mr. H.K. Kaul, Librarian, Indian International Centre, New Delhi, Mr. Waris Sarhandi of Kanjrur Dattan in Pakistan, the authorities of National Archives of India and Nehru Memorial Museum and Library, New Delhi.

For about a decade I have had many occasions to interchange ideas with Professor S. Gopal and Professor Bipan Chandra on the problems treated in this book. I have greatly profited from their understanding of India's struggle for freedom. I acknowledge my debt of gratitude to them. I warmly thank Professor Mushirul Hasan for his continuing interest in this work. I must set down my gratitude to my publisher Mr. Ramesh Jain for his help, encouragement and patience in seeing the book through by his painstaking efforts.

At home in Kurukshetra I owe much to my colleagues in the History Department who provided me much incentive for independent research work for which I am grateful.

Professor O.P. Grewal undertook the tedious task of reading through the manuscript and I am deeply obliged to him for his criticisms which were both constructive and helpful. As for my wife's unfailing support and devotion, I can only repeat what Wittgenstein said in a different context "Whereof one cannot speak, thereof one must remain silent."

# ABBREVIATIONS

| | |
|---|---|
| Douglas | Ian Handerson Douglas, *Abul Kalam Azad* |
| GK | Azad, *Ghubar-e-Khatir* |
| Home Political Department | *Home Pol* |
| IWF | *India Wins Freedom* |
| Kahani | Azad, compiled by Abdur Razzaq, Malihabadi, *Azad Ki Kahani Khud Azad Ki Zabani* |
| Tazkira | Azad, produced by Fazluddin Ahmad |
| T.P. | Nicholas Mansergh *et al.*, ed.; *The Transfer of Power*, 1942-47 |
| TQ (ET) | Azad, *Tarjuman al-Quran* (English translation by Syed Ahmad Latif) |
| TQ (SA) | Azad, *Tarjuman-al-Quran* (Sahitya Akademi edition) |
| Zikr | Abdur Razzaq Malihabadi, *Zikr-e-Azad* |

1

# EARLY LIFE

In order to understand the question how Maulana Azad came to adopt the role of a great scholar, a profound religious thinker and an intrepid freedom fighter we have to identify the influences which worked on him in his early life to make him a multi-faceted personality. Had he been asked to tell about the influences he had imbibed, he would most probably have only smiled without giving us any clues in this regard. In an autobiography a writer is likely to dwell at length upon various influences working on him in the formative stage of his growth. That is what Mahatma Gandhi and Jawaharlal Nehru have done in their famous autobiographies. In the absence of such a work in the case of Azad the task of tracing the course of these influences is rather difficult.

Azad does not say anything about his social and intellectual development, and far less about the early stages of his growth. The only option left for his biographer is to trace from his writings and public actions various influences which left their mark on his life. Such an exercise involves some risk as the biographer would be inclined to see more than what meets the eye. The process by which a great man's personality is moulded is too complicated to allow simple reading. A man like Azad derives his strength from many sources. At times irrational impulses push men into sublime regions of creative activity and all attempts to uncover hidden springs of actions are only wishful fancies rather than accurate appraisal. In Azad's case it is his literary and religious works which provide us the most authentic source for understanding his ideas, feelings, inclinations, choices and manners.

H.A. Taine (1828-93), a French historian, philosopher and critic, in his famous *History of English Literature* suggests that any literary work, under critical scrutiny, would reveal the writer's mode of thinking and experience of life but also his inherited beliefs and ways of life, the temper of his time and the general social and intellectual state of his people and country. According to him, diction and style, choice of metaphors, similies and turns of phrases, and the logical order of reasoning adopted by the writer are all outward manifestations of his impressions and the impact of environment on his mind and sensibility. On the model indicated by Taine, one can use the analysis of literature to understand the psychology, thinking, beliefs and sentiments of the man, the period to which he belongs and also the heritage from the past to which he is heir and in this way lay bare the motivations and springs of his actions. To use F.W. Maitland's words relating to Leslie Stephen's commemorative biography, we can illustrate Azad's life by 'his books and his books by his life and both by their environment.'

To understand the various influences of Azad's personality let us first of all look at the influences that led to the formation of his intellectual and emotional identity in his early childhood. It is in childhood that the foundations of a man's entire life are laid and the basic character of his inclinations and perceptions is determined. John Milton wrote:

> The childhood shows the man
> As morning shows the day.

Azad had a rather extraordinary family background. He had roots in Mughal India. His forefathers had migrated to India from Herat in Babur's time, and settled first in Agra and moved later to Delhi.[1] He traces in *Tazkira* the origins of some of the leading families of India and Arabia. He narrates the religious and literary accomplishment of three branches of his family that were closely interconnected with each other. In the opening paragraph of *Tazkira* he wrote:

> In my families three families were joined and all three are famous and learned families of India and the Hejaz. Although none of them sought it, the world has always offered them its honour and glory which sometimes they accepted, sometimes they declined.[2]

Azad does extol the achievements of some of his ancestors but he firmly believes that the rich heritage that has descended on him should not fill him with vanity or blind him to his responsibility for shaping his own destiny. He states that eventually man has to build his own future exclusively by his own efforts and not by seeking favours from others. He hopes that by drawing inspiration from the examples set by his ancestors who combined in them the excellence of erudition and virtues of piety, he would try to prove himself worthy of the name given to him as their descendent.[3]

Azad conjures up the image of his profoundly religious, learned and high-minded ancestors who boldly stood up to fight against injustice in order to draw inspiration from their examples. They were respected for the simplicity of their character and piety. These men had a fearless spirit and would not give in even when placed in most trying situations. Some of them came to occupy high civil positions. The most notable among his forefathers was Shaikh Jamaluddin (popularly known as Shaikh Bahlul of Delhi and described in Muslim annals as Rahemtullah) reputed for his erudition and independence of character.[4] Abdul Qadir Badauni in his *Muntakhab-ut-Tawarikh* has paid him an eloquent tribute for his deep religious fervour, wide learning and self-abnegation. According to Badauni, Jamaluddin was a dedicated scholar completely detached from worldly affairs. Khan-i-Azam Mirza Aziz Koka, Akbar's foster-brother, was his disciple.[5] He was acknowledged as unrivalled in the knowledge of *Hadith* (Islamic traditions).[6] The renowned scholar Shah Abdul Haq (1557-1642) in his *Tazkiratul Waslin* recognised his authority on *Hadith* and praised his disinterested pursuit of knowledge.[7] Jamaluddin translated *Sahih Bukhari* up to *Kitab al Nikah* in Persian which became popular in scholarly circles and served as a textbook for courses of studies.[8] He also translated *Asool-i-Baidwi*.[9]

Jamaluddin had the courage to defy even Emperor Akbar by opposing his claim as *Imam* and refused to sign the document which is conveniently called the Infallibility Decree acknowledging the Emperor as the spiritual as well the temporal head of the people.[10] He also disagreed with the Emperor's supporters over the teachings of Sayyid Muhammad Jaunpuri, a self-proclaimed *Mehdi*.[11] Jamaluddin was so disgusted with the royal authorities that he migrated to Mecca and remained there in self-imposed exile for about thirteen years. Shaikh Jamaluddin's son, Shaikh Muhammad refused to prostrate himself (koarnish) before Emperor Jahangir which the Court Statute required him to do. He believed that the kind of obeisance offered was only reserved for God. As the *Khalifa* in Delhi of Shaikh Ahmad Sirhandi (1564-1624), Shaikh Muhammad supported him when the royal court suspected his *bona fide*. For this he earned Jahangir's wrath and was imprisoned in Gwalior fort for about four years. Maulana Sirajuddin (Azad's father's maternal grandfather's father) had accompanied Ahmed Shah Abdali (1747-73) from Herat and was made Chief Qazi and Counsellor to the Governor of Punjab.[12] He died fighting the Sikhs in Punjab.

Manawwaruddin (1787-1861), Azad's father's maternal grandfather was taught under the tutelage of the famed Shah Abdul Aziz and rose to the high Mughal position of *Rukun-u-Madarassin* (equivalent to the Director of Education), an office which was intended to give financial aid to teachers and scholars, to encourage learning and to supervise the state activities concerning education. A great preacher, calligraphist and orator, Munawwaruddin's scholarly works included the one on *Sirat-u-Nabi*.[13] At the suggestion of Shah Abdul Aziz he married off his elder daughter to Muhammad Hadi (Azad's paternal grandfather), the Governor of Agra fort.[14] Muhammad Hadi was the youngest son of Mohammad Ahsan who was related to Shaikh Jamaluddin. Mohammad Hadi was taught by Mufti Sadduruddin. He died at 25 leaving behind a son, a lad of about 3 years, Khairuddin, who was to be Azad's father. With the death of his son-in-law at such a young age the responsibility of bringing up Khairuddin fell on his maternal grandfather Munawwaruddin.

Munawwaruddin had an easy access to the Mughal Court. A simple-hearted man, he shunned ostentation. He had a wide circle of friends and admirers in the country. Shah Abdul Aziz from whom he received his early education took personal interest in his family affairs. An orthodox *sunni* he was widely respected for his learning and integrity of character. He had the courage to criticize the royal practice of private marriage to low-bred Hindu women in King's presence at the risk of offending him.[15] He also condemned in the royal presence the *shia* tract which was spreading unorthodox influence of the Lucknow Court.[16]

Munawwaruddin felt unhappy over the deteriorating political situation in India and sometime towards the end of 1855 decided to migrate to Mecca where he thought he would pass the rest of his life in the contemplation of religious ideas he had cherished. To set sail to Mecca from Bombay he went first to Bhopal where Nawab Sikandra Jehan Begum treated him as his guest and detained him in Bombay for about a year as the revolt of 1857 had engulfed the country. When the political situation improved, Munawwaruddin went to Bombay and then to Mecca probably in early 1858 accompanied by Khairuddin who was then about twenty-five.[17]

Maulana Khairuddin (1831-1908) was a reputed Arabic scholar known throughout the Islamic world, a religious divine and a *sufi* of the Qadriya school. Born in 1831 he received his early education under the tutelage of Mufti Sadruddin, a great authority on the *Hadith.*[18] Along with the Mughal princes he was imparted academic and physical instruction under able instructors.[19] Mufti Sadruddin performed the ceremony of his *Dastar Bandi.*[20] Shah Abdul Gani, another scholar, took him to the (*masnad*) of Jama Masjid, Delhi, where he began to impart instruction to the students. Thus Khairuddin was initiated into taking up his role as a teacher and preacher. Because of Munawwaruddin's influential position and access to the Mughal Court, Khairuddin had the advantage of cultivating the Delhi elite and taking part in literary activities.[21] At the *Diwankhana* of Mufti Sadruddin, Khairuddin used to participate in literary discussions. It is likely that he encountered Sayyid Ahmad Khan there.[22] Both Khairuddin and Sayyid Ahmad Khan later recollected nostalgically these delightful literary assemblies which became things of the past, gone for ever.[23] Ghalib has also lamented over this literary loss in some of his moving verses.

At Mecca Khairuddin was married to Aliya, the niece of Shaikh Mohammad Bin Zaher Watri, the Mufti of Mecca, a renowned scholar whose fame travelled outside Arabia.[24] A strict orthodox Muslim, Khairuddin had a firm grasp of the Quran and Islamic theology. He led a simple and austere life in accordance with the injunctions of Islam. He had mastered several languages including Turkish, Arabic, Persian and Urdu. He had travelled widely in the Middle East countries, including Iraq, Syria and Turkey and established close contacts with the ruling authorities in several countries where he had a large following.

Khairuddin took steps to repair the hitherto neglected Nahr Zubeda built by Zubeda (762-831 c.), queen of the fifth Abbaside Caliph Harun al Rashid (786-809). The lack of maintenance of the canal caused shortage in the supply of water which became acutest at the time of the *Haj* when a large number of pilgrims came to the holy shrine. The pilgrims had to pay a high price even for a glass of water. By his own initiative Khairuddin raised a fund of about twenty lakhs with the help of his disciples from India, Egypt, Syria and Turkey.[25] Sultan Abdul Majid, the Emperor of Turkey, was greatly impressed by Khairuddin's zeal for public causes and he awarded Khairuddin the coveted first class Majidi medal in recognition of his services.[26] Because of his mediation the Sultan of Turkey released the Sharif of Mecca and reinstated him.[27]

Khairuddin wrote several works. He is stated to have produced an Arabic work in ten volumes which were published in Egypt.[28] The name of the publication is not given in *India Wins Freedom*. This work has so far not been traced or identified.[29] According to *Kahani*, this was Khairuddin's biggest work in ten volumes of which only two were published from Mecca.[30] This work was entitled *Najm.-al-rajm al-Shayyatin.*[31] Another scholar has identified it as *Najm-al-Mubin fil Rajm al-Shayatin.*[32] Khairuddin's other works included – (1) a grammar of Turkish language and a dictionary giving the Arabic, Persian and Turkish equivalents up to the letter Qaf; (2) *Khayr-al-Amsar-Madnat-al-Amsar*; (3) *Dur-al-Durur Bahaiyya Fi-Iman-al-Aha-wa-Al-Umahat-al-Mustaawiya*; (4) *Ashab al Surur al-Ashab-al-Khayur*; and (5) *Aquaid-i-Alfiriqain.*[33] Khairuddin never wrote anything discreditable that could be easily dismissed but his writings do not seem to have made any strong impact on Azad's mind. It is interesting to note that Azad never reprinted any of his father's works. Was it not worth doing?

Khairuddin had stayed in Mecca for about thirty years before returning to India. He had built his own house there. He had assimilated in Mecca the essence of the Islamic doctrines and way of life. Nothing mattered to him more than Islam which governed his thinking and habits of life. He turned into an eloquent preacher who brought tears to his audience by the moving quality of his discourses. Being a *Sufi*, he experienced spiritual ecstasy. Living in Mecca for so long and being married to an Arab woman connected with a family with highly scholarly and religious tradition, Khairuddin naturally imbibed the cultural values of Arab heritage. Although he seemed to be more than an Arab in religious and literary outlook, he did not cut himself off from the streams of Indian culture. He came to India thrice during his stay in Mecca.

Khairuddin had no intention of returning to India and wanted to stay on for the rest of his life in Mecca but Nature willed it otherwise. He fell down and broke his shin bone. For treatment he was persuaded by his disciples to go to Calcutta where he reached in 1890 and was prevailed upon to stay there.[34] A year later his family joined him. It is not clear when Khairuddin reached Calcutta and how old Azad was at that time. It was probably around 1895 that Khairuddin arrived in Calcutta. Azad was then about four years old. Khairuddin had three daughters, Zainab, the eldest born in Constantinople had died. Fatima and Hanifa were about four and three years senior to Azad and his elder brother Abu Nasr was older to him by about two years.[35] A year after the family's arrival in Calcutta, Khairuddin's wife died.

There is no certainty about the date of Azad's birth. Humayun

Kabir says that Azad's seventieth birthday fell in November, 1958.[36] The Government of India went a step further and for reasons still unknown fixed 11 November as Azad's birthdate. Azad mentions 1888 as the year of his birth but does not give the precise date.[37] It seems that he did not remember it. According to Ghulam Rasul Mihr, Azad was born on 17 or 18 August, 1888.[38] Malik Ram regards 22 August, 1888 as the date of his birth on Rasul's calculations.[39] On the basis of Azad's own statement in the *Tazkira*, Malik Ram calculates that Azad was born some time between 9 August and 6 September, 1888.[40] Azad was about four years when his mother died. This was the greatest blow that could fall on him. He was the youngest of the family. A mother's death is a great calamity for children who are not mature enough. The death of Azad's mother left a vacuum for him for all time to come. His father was not temperamentally the sort of person who could give him comfort or solace.

When Khairuddin returned to India he was about sixty. He was tall, good-looking, athletic in youth, patriarchal in his old age with his head bent, shoulders slumped and forehead lined with furrows. Due to his injured knee he was a bit lame and walked slowly with the support of a stick. A man of simple habits, he had no conceit about his learning. Islam governed his life and he accepted its moral code without question whenever the situation demanded from him. Always serious and dignified he knew how to render himself agreeable. He claimed that the whole world contained two and a half Muslims, himself, Abdul Qadir Badauni and Ahmad Raza Khan.[41] His status as a *Pir* brought him social position, influence and money.

Not by any means fabulously rich, Khairuddin contrived to keep a comfortable establishment. His house was open to his disciples who flocked to pay obeisance to him. He never sought to move outside his house except on Fridays to address the congregation, or on *Moulid Shareef* (the Prophet's birthday), the *ID* day and other occasions in fulfilment of his religious obligations.[43] But though he visited people rarely he would expect them to call on him.[44] He had no furniture in his chamber but only a mat where people sat reclining on large multicoloured pillows. Proud, free of ambition and envy, Khairuddin was sensitive to criticism. He would not sulk but explode in rage on matters that offended his moral sensibility. He never procrastinated. He answered letters on receiving them and answered even when they did not need any answer. In private life he acted with the greatest virtuosity. He was munificent and generous to the extent his means allowed. He showed no interest in the burning questions of contemporary politics, foreign affairs or economics. His family comprised his social world.

Khairuddin moulded Azad's religious thinking and habits of life. Khairuddin's religious commitments consumed his entire time : *namaz* five times a day, prayers, visitors and large correspondence, and supervision over charitable institutions. He also found time to do some private reading of religious nature and verses for the Friday congregation. He needed preparation for the interpretation of the Quranic text and its communication to his audience. He also prescribed medicines for his needy patients. Thus his daily timetable was tight and he had hardly any time left for relaxation or entertainment. Life was not to be loved or enjoyed but was meant only for duty and labour. That was Khairuddin's life-style. And above all, he took upon himself the responsibility of educating his children under his close supervision. This was to have profound influence on their development.

About one thing Khairuddin was very clear and firm in his mind. He wanted his sons to succeed him as *Pirs*. Learning and devotion to Islam and its propagation had been family's *raison d'etre* for generations. *Piri* and *Muridi* had their own charms which could hardly be compared with material gains. Accordingly Khairuddin planned an elaborate programme for the education of his sons whom he decided to educate at home. He firmly believed that outside influence would corrupt the habits and manners of his children and mislead them. Calcutta had a famous *Madrassa*, a theological centre of higher learning, founded by Warren Hastings in 1781 where instruction was given in Oriental studies, particularly in Arabic and Persian, but this did not induce him to send his sons there. Khairuddin did not think well of the *Madrassa* as an educational institution.[45] The idea of imparting English education to his sons was abhorrent to him. Khairuddin hated things modern. He preferred to live in the medieval world. Hindus had advanced far ahead of Muslims in developing proficiency in English language and acquisition of modern knowledge. Sayyid Ahmad Khan had started his campaign for the diffusion of modern knowledge among his community but this hardly interested Khairuddin. To him only Islam, the Quran, *Hadith* and *Shariah* mattered and he wanted his sons to live in that world.

In Mecca both the sons had finished the Quran and had learned some portions of it by heart. They went to the *haram shrif* for their lessons in *Qurat* from Shaikh Hasan.[46] When the family moved to Calcutta, Khairuddin himself began to teach his children. Though conservative in outlook in the matter of education, he made no distinction between boys and girls.[47] As their mother was an Arab, the boys had started picking up Arabic by instinct. Urdu was treated as mismash not to be taken seriously as a literary language. They began to be taught Persian and Arabic languages but the main focus of their study was to master the Quran, *Hadith* and other Islamic religious literature. Due to heavy pressure of work and his failing health however, Khairuddin could not teach the entire course of studies to his sons. So he had to engage some eminent teachers to share his load of work.

Under the guidance of Maulvi Yakub Khan and Maulvi Nazir-ul-Hasan the children studied Persian and Arabic languages. Saadat Hasan, who was awarded the title of *Shams-ul-Ulema* later and was the second master in Calcutta Madrassa taught the fundamentals of *Hadith* to Azad.[48] Azad's association with Mirza Mohammad Husain ( a profound Persian and Arabic scholar), who had come to Calcutta from Iran, brought him in close touch with classical Persian literature.[49] Azad started preparing a Persian Dictionary before he was ten.[50] This amazing feat is similar to that of young Thomas Babington Macaulay who had begun to write compendium of universal history at the age of eight.[51] Azad wrote later that Hafiz Wali Ullah had taught him Urdu alphabet and that with a little proficiency in Urdu he had started reading *Yadgar-e-Ghalib* and *Qaitay-e-Burhan*.[52]

Intellectually Azad derived great benefit from his year-long association with Shaikh-ul-Rais, an outstanding Arabic and Persian scholar, who guided him in the study of *Sharih Hikmit-i-ul-Ishraq*.[53] He learnt the subtleties and nuances of classical Persian literature from Mirza Shirazi, a Persian scholar who was well-versed in French, German and English literature.[54] He also took lessons in Turkish language from one Tahira Beck but could not make any headway in it.[55] He learnt the English alphabet from Mohammad Yusuf Jafri, chief examiner of the Oriental course of studies, who gave him Pyarechand Sarkar's first book to read. He then took up the Bible in English and compared it with its Urdu and Persian versions.[56] Such a comparative study combined with his reading of English newspapers enabled him to read English books in history and philosophy.[57]

Due to the rigorous teaching imparted to Azad he was able to complete the highly specialized *Dars-e-Nizami* (framed by the great teacher Mullah Nizamuddin and prevalent since the eighteenth century) when he was only fifteen, taking one third of the normal time for completing it.[58] This was indeed a remarkable performance for a young boy at that age. Sir Sayyid Ahmad Khan has given details about the features of the *Dars-i-Nizami* in his *Tahzib Al-Akhlaq*.[59] The course included study of physics, metaphysics, arithmetic, geometry, astronomy, scholastics, Muslim law and its principles, *Hadith* and its principles, lexicography, medicine and *Tafsir*. After completing *Dars-e-Nizami*, as was the custom, Azad was required to teach a batch of students and he taught higher philosophy, mathematics and logic to fifteen students.[60]

About forty years later Azad assailed the *Dars-e-Nizami* as antiquated and worthless because it encouraged memorization of the text without giving any insight or developing the thinking faculty.[61] He also criticized his father's method of teaching which started with the memorization of some text because that was the method of teaching in the family of Shah Waliullah.[62] Khairuddin was not content with *Dars-e-Nizami* for Azad. So he went beyond it and included in his course of study other subjects like medicine, mathematics, astronomy and astrology. He taught the whole of *Baidawi*, some sufi texts of Ibn Arbi and Suhrawardi. He also initiated Azad into the study of the principles of logic. But the main focus throughout remained on the study of Quran, *Hadis*, *Tafsir*, *Fiqa* and Islamic religious literature.[63]

It was indeed a very hard experience to be taught by Khairuddin who would give lessons to his sons thrice a day, in the early morning, afternoon and at night. The children also said their prayers five times a day like devout Muslims. They had to get up first at 4 a.m. for their *namaz*, and this habit of rising early became a permanent feature of Azad's life. In the course of his teaching exercises to his sons, Khairuddin would examine them to see how far they had grasped what had been taught them. In this face to face encounter Azad would prefer to remain silent. When compelled to give an answer he would falter out of nervousness. But the doting father would insist on a straight answer. Failure to give an answer would bring in a sharp rebuke from the father. At such unhappy moments Azad's cheeks turned pale with tears streaming down and hands turning cold. Such gloomy scenes of dejection were not infrequent.

Azad suffered heavily under this sort of domineering parental authority. He had to accept, obey and comply with all that he was asked to do. This kind of oppressive control to which Azad was subjected filled him with anguish. As a father Khairuddin had set his hopes rather too high about the future of his sons and expected them to touch the skies. When Azad's performance in studies did not measure up to his exacting standards he exploded in rage. A parent can seldom be a good teacher for his children. Often it has been seen that the children's natural faculties of creativity have been smothered if not totally extinguished under the dead-weight of parental tutelage.

Khairuddin had lost his father when he was a child but through his dedication to religious work and hard toil he had made a considerable mark in literary and social fields. Both wealth and name came to him in abundance. Self-made men like Khairuddin tend to be rather conservative in outlook, overconfident, inflexible and self-righteous. Khairuddin's wife had died when his sons were growing up and the paternal solicitude of rearing them became almost an obsession with him. The death of a wife and a mother makes a world of difference to the pattern of Indian domestic life. There were no elderly ladies to look after the household; Khairuddin had to do almost everything. With the fanatical devotion of an overzealous father reminiscent of Lord Chesterfield, Khairuddin concentrated his time and energy on the casting of his sons in the image of traditional Muslim religious divines.

Nothing is more striking in Azad's childhood than unremitting study. In his extraordinary precocity he shows a curious parallel to John Stuart Mill who began learning Greek at three and read Herodotus, Xenophon, Lucian and the first eight dialogues of Plato at eight. Azad spent most of his time in the company of his father, his teachers, the visitors who called on his father, and of course, with his sisters and brother. He had no friends or companions of his own age to talk to or play with. Azad wrote, "I never got an opportunity of moving out of my house so far as my education was concerned."[65] He associated with men almost twice his age. Later he recalled his friendship with Shibli Numani who was thirty-one years senior to him and Maulana Habibur Rahman Khan Sherwani who was his elder by twenty-one years.

Azad never learnt to play or to go to a school. He knew not what entertainment or relaxation were! Cut off from companions of his own age and leading a solitary life buried in books, one wonders how young Azad could hear obscenity or know about the process of reproduction, sexual act or maternity–the mysteries that arouse natural curiosity during one's adolescence. In Azad's house one could seldom hear a guffaw of laughter. He found some satisfaction in idle day-dreaming or in talking to himself in a flamboyant declamation before an imaginary audience. He felt unhappy and utterly lonely. There was no one around to whom he could pour out the pent-up feelings raging like a storm in his heart.

Reading became with Azad almost a passion and he began to devour books. He had the free run of his father's library which had a big collection of books bought largely from Turkey, Egypt, Persia and from Bombay. Like young Macaulay, Azad read voraciously with guidance and also independently with far from complete comprehension of what he read. He mastered the whole of *Fiqa-i-Akbar*, *Tehzib* and *Khulasa-i-Kaidani* when he was only twelve years old, which astounded the scholars and religious divines.[66] His teachers could not keep pace with Azad's progress and had to teach him separately from other students.[67] Later Azad wrote that his teacher who taught him Rational Sciences used to say in light humour while referring to his amazing intellectual power: "This youngster Azad expounds to me the *Sadra* but is under the fond illusion that I was teaching him."[68] In his exposition of the principles of logic and astrology he would leave even well-trained teachers flabbergasted. He read with diligence the works of Imam Ghazali, Imam Razi, Shah Waliullah of Delhi and the Ain-i-Akbari (Akbar's edicts). The Persian poetical works of Rumi, Sadi, Hafiz, Bedil, Khayyam and Ghalib were at his finger tips. His favourites in Urdu were Mir, Ghalib, Sayyid Ahmad Khan, Hali, Shibli, Mohammad Nazir Ahmad and Muhammad Husain Azad.

Azad possessed a phenomenal memory and could assimilate passage after passage and reproduce them effortlessly. He claimed later that whatever he read once sank down and settled in his mind and he could remember much of it. Admiring the prodigious memory of Napoleon Bonaparte who fascinated Azad greatly, he wrote about the working of his mind as follows :

> So I too have made compartments in my brain, hundreds and thousands of compartments. This compartment for law, this for international politics, this for historical knowledge, this for mathematics, this for military science. I accumulate a variety of information in an orderly and systematic fashion like a discriminating and expert store-keeper in separate compartments. I open the appropriate compartment whenever I need it and keep the other compartments closed. Everyone can do so.... My case is not so simple. Napoleon had one compartment. At one and the same time I have to open many compartments.[69]

Azad's curiosity eventually took him outside the sphere of

religious literature much against the wishes of his father. Because of the joylessness at home and the kind of severe teaching administered under the eagle eye of his father which lacked *vividus visanimi* that excites and exalts young men to shine on their own, Azad began to look serious-minded, grave and far too nature for his age. That is why Sarojini Naidu quipped, "Do not talk of Maulana's age. He was fifty the day he was born."[70] Azad's editing of *Lisan al-Sidq* at fifteen shows the high level of scholarship and literary taste he had acquired so early in life.

By the time Azad finished his *Dars-e-Nizami* his phenomenal memory had become a vast storehouse of knowledge, which he had assembled through an assiduous study of the masterpieces of classical Arabic, Persian and Urdu literatures. Because of his extensive reading combined with great memory there grew on him a habit of quoting from books which became an integral part of his diction both in his speech and literary compositions. From reading to writing was just a step and his pen began to flow incessantly with effortless ease.

It would be clear from the foregoing account that Azad went beyond the *Dars-e-Nizami* and extended his range of study through his strenuous efforts. But what kept rankling in his heart was the type of education administered to him under the magisterial parental authority. Azad has given a vivid account of the type of education he received from his father and of the bold resistance he was compelled to offer against the system so ruthlessly imposed on him.[71]

Azad makes it clear that his father and teachers moulded in the medieval cast of mind clung tenaciously to obsolete tradition and were antagonistic to new ideas.[72] Because of the hardening of their arteries and coarsening and thickening of their intellectual fibres, Azad felt that his teachers had lost the elasticity of mind and suffered from intellectual arrogance.[73] To Azad they were like the Medieval Schoolmen in Europe before Francis Bacon, the founder of the inductive sciences appeared on the scene. Azad states that his father would appoint only such teachers for him as would measure up to his exacting standards of scholarship after thorough examination.[74] But Azad regarded his father's standards of judgement as narrow and obsolete.

Knowledge is like water, which however pure, loses its savour and becomes stagnant, unless refreshing water is made to flow into the old channels. In the case of Azad no such body of fresh and stimulating water from tributary streams was brought to enrich the old course. Thus the content of knowledge passed on to him remained stagnant.

Azad wrote:

> The intellectual world in which my family lived was totally irrelevant to the needs of the time. I felt as though I were living in the India of a hundred years past.[75]

Azad's father always assumed that anything new was likely to be nasty. He disapproved of wasting time over the study of nonreligious works. Reading or writing poetry he regarded as fatuous. He had a strong prejudice against English education and the question of imparting it to his son did not arise at all.[76] Azad later assailed the whole spurious mode of instruction imparted to him.[77] Mentioning the various courses of study that he followed he repeats the same verdict: *'nakis'* (worthless).[78] He writes that looked at from every angle, whether it was the selection of books or choice of themes and mode of instruction and discussion, the system of education to which he was subjected was totally fruitless.[79]

Azad's course of studies consisting of old categories *Ulum-e-diniya* (religious sciences) covered revealed sciences, the Quranic *tafsir*, *Hadith*, *fiqh* and *maqulat* (rational sciences) including grammar, logic, philosophy and mathematics.[80] According to Azad, the study of *Ulum-e-diniya* confined as it was to the study of a few texts, gave information on the content and meaning of words and stimulated the art of narrative writing without cultivating the powers of ratiocinative analysis and perception. Thus the learning imparted to students deprived them of gaining any insight into the problems of matter and mind. As to *muqulat* (rational sciences), exclusive of astronomy, they gave some notion of the intellectual trends in the classical ancient philosophy but said little about the recently advanced history of ideas.[81] The kind of mathematics he was taught bore no comparison with modern mathematics.[82] The net impact of the whole course was that matter was sacrificed to style. In fact the teachers minded words, not matter, and set manner over content.

Azad says that his teachers by exercising their ingenuity upon a very limited data spun an endless but worthless web of philosophy and contentious metaphysics dealing with trifles. The Muslim learning depended on *a priori* ideas and comprised endless syllogisms from a few unverified premises and led to the development among the students of a habit to give assent to any proposition sanctified by some authority or the other. Even the authorities in the text prescribed for the students were limited. The object of this Muslim mode of learning was to produce a squadron of well-versed likeminded theologians. Azad felt that Muslim scholasticism diverted men's attention from more useful scholarly pursuits. In short, to Azad the Muslim mode of education was a failure because it had no reference to contemporary experience and because it was faulty in method. Any expansion or growth of knowledge must rest on a wide data and a large and well-considered experience. This was the point which Azad constantly emphasised whenever he talked about improving the quality of education.

Khairuddin continued his tirade against the 'Wahhabis'. He could not even bear their sight. This strong and persistent prejudice he had nursed since his Hejas days. He never missed an opportunity of inveighing against them in the severest terms. The Wahhabis were Muslim sect that followed strictly the doctrine of Abdul Wahhab, an eighteenth century Arab reformer. Being puritanical, they rejected all aberrations and deviations from pure Islam.[83] They desired to save souls from the sin of error. They wanted to revive the true spirit of Islam in its pristine glory and to return to the 'simplicity of faith (society) of the Prophet's Arabia.' They attacked the blind reverence shown to the *Pirs*, tombs and other common rituals practised mechanically. Their avowed object was to establish an independent Muslim state through *Jihad* (holy war) in which true Islam could be preached and followed. The Wahhabis in India organised rebellions against the Sikhs and the British in Bengal, Punjab and in the North.

The Wahhabis were in fact the followers of Shah Waliullah of Delhi because they opposed *taqlid* (to follow authority without reflection) and favoured renewed *ijtihad* but they were branded as 'Wahhabis' by their opponents in the nineteenth century. In fact the use of the term 'Wahhabi' was a misnomer for them.

Azad has given a detailed account of the Wahhabis and the crusade his father launched against them in Mecca. Considerable evidence of their complicity in waging *Jihad* against the British had come to light which convinced the British of their well-planned conspiracy to topple their rule in India. The British Government in India took strong measures against the Wahhabis, arresting a number of them and confiscating their property. Because of the hostility of the Government, the 'Wahhabis' fled the country and sought refuge in Mecca but their hopes to get respite from their suffering were belied. The Wahhabis aroused strong antipathy among the local Indian residents of Mecca. The Egyptian Government too condemned them as violent people always ready to use force on the slightest pretext.[85]

Azad states that it was mainly his father who aroused against the Wahhabis the wrath of the Egyptian Government and the Sultan of Turkey with whom he was on the best of terms.[86] How could his father tolerate the 'Wahhabis' who opposed almost everything that he held dear to his heart? Khairuddin was a *sufi pir* of Qadiri and Naqshabandi order who followed tenaciously the injunctions of *taqlid* and sufi preachers which were the essential element of the life of a *pir*. His father constantly upbraided the Wahhabis saying that these Wahhabis unlike the Jews and Christians deny even their Prophet.[87] At the orders of the Shaikh al-Haram, thirty-three Wahhabis were arrested out of whom thirty were released. Three of them were whipped severely thirty-nine times each.[88] Azad says sarcastically that these three pleaded guilty to the crime of following the Quran and the traditions of the Prophet while others escaped through the practice of *taqiya* (dissimulation or concealment permitted according to Shia doctrine).[89] Due to the British Government's intervention these Wahhabis were sent back to India where too they found it hard to lead a peaceful life because of the hostility of the government.

Khairuddin wrote a work called *Najm-al-Mubin fil Rajm-al-Shyatin* in ten volumes on the Wahhabis to denounce their doctrines. Only two volumes of this work actually appeared.[90] Azad also describes how his father was responsible for the trial of a distinguished *hadith* scholar Syed Nazir Husain for his Wahhabi leanings. He was confined to jail for nine days and ultimately released due to the British mediation.[91] He notes the narrowness of his father's condemnation of Waliullah refusal to follow *taqlid* according to any one juristic scholar but he finds his father inconsistent in encouraging Shaikh Ahmad, who became later *Shaikh-ul-Haram* to change from the Shafi to the Hanifi juristic school.[92] Thus, according to Azad, his father preferred one *taqlid* to another.[93] Khairuddin also produced a journal in defence of his action.[94]

Khairuddin's prejudice against the Wahhabis did not diminish after his return to India. Because of his father's hostility, Azad too built in his mind the image of a 'Wahhabi' as a monster, a *kafir* who repudiated the Prophet, a one-eyed ugly man with a mutilated forehead, who struck terror in him.[95] In Azad's house these Wahhabis were referred to as mosquitoes and mice. Azad narrates how his father treated an elderly bearded man, sitting respectfully in his chamber harshly. Azad asked who the man was.[96] 'The Wahhabi' was his cryptic reply. His father exploded in rage at the sight of this man who exhibited Wahhabi leanings. Azad took up courage and asked his father whether this màn had a black face. His father said emphatically that he had a black heart dotted with so many black and sinful spots.[97] The treatment meted out to the man by his father filled Azad's heart with compassion for him and he saw no justification for his father's treatment of him in such an odious manner. On reading the literature ascribed to the Wahhabis Azad felt that his father's vilification of the Wahhabis was gratuitous, because the Wahhabis did not deny the tenets of Islam and the Prophet. Azad freed himself from this prejudice against the Wahhabis and began to feel sympathetic to their belief and ways of life. He argued with his teachers about the Wahhabis but they too poured scorn on them and failed to satisfy Azad when he tried to defend them. Doubts gradually began to stir within Azad about his father's beliefs, convictions, and outlook. A point eventually came when Azad began to break the traditional chains that bound him.

Azad passed through an emotional and mental crisis at the age of twelve.[98] There was none to share his agony. He felt utterly lonely at heart and did not know where to go for sympathy. Perhaps his mother could have shared his load of sorrow but she was no more. Except for observing strictly the Muslim religious practices and the reading of books mostly of Islamic literature, there was very little in his house for Azad to do. He felt an immeasurable gulf separating him from his father.

Khairuddin believed that the relation of the human mind with the world was only moral and intellectual, not emotional and imaginative. But Azad apprehended more than what religious rituals and the bookish knowledge comprehended. He wanted another kind of existence and therefore there commenced in him a strong reaction against what his father valued and stood for. Azad acknowledged that at this stage he was intoxicated with Sayyid Ahmad Khan's writings which opened a new vista of thought for him.[99] He found Sayyid Ahmad Khan totally opposed to his father's traditional orthodoxy, which gave him satisfaction. Thus Sayyid Ahmad Khan became for him a sheet-anchor, a counterpoise against his father who was so obsequious in observing religious practices that his faith almost verged on fanaticism and superstition. He reacted against the whole religious mode of thinking which his father expounded and preached with zeal.

Azad argued within himself that there were two courses open to him, one to flee from his house for good and lead an independent life, and the other to continue chafing under the restraints imposed by his nagging father who wanted to govern and mould every aspect of his son's life according to his own lights. The life-programme which his father designed for him began to look to Azad odious and vulgar. So he summoned up courage to free himself from the traditional religious orthodoxy. He wanted to escape from a life marked by painful crudities and hopeless dreariness under which he constantly groaned. Such an impulse to take a crucial decision at a critical moment in life could come from sources which are inside ourselves or from some extraordinary push given by the force of circumstances outside. Azad began to think and plan his actions in a new way. With the change in thought came the change in the selection of literature that he began to read. Azad points out that he dared not oppose his father even when his behaviour offended him. In such moments being completely humble, he kept cool and bowed his head in submission like an obedient son.[100] He knew that an expression of even the slightest difference of opinion with his father would throw him into a paroxysm of rage.

Azad gives a moving account of his encounter with his father.[101] One day his father detained him for a while and patting him affectionately on the head said to him, "What is the matter, what ails you? Why are you so sad and mute? Why do you get lost? Why don't you open up?" As was his wont, Azad kept quiet but when his father insisted on a straight answer, tears trickled down his eyes and with a choked voice he mumbled, "I am not on the wrong path. Nor am I a Wahhabi or a Nachari. I am not a rebel against my family as you take me to be. I seek peace from wherever I find it."[102] The father asked him straight, 'Who gives you peace?' "Sayyid Ahmad Khan's works" was Azad's answer. Azad made it clear to his father that he would not like to succeed him as a *pir*; his brother was more suitable for it and he could carry on the family tradition. This rebellion on Azad's part made his father terribly angry.[103] It was a parting of the ways between the father and the son for all times.

To his chagrin Azad saw a large number of people crowding round his father, kissing his hands, feet and head and prostrating themselves before him. To Azad these daily scenes of servile obeisance were obnoxious. As a *Pir zada* (*Pir*'s son) people did not spare even the young Azad.[104] Respectable people would appear before him with folded hands, kiss his feet, hands and sometimes even his shoes, and then sit back quietly on the floor as a mark of deference to him.[105] By nature Azad was not strong enough to stop these garish demonstrations. But he tried to prevent them politely from indulging in this type of behaviour. Azad wrote later: "These disciples regarded me as a *murshid* and wanted me to give a discourse to them but they had no courage to utter a word about it due to my forbidding silence."[106] Azad thought that the whole exercise of *Piri-muridi* was an unsavoury ordeal performed as a ritual which signified nothing.[107] He felt that he was an ordinary man like his father's disciples and had done nothing to deserve the honour they tried to give him. Only because *Piri-muridi* was the *taqlid* of his ancestors, it was followed blindly for some time.

On the first death anniversary of his father quite a number of influential people approached Azad and tried to persuade him to assume the role of a *Pir* like his father but he firmly repudiated the suggestion.[108] In rejecting the life of a *Pir* he broke off from the family tradition. Azad had turned back on his father. We find that Azad, himself being a distinguished scholar, never published any one of his father's manuscripts or reprints of his work. This shows that he did not want to circulate his father's ideas. It would have been indeed a blessing for Azad to be a *Pir*. He had learning, eloquence, firm grasp of the fundamentals of Islam, a pleasant personality and family name. *Piri* would have brought him social status, fame and wealth. But Azad was made of different stuff. He chose a new path, hard and independent. All through his life he attacked the veneration shown to *Pirs*, tombs and other fanatical practices performed in the name of Islam.[109]

Sayyid Ahmad Khan's religious writings brought Azad closer to the true spirit of Islam which had been obscured by the juristic sects and meaningless controversies raised by the contentious *Ulama* in the interpretation of the Quran.[110] Sayyid Ahmad Khan had subjected the Quran to rational criticism and rejected all that was opposed to logic and nature.[111] He was not enslaved to *taqlid* and common law. By analysing his religious thought Azad wanted to write a commentary on Sayyid Ahmad Khan's theology. He also wished to edit the text of his writings. He greatly admired Sayyid Ahmad Khan for his strong defence of Islam on rational grounds against the secular criticism which aimed at undermining the traditional foundations of belief.

Azad used the term of *mujtahid-e-mutlaq* (the absolute interpreter) for Sayyid Ahmad Khan indicating the intellectual debt that he owed to him. He described himself at that stage of his religious development as *mujitahid fil mazhab* (interpreter within a juristic school).[112] He believed that nothing was more inimical to man's moral and spiritual development than to be bound by the chains of *taqlid*.[113] He felt that the notion of religion he had imbibed began to be shaken by the new way opened to him by Sayyid Ahmad Khan in the interpretation of Islam. Azad later wrote that the family tradition and education that had governed his boyhood could not take him in the direction they had intended to.[114] In other words, he could not be bent or moulded to their purpose. The impact of Sayyid Ahmad Khan's writings resulted in the repudiation of his family's traditional orthodoxy and a complete refocusing of his ideas about Islam.[115]

Azad faced the agonizing task of rethinking about his whole religious outlook. Sayyid Ahmad Khan's ideas, it turned out, could not satisfy Azad for long. His mind was further assailed by intellectual doubts and vague forebodings. He began to question the entire basis of religion and its place in life. His restless and insatiable curiosity began to probe deeper into the accepted system of religious beliefs. Azad points out that from the age of fourteen he was torn by religious conflicts for about nine years.[116] He regards this period of nine years as the darkest in his life.[117] About the state of his mental tension, Azad wrote:

> Then began the hangover. I reached the stage which normally occurs: denial of the tenets of the faith. The result of all the involvement in scholastic theology, in criticism of basic dogma and the study of the rival schools of thought all this produced a new restlessness. The intervening peace derived by following Sayyid Ahmad Khan's direction was only delusion of mind. Underneath, I never found peace.[118]

Azad's religious outlook had changed due to Sayyid Ahmad Khan who had shown him that the reality of Islam was different from what his ancestors had believed it to be. This freed Azad from the fetters of his parental religious orthodoxy. But now fresh doubts began to rise in his mind. Being extremely curious and asking perpetually the how and why of things like Ram Mohun Roy, he began to question the validity and justification of conventional and customary religion and would not be content with facile answers.[119] He thought that religion with its elaborate and complex paraphernalia was only a creation of man.[120] These doubts led him to question the existence of God, prophethood, revelation, the immortality of soul, etc. He became a heretic and religion ceased to appeal to him.[121] He was longing to find something new.[122] In his quest for the true nature and essence of reality, he applied the methods of rationality.

Azad read with passionate interest a great deal of religious literature, particularly the works written by Western writers and translated into Arabic and Urdu. This made him familiar with the nature, character and history of different religions. He also became aware of the debate on science and religion in the West which shocked men into realizing that many things in religion were not as they had always seemed and that the world was quite different from what they had been taught to suppose it was. He also held discussions with the followers of different religions, Christians, Jews, Hindus and Parsees to understand their viewpoints. It seems that in his denial of the existence of God, Azad was influenced by the ideas of Western sceptics. The old world view built in his mind lay in ruins.

Under Sayyid Ahmad Khan's influence Azad had repudiated deviations and aberrations from Islam but now he rejected Islam itself. He had come to the realisation that religion itself, although it was supposed to create a spirit of harmony, was the greatest cause of strife in the social history of man. There cannot be either multiplicity or contradiction in truth. Where there is opposition and dispute, there is no truth.[124] Azad differed with Sayyid Ahmad Khan in his ideas of Prophethood which meant to him an extraordinary perception and insight given to discerning men to see things hidden from others. He points out how he passed through a period of mental anguish when he gave up *namaz*.[125] He also abandoned celebrating the *Id*. He could not sleep the whole night and was emotionally disturbed. He never ceased to question and continued his quest for further enquiry into the purpose of human existence. He carried his reflections much further, and surrendered himself to the philosophical questions like, 'What is life and its meaning?', 'the beginning and end of it', 'how to apprehend reality and truth', and 'how do we determine that the method of finding Truth is valid?'[126]

Three basic questions dominated Azad's mind:

(i) Firstly, does God exist, and if so, what is the evidence of his wisdom and power in Creation?
(ii) Secondly, if reality is one, why are there different religions professed in the world by various communities and why are there differences in the world among communities concerning beliefs, traditions, religious practices and laws, etc.? and
(iii) Thirdly, if religions promotes peace and tranquillity, why does

> it lead to religious controversies and sectarian intolerance between Christians and Jews, Muslims and Hindus, and Shias and Sunnis?

Azad is puzzled over the fact that each adherent of religion thinks his own brand to be the best. This made it difficult for him to understand how differences between one religion and the other could be explained. Religion being riddled with inner conflicts, it was hard to decide what one should believe or disbelieve. As a Muslim born in a strictly orthodox family, Azad had to observe certain outward religious forms when his father was alive but inwardly he decried all forms of religion.[127] About this sharp conflict simmering in his mind, he wrote:

> My outward appearance was that of a man who wanted to reconcile religion with reason and intellectual discussion but within I had renounced all beliefs and in practice was a sinner. This was the final stage of my despair.[128]

Azad says that these eight or nine years of his life were a period of great mental tension for him. He sought peace but peace was not to be found. He battled with his own self and indulged in self-introspection to probe deeper into the state of his mind. His experiences in life and reflections on the vast reading of religious literature he had done made him feel that he was merely a puppet, a mere victim of circumstances. But with the passage of time he plunged himself into his literary and journalistic work and this distracted him to a certain extent from the agitations of religious conflicts that had been disturbing him.

Azad put under question all things, even scepticism. However, in his scepticism there was no touch of violence or hatred.[129] Doubts and questions about the existence of God were expressed in *Kahani* and *Zikr* published after Azad's death; while helping Abdur Razzaq Malihabadi to prepare *Kahani*, Azad reconstructed in 1921 the story of the renunciation of his religious faith during 1902-1910. It is unlikely that the questions about God and religion which agitated Azad's mind could have been framed in such a concrete and systematic manner by Azad when he was about 15 or 16 years old. But it is plausible that in general terms these questions had arisen as they are bound to do in curious and inquiring minds. Looking back on the period of his early youth, Azad says that he lost at that point of time everything in life, including his religious faith.[130]

After the death of his elder son Abu Nasr, Khairuddin insisted in Azad that he should succeed him as *Pir*. To build up his image, he sent Azad to various places in the country, Amritsar, Lahore, Lucknow, Bombay and Poona. If Khairuddin had lived for a few years more, it is likely that he might have succeeded in establishing Azad as *Pir* in his place, but he died in 1908. Sayyid Sulaiman Nadwi wrote that Azad succeeded his father as *Pir*. Assuming that this view is correct, he abandoned this vocation soon after.[131] That left Azad free to choose his course. On the first death anniversary of his father, quite a large number of people including Khairuddin's disciples tried to persuade Azad to assume the office of *Pir* but he declined.[132] Though outwardly Azad conformed to the life-style of a devout Muslim, he was inwardly devoid of all religious sentiments. There was a striking dichotomy in those days between his outward and inner life. Azad continued to be a convinced heretic between the age of fourteen and twenty-two (1902-1910).

After his father's death in 1908 Azad visited the West Asian countries and also France. This increased his knowledge of men and he became a man of the world. We get scant information about him in the interlude between the death of his father and his launching of '*al-Hilal*' in 1912. Douglas states that from the time of his father's death until 1910, Azad's time was taken up, as he testifies, in the pursuit of sexual indulgences.[133] The implication in this statement is that Azad had nothing to do except gratification of his enormous sexual appetites in this period of his life. In the formation of this opinion, Douglas seems to have been influenced by Azad's letter to Sayyid Sulaiman Nadwi which is Azad's unequivocal confession of his youthful licentiousness. In this period of his life Azad was actually concerned about the fundamental question regarding the course of action he should adopt. He had turned his back on taking up the role of the *Pir*. His foreign tour had opened a new world to him. Being young he had natural sexual urges which needed an outlet, but to blow this out of proportion, as Douglas has done, is to misunderstand Azad and the changes he was undergoing in personality and outlook.

The basis of Douglas' contention about Azad's habitual sexual indulgences in his youth is Sayyid Sulaiman Nadwi's letter of 21 February, 1914 addressed to Azad which condemned him as a hypocrite, a plagiarist and a reprobate.[134] Nadwi was staying with Azad in Calcutta to assist him in the editing of *Al-Hilal*. He saw Azad from close quarters and found him leading a sinful life contrary to the injunctions of Islam. Nadwi laments that regrettably Azad showed no trace of the influence of his family's religious life on his personality; so his claims of being a true votary of Islam were pretentious.

In his dignified reply which reflected his nobility of mind, Azad confessed with frankness his failings as a human being. To the charge that he was addicted to drinking alcohol, Azad said that drinking was a minor affair as compared to the serious misdeeds to which he had been driven by his youthful indiscretions. Azad wrote:

> I am not an abstemious man of saintly life.... I used to drink. Why single out drinking? I did every kind of hateful deed.[135]

In a private letter to Abdul Majid Daryabadi, dated 26 October 1913, Nadwi likened Azad to flowers that look pretty but lack fragrance.[136] Recalling his period of early youth, Azad stated that whatever he did, he did in extremes; be it virtuous deeds or sinful life, he never held back.[137]

In his letter to Nadwi, Azad stresses that in an imperfect world nothing can be wholly good and being imperfect himself, he faltered at the thought of perfection. Flagellating himself with accusations of unworthiness he tried to arouse pity by projecting himself as a lamentable spectacle, a wrong-doer who was a victim of misfortunes.[138] This frank and forthright letter is a remarkable document which actually reflects his aspiration to be good and to win back what he had lost. He would not like to be downed by his shortcomings. His will and determination were unfaltering. His sincerity in this regard is evident from the following extract.

> I then became involved in various forms of misconduct and there was scarcely any degree of sinfulness which escaped the poor wretch that I was. This was the condition of my behaviour, and as far as belief was concerned, I was a heretic, a virtual heretic. This remained for some time, but at least in this situation there were occasional strong spells of remorse and revulsion, although they did not last.[139]

Douglas has given a psychological explanation about Azad's recovery of his faith. He seizes on a glittering passage in *Tazkira* loaded with surfeit of metaphors and similies in which Azad confesses in allusive fashion his experience of rejected love affair. In *Tazkira*

Azad looks into the mirror of his soul and makes himself the subject of his contemplation. There is no reason to doubt the genuineness of this love-experience. Such experiences happen to many people who receive illumination from women.

It is in the concluding portion of Azad's *Tazkira* that we find oblique references to his rejected love affair disguised in poetic flights and passionate declamation.[140] It was on Abdul Razzaq Malihabadi's insistence that Azad wrote the last part of *Tazkira* in order to give a brief account of his personal life. Malihabadi tells us that Azad wrote an independent piece on his love affair which he withdrew later on the pretext of revising it.[141] As pointed out, Malihabadi produced both *Kahani* and *Zikr* after Azad's death. Malihabadi could have easily reproduced from his memory at least some account of Azad's love affair, but he did not because, as he says, he refused to divulge the secret of Azad's life without obtaining his permission. This argument is unconvincing. In his books Malihabadi has written on some sensitive issues relating to Azad's life.

Malihabadi's knowledge of Azad's involvement was a valuable card up his sleeve which he could have used to his own benefit in his works as well as for others interested in understanding Azad. To know such secrets and then to suppress them particularly about the celebrities is to do grave injustice both to posterity and to history. It is quite possible that Malihabadi knew no details about this love episode for which he made tall claims. So we have to depend on Azad's *Tazkira* for our knowledge of his love affair.

Azad gives no details about his attachment to the woman he loved. He was no Rousseau to lay bare his heart! Nor does he tell us the name of the woman for whom he fell. That should not really matter! It could not have been the famous Attiya Begum who had infatuated Shibli and for whom the poet Iqbal was sighing as a lover.[142] Iqbal wanted to marry her and was willing to divorce his wife. There is no evidence to suggest Azad's association with Attiya Begum. She was also older to him by eleven years which, however, may be taken as immaterial. Love knows no age: Young men are known to develop fascination for older women. But a polished and sophisticated woman like Attiya Begum educated in England, widely travelled in Europe and anxious to imbibe Western influences would shudder to befriend a sombre and unsmiling youth like Azad descended from the family of religious divines with little ability to converse in English.

Azad's love episode took place in Bombay around 1909 when he was already a married man. He had married Zulaikha, the daughter of Aftab Ahmad, his father's disciple in Calcutta when he was about thirteen and his wife seven. They had lived together since 1907, as after her death Azad refers to their thirty-six years of life together.[143]

It is not clear whether Azad's love affair was one-sided or it ruptured at its initial stage. The question is whether Azad would have renounced his wife, contemplated another marriage with a new woman or carried on his intimacy with her clandestinely. Azad points out that it was the physical aspect of love which aroused first the intensity of his passion.[144] He wrote that it is the physical manifestation of love that governs the entire universe.[145] According to Azad nothing matters in love except its object; everything else is irrelevant, and by opening one door, all other doors are closed. Of his passion for physical love, Azad burst into a flame of poetic prose in the following passage:

> When I opened my eyes, adolescence had already dawned, every thorn in the wilderness of my world was gay as a flower with the dews of ambition and desire. When I looked at myself, I saw a heart filled with quicksilver instead of blood. Heedlessness and inebriation chanted their magic spells, passions filled with the cups, the madness of youth caught me by the hands, my heart, loving to surrender itself, accepted as its goal the way shown to it by impulses and desire. In reality there are three stages, desire, love and truth: what I mean by love is love in the narrow, impure physical sense, not the absolute love, which embraces all creation. No doubt the (love of mine) was also a lapse. But what shall we say of lapse that casts on the feet of the beloved. The end of all effort is to reach Him. If lapses and intoxication lead us there, why should not a thousand forms of constancy and sobriety be offered up on their altar.[146]

A lover endowed with fiery imagination and refined sensibility like Azad who knew the experience of violent passion for a woman regarded love as a life-giving inspiration. John Keats had carried this emotion to a higher degree of intensity when he wrote, 'Beauty is truth, truth beauty. ...' Iqbal, the poet-philosopher, too looked for the manifestation of truth in the form of physical beauty. He wrote:

*Kabhi aiy hakikat-e-muntzar nazar a labas-e-majaz main*

*Key hazaron sajdeh tarap rahe ik jabin-e-niaz main.*
O,Truth, that is to be apprehended, manifest thyself in the form of physical beauty
Because hundreds of protestations in my forehead are struggling to fall in stark humility at thy feet.

At this stage of Azad's life two strong passions dominated his life, curiosity and love – curiosity to know, understand and pierce through to the heart of things, and passionate rapture of love itself with extremes of bliss, insatiableness and suffering.

This experience of thwarted love brought him the anguish of despair and he wandered into a blind alley.[147] Azad would often weep over his plight in those days and felt the agony of utter loneliness in the universe. He wrote that for the fulfilment of his dreams he had to 'burn the offices of his hopes and aspirations.'[148] Rejected love tends to stir suicidal tendencies but Azad was not the man to succumb to them. He was made of sterner stuff. The essence of suffering makes for wisdom and illumination. It opens new vistas, and there is a positive side of beatitude in it. 'Where there is suffering there is holy ground,' wrote Oscar Wilde.

It was the insatiate hunger of sensual love which seized Azad. He seems to have set high hopes for the attainment of his object. But these were shattered because the woman he loved spurned him. The torment of failure in love was allayed by his repose in God. Faiz, the Urdu poet, in his poem on 'Raqib' waxes lyrical about the broken loves' gifts to man; humility, compassion for the poor and insight into the meaning of human sorrow.

Azad wrote that 'failure in love opened my eyes.'[149] This awakening of the mind and soul through thwarted love has been the experience of some of the greatest minds in history. It was Beatrice, the fount of Dante's inspiration and his poetry that inspired him to compose *Vita Nuova*. To Leonardo da Vinci, the secret of the universe was the secret of Mona Lisa, the wife of a Florentine banker whose ethereal charm captured him and inspired him to produce his masterpiece, one of the most celebrated portraits of the world, 'Mona Lisa Gioconda'.

When Azad launched *al-Hilal* in 1912 he was already a deeply religious man with his faith firmly established in God and Islam. His rejection of scepticism and embracing of Islam had not been easy. Azad had to battle with himself. Though Nadwi accused him of being a hypocrite in 1914, it is evident from the pages of *al-Hilal* that he was a devout Muslim committed to the propagation of Islam not only in India but also abroad. It was during his confinememt in Ranchi in 1919 that Nadwi was delighted to see Azad in the mould of a firm Muslim adopting the ways of Ibn Taimiya and Ibn Qayyim.[150]

According to Azad, this love episode gave him a new vision of life.[151] He regarded despair in love as necessary for real advancement in life. The woman who rejected him became for Azad a personification of distinct moral and intellectual values. Swayed by the flood of emotions, Azad wrote with pardonable exaggaration that it was this experience which entirely shaped his personality to the exclusion of all other influences including his education and family traditions. He wrote what came to him as pain became for him eventually a medicine and a healing power for his wounds.[152] The following extract from *Tazkira* shows how similar to Wordsworth was his unfaltering faith in mystical pantheism:

> The world, that tavern of oblivion where I had tasted the wine of heedlessness, whose visions tempted my eyes, whose melodies charmed my ears, that same world now so transformed itself that every bit of it was picture of sobriety and wisdom, a lesson for the seeking eye and the knowing mind; every particle was eager for dialogue, every leaf was a document, flowers opened their lips, stones raised themselves and beckoned, the downtrodden dust rose up to come down as a shower of pearls, the heavens descended to answer questions, the earth lifted itself up so that the stars might be plucked from the sky, angels held my arms to prevent me from falling, the lamp of the sun shone to prevent me from stumbling; all veils were thrown off, all curtains riddled with holes, every eyebrow gave a message, every eye had a story to tell.[153]

Again explaining how he entertained doubts which were dispelled about the existence of God, Azad wrote:

> Suddenly the light of hope dawned. Just as I cannot say how I was pushed into darkness, so I cannot say how suddenly I was pulled out into the light. Nevertheless, the fact is that the light shown bright and after nine years of groping in the dark I found that I was seeing light in front of me. All doubts disappeared, all disappointments ended and I found the certainty of faith and peace I had been seeking.[154]

In another poetic image, expressing the state of bliss that he had attained, Azad wrote: "Suddenly the dark curtain was parted. I lifted my eyes and there was the face of lost truth unveiled before me."[155] In his letter to Nadwi, Azad professes his complete allegiance to Islam. He wrote:

> About five years ago when I was in Bombay such tragic events intervened that there was a complete revolution in my condition, and God granted me the grace of repentance. I determined that I would keep myself from anything forbidden and would act upon the injunctions (of the Sharia).[156]

The *Tazkira* and *Ghubar-e-Khatir* show his firm faith in Islam which drew him to contemplate mystical ecstasies the glow of which illuminates his works and the rest of his life. Azad saw no conflicts between religion and rigid rationality. Like John Stuart Mill he thought that most of the highest truths were intuitive and that analytic habits undermine all feelings and passions. He believed that as truth is one so there could not be differences in the eternal values of religion. Islam resolves all conflicts and allows the followers of other religions to practise their own faith freely.[157] For Azad religion answers a permanent need in man. His fate was that of John Bunyan's famous pilgrim who passed through the 'slough of despair', journeyed through the 'caravan of doubt' and ultimately emerged through surrender to the Omnipresent and Omniscient power that governs and guides all creations.

Because of joylessness at home, music alone brought real consolation to Azad and created in him a body of feelings strong enough to resist the disintegrating influences of excessive restrictions imposed on him. To John Stuart Mill too deliverance had come through the reading of Wordsworth's poetry which acted as a medicine for his 'state of mind'.[158] Mill wrote, "They (Wordsworth's poems) seemed to be the very culture of feelings."[159]

Like Martin Luther, Azad gave next to theology the highest place to music and honour. Lord Bacon had music placed next in the room adjoining his study. The account of Azad's early life is incomplete without mentioning his passion for music which persisted throughout his life. During his prison days in Ahmadnagar Azad wrote in 1943 that he could not live without music.[160] Azad had received his instruction in music from Masita Khan, a frequent visitor to his father with the intention of becoming his disciple.[161] Masita Khan had been trained in music in Delhi and Jaunpur. Knowing his father's antipathy to Masita Khan for giving musical lessons to some local prostitutes in Calcutta Azad managed to meet Masita Khan at somebody else's house for about two hours daily.[162]

Azad played on the flute and *sitar*. He practiced on these musical instruments for about four years.[163] Azad recalled that in his childhood the melody of the *muazzin* Shaikh Hasan's voice in *haram sharif* moved him deeply. He tells us in pictorial imagery that he used to go alone with his sitar in hand to the Taj on moonlit nights at Agra and play on it with his face turned towards the silvery waters of the Jamuna. His soul was uplifted in such moments.[164] Mirza Hadi, an expert on music, acquainted Azad with some valuable musical literature during his stay at Lucknow in 1905. During his visit to Egypt, Azad heard some of the famous singers including Tahira in Cairo.[165] He used his Radio set to hear the Persian and Arabic melodies. He would not miss the opportunity of listening to the moving lyrics of Um Kilyam, perhaps the greatest of singers in her time in Egypt. But his chief passion was the haunting melody of Arab music which stirred sad thoughts in him.

It would be seen from our study that in his religious and intellectual development Azad had behind him his father and Sayyid Ahmad Khan but it must be emphaised that his own thinking and work does not correspond point for point with either of them or any one of their compositions. This is because he did his own thinking and this produced vital differences in the pattern of his thought. To him doubt was essential for the progress of intellectual development. He became a questioner of things established.

Azad's father drew him to the Quran and to the whole gamut of Islamic doctrines. He owed his passion for reading also to his father but this was greatly strengthened by the awakening of new interest aroused by Sayyid Ahmad Khan. It is hardly too much to say that Sayyid Ahmad Khan is one of the most important references if we wish to understand Azad's mind in its early stages of development.

After his father's death Azad had decided not to be a *Pir*, but the experience of thwarted love seemed to reinforce his faith in Islam. By the opening of the twentieth century when he was about thirteen years, he had started writing on serious religious and literary themes. His scholarship had begun to be recognised in literary circles. Nothing could be more favourable to his literary and religious bent of mind than journalism to which he came like a duck to water.

## REFERENCES

1. Herat, a city in Afghanistan, Babur, a Central Asian ruler (1483-1530) who founded the Mughal dynasty in India; see Abul Kalam Azad, *India Wins Freedom*, P. I. and *Tazkira*, ed. by Malik Ram, pp. 31-33.
2. *Tazkira*, p. 25. Among his ancestors he selects his mother's uncle Shaikh Muhammad Watri, the Mufti of Medina, his own maternal grandfather, Maulana Munawwaruddin and an ancestor from his father's side, his paternal grandfather, Shaikh Jamaluddin Dehlawi.
3. *Tazkira*, pp.25-30. Azad has been accused of elevating some of his ancestors. Certain discrepancies have been pointed out in the accounts of his ancestors in *Azad Ki Kahani Khud Azad Ki Zubani* ed. by Abdur Razzaq Malihbadi, *Tazkira* and *India Wins Freedom.* To attribute motives to Azad for misleading his readers by exaggerating the achievements of his ancestors would be totally unjust. *Azad Ki Kahani Khud Azad Ki Zubani* was published after Azad's death and Azad did not know about its contents. *Tazkira* appeared without his approval and he had no opportunity to revise it or correct its mistakes. *India Wins Freedom* is a work of doubtful authenticity which we will discuss later. In such a situation when Azad had no control over the texts attributed to him and when books ascribed to him were published without his approval, some confusion with regard to details on his life is bound to occur. Further, in recollecting the past, an exercise in which Azad seems to have indulged, memory is also likely to play its tricks. See Mushirul Haq, *Muslim Politics in Modern India*, 1857-1947, pp. 60-63.
4. Azad is the ninth or tenth in paternal descendant from Jamaluddin.
5. *Tazkira*, p. 37.
6. *Ibid.*
7. *Ibid.*, p. 303.
8. *Ibid.*,.p. 304.
9. *Ibid.*
10. *Ibid.*, pp. 45-52.
11. *Ibid.*
12. *Ibid.*, p. 26.
13. *Kahani*, p. 44.
14. *IWF*, p. 1.
15. *Kahani*, pp. 38-41.
16. *Ibid.*, pp. 41-44.
17. In *India Wins Freedom* it is stated that Munawwaruddin died in Bombay and could not go to Mecca, but according to *Kahani*, he went to Mecca where he died after about four years. It seems unlikely that Khairuddin went alone because he could not have gained influence in Mecca in the initial stage without Munawwaruddin's wide contacts.
18. *Kahani*, p. 54.

19. *Ibid.*, pp. 54-55.
20. *Dastar Bandi*, meaning the ceremony of tying a shash around the turban on an auspicious occasion.
21. *Kahani*, p. 54.
22. Khaliq Ahmed Nizami, 'Maulana Azad Par Sir Sayyid Kay Asrat' in *Ajkal, Maulana Azad Number*, November, 1988, p. 58. *Dewan Khana*, meaning main audience chamber in Muslim household.
23. *Ibid.*
24. *Tazkira*, p. 2. *IWF*, p. 2. There is a discrepancy in both these accounts; In *Tazkira*, Aliya is regarded as Watri's niece but in *IWF* his daughter.
25. *IWF*, p. 2.
26. *Ibid.*
27. *al-Hilal*, 13 July, 1912.
28. *IWF*, p. 2.
29. Mushirul Haq has questioned Khairuddin's authorship of these ten volumes. He has not found any of Khairuddin's works except on the religious life of the forefathers of Prophet Mohammad. See Mushirul Haq, *op. cit.*, p. 63.
30. *Kahani*, p. 77.
31. *Ibid.*
32. Dr. Safia Muzzammil, *Abul Kalam Azad, Islam and Humanity*, p. 5.
33. *Ibid.*, p. 7.
34. *IWF*, p. 2. Douglas thinks it 1898. See Ian Henderson Douglas, *Abul Kalam Azad*, p. 38.
35. *GK*, p. 98.
36. *IWF*, p. VIII.
37. *Tazkira*, p. 310.
38. Ghulam Rasul Mihr to Riaz ur Rahman Sherwani, 29. Jan., 1963 in *Jamia*, Feb., 1988, No. 2, Vol. 85, p. 36.
39. Malik Ram in *Ajkal, Maulana Azad Number*, November, 1988, p. 38.
40. *Ibid.*
41. Abdur Razzaq Malihabadi, *Zikr-e-Azad*, p. 121.
42. Mahadev Desai, *Maulana Abul Kalam Azad*, p. 12.
43. *Kahani*, p. 173.
44. *Ibid.*
45. *GK*, p. 96.
46. *Qurat* is the science of reading and chanting the Quran. See *Kahani*, p. 169.
47. *Kahani*, pp. 59-63, 180
48. *Ibid.*, pp. 170, 180 and 188.
49. *Ibid.*, p. 173.
50. *Ibid.*, pp. 203-04.
51. Sir George Otto Trevelyan, *The Life and Letters of Lord Macaulay*, p. 21.
52. *Naqsh-e-Azad*, ed. by Ghulam Rasul Mihr, p. 330.
53. *Kahani*, p. 205.
54. *Ibid.*, pp. 209-19.
55. *Ibid.*, p. 213.
56. *IWF*, pp. 3-4.
57. *Ibid.*
58. *GK*, p. 99.

59. G.M.D. Sufi, *Al-Minhaj*. Being the Evolution of Curriculum in the Muslim Institutions of India, pp. 120-25.
60. *IWF*, p.3.
61. *GK*, p. 97.
62. *Ibid.*, p. 88.
63. *Kahani*, pp. 177-78, 353-54.
64. *GK*, p. 96.
65. *Ibid.*
66. *Ibid.*, p.98
67. *Ibid.*, p. 99.
68. *Ibid.*, p.98.
69. *Zikr*, pp. 116-18.
70. Humayun Kabir ed., *Maulana Abul Kalam Azad*, p. 69.
71. *GK*, pp. 94-105.
72. *Ibid.*, p. 95
73. *Ibid.*
74. *Ibid.*
75. *Ibid.*
76. *Ibid.*
77. *Ibid.*, p. 97.
78. *Ibid.*
79. *Ibid.*
80. *Ibid.* Douglas has completely misunderstood Azad's account with respect to the study of rational sciences in *Ghubar-e-Khatir*. It is not the memorization of the text that Azad comments on but the limited nature of knowledge promoted and imparted by these sciences. See Douglas, *op. cit.*, p. 40, *GK*, p. 97.
81. *GK*, p. 97.
82. *Ibid.*
83. Wilfred Cantwell Smith, *Modern Islam in India*, p.11.
84. *Kahani*, pp. 71-79.
85. *Ibid.*, p. 72.
86. *Ibid.*, p. 73.
87. *Ibid.*, p. 74.
88. *Ibid.*
89. *Ibid.*
90. *Ibid.*, p. 77. This has been disputed as discussed earlier.
91. *Ibid.*, pp. 88-91.
92. *Ibid.*, pp. 78-79; Douglas is wrong in saying that Shaikh-ul-Haram adopted Hanifi faith. Shaikh Ahmad was not the Shaikh-ul-Haram; see *Douglas*. p. 34.
93. *Kahani*, pp. 78-79.
94. *Ibid.*
95. *Ibid.*, p. 338.
96. *Ibid.*, p. 340.
97. *Ibid.*
98. *Ibid.*, pp. 371-92.
99. *Ibid.*, pp. 361-62.
100. *Ibid.*, p. 373.
101. *Ibid.*

102. *Nechari* is derived from Nechariyat, the worship of nature, an accusation levelled at Sayyid Ahmad Khan's followers by his opponents. Sayyid Ahmad Khan's followers were labelled *necharis* (followers of nature).
103. *Ibid.*, p. 375.
104. *Zikr*, p. 253.
105. *GK*, p. 96.
106. *Ibid.*
107. *Kahani*, p. 332.
108. *Zikr*, p. 424.
109. See Azad's article on '*Fitnae-Qabr*' in *Zikr*, pp. 460-76.
110. *Kahani*, pp. 359-61.
111. Smith, *op. cit.*, p. 20.
112. Douglas, *op. cit.*, pp. 56-57, n. 74.
113. *GK*, p. 100.
114. *Ibid.*
115. *Ibid.*, p. 102.
116. *Zikr*, p. 289.
117. *Kahani*, p. 398.
118. *Ibid.*, p. 382.
119. *Ibid.*, p. 259, *Zikr*, p. 252.
120. *Ibid.*, p. 398.
121. *Ibid.*, pp. 39, 297; *Zikr*, p. 252.
122. *GK*, p. 100.
123. *Kahani*, p. 393.
124. *Ibid.*
125. *Ibid.*
126. *Ibid.*
127. *Ibid.*, pp. 259-60.
128. *Ibid.*
129. *Zikr*, p. 252.
130. *Kahani*, pp. 397-98.
131. Sayyid Sulaiman Nadwi, *Hayat-e-Shibli*, p. 445.
132. *Zikr*, p. 259.
133. Douglas, *op. cit.*, p. 95.
134. For the original letter, Azad to Sulaiman Nadwi, see Abdul Majid Daryabadi, *Maktubat-e-Sulemani*, Vol. I, *op. cit.*, pp. 182-88.
135. Daryabadi, *op. cit.*, pp. 13-15.
136. *Ibid.*
137. *GK*, p. 256.
138. *Zikr*, *op. cit.*, p. 18.
139. *Maktubat-e-Sulemani*, Vol. I, *op. cit.*, p. 27.
140. *Tazkira*, p. 317.
141. *Zikr*, pp. 270-71.
142. Syed Shahabuddin Dasnawi, *Shibli*; see the chapter on Attiya, 'Iqbal and Shibli', pp. 57-62.
143. *GK*, p. 241.
144. *Tazkira*, p. 318.
145. *Ibid.*, pp. 319-20.

146. *Ibid.*, pp. 314-18, cf. Mujeeb, 'The Tadhkirah' in Humayun Kabir, *op. cit.*, pp. 142-45.
147. *Tazkira*, p. 318.
148. *Ibid.*, p. 331.
149. *Tazkira*, p. 324.
150. *Maktubat-e-Sulemani*, *op. cit.*, p. 115.
151. *Tazkira*, p. 330.
152. *Ibid.*
153. *Ibid.*, pp. 321-26, cf. Mujeeb, *op. cit.*, pp. 147-48 in Humayun Kabir, *op. cit.*
154. *Kahani*, p. 400.
155. *Zikr*, p. 252.
156. Abdul Majid Daryabadi, *Maktubat-e-Sulemani*, Vol. I, pp. 20-27.
157. *Zikr*, pp. 261-62.
158. John Stuart Mill, *Autobiography*, p. 125.
159. *Ibid.*
160. *GK*, p. 258.
161. *Ibid.*, p. 255.
162. *Ibid.*, p. 256.
163. *Ibid.*, p. 257.
164. *Ibid.*, p. 258.
165. *Ibid.*, p. 262.

## 2

# AZAD AS A JOURNALIST

By the beginning of the twentieth century Indian journalism had become a strong vehicle of nationalist opinion. Through the instrumentality of journalism, the attention of Indian public was directed to the conduct of the Government. Newspapers like the *Amrit Bazar Patrika*, *Bande Mataram*, *Kesari*, *Mahratta* and the *Tribune* courted displeasure of the Government by their strong criticism of some of its policies. Bal Gangadhar Tilak, Gopala Krishna Gokhale and Aurobindo Ghosh continued to defend the Press against the restrictions imposed by the Government.

After the rebellion of 1857 the number of Urdu journals increased. By the beginning of the twentieth century there were seventy Urdu journals published regularly.[1] Some of the important papers were the *Oudh Akhbar*, *Paisa Akhbar*, *Sulh-e-Kul*, *Zamindar* and *Wakil*. In the growth of Urdu journalism Sayyid Ahmad Khan's *Tahzib al-Akhlaq* (Social Reformer) proved a landmark. Published with the avowed object of ameliorating the social, educational and religious conditions of the Muslim community, it also criticised their social stagnation and religious orthodoxy and greatly influenced their thinking.

Broadly speaking, Azad's journalistic career can be divided into two parts, first from 1900 to the pre-*al-Hilal* period, and second, from his starting of *al-Hilal* in 1912 to its renewal in 1927 when he made his last effort to publish it.

In the pre-*al-Hilal* period we find the striking influence of Sayyid Ahmad Khan, Altaf Husain Hali and Shibli Numani upon the thoughts of Azad or to be more precise, upon his attitude towards Muslim society, religion and literature, a subject still to be explored. Azad learnt of the system of ideas of these three exponents of humanized puritanism though he added by his own lights some extra – or ultra intellectual knowledge to what he had received from them. Sayyid Ahmad Khan was the first critical thinker of the Muslim community in the modern period. Sayyid Ahmad Khan's writings had aroused Azad's interest in social reforms and convinced him that no social and intellectual development of the Muslim community could be possible without acquiring Western learning and knowledge of the science. Sayyid Ahmad Khan firmly believed that if the Muslims did not take to Western learning they would be outdistanced by the Hindus in their race for social and material advancement. Azad also owed to Sayyid Ahmad Khan his quest for modern knowledge as a key for emancipating Muslim society from the fetters of bigotry, superstition and obsolete customs. Sayyid Ahmad Khan's writings may have provoked him to rationalize the Quran and challenge Muslim orthodoxy and dogmatism. In many ways Azad's *Lisan Al-Sidq* carried Sayyid Ahmad Khan's echoes.

Sayyid Ahmad Khan had started the Translation Society at Ghazipur in 1857 with its journal published in 1866 as *Aligarh Institute Gazette*. He launched his weekly *Tahzib-al-Akhlaq* (modelled on the *Tatler* and the *Spectator*) on 24 December, 1870. According to Shibli, the distinguished scholar, Urdu literature was generally influenced by Sayyid Ahmad Khan's 'reformation and reform'.[2] Shibli called Ghalib, the great poet, and Sayyid Ahmad Khan, the *Imam* and *Mujadid* of modern prose writing.[3]

Altaf Husain Hali (1837-1914), a poet, critic and biographer was one of the most resourceful of authors who had captured the imagination of the Muslim community by coaxing and persuading it to reflect on its plight. He constantly took up such themes of social reforms as deeply concerned the welfare of the community. He was not much a mystic and was primarily interested in the advancement of Muslims as a community. He was less traditional and more forward-looking than many other social reformers and thinkers of his time. His *Musaddas* published in June, 1879, a landmark in Urdu literature, took the public by storm. It was in tune with the spirit of *Tahzib al-Akhlaq* and gave a most trenchant expressions to the aims and ideals that should govern the reforms needed for the advancement of Muslim society.[4]

In *Musaddas*, a moving elegy, Hali portrayed in sweet melancholy the decline and fall of Islam in India and depicted the sad plight of his compatriots. The *Musaddas* had a profound impact on the awakening of the Muslim mind. In a flowing verse Hali exhorted the Muslims to give up their ignorance, lethargy and disunity and restore their lost glory.[5] His *Shikwa-e-Hind* (the complaint of India) a tribute to India's past heritage, is an outcry against the humiliations suffered by her in the present circumstances. It is a precursor of Iqbal's famous *Shiqwa*. Hali was the founder of a new mode of literary writing, simple and manly, and free from artificial embellishments. He spoke from the heart. He was a poet with a new message for the Muslims. When Hali sent a copy of *Musaddas* to Sayyid Ahmad Khan, the latter wrote to him:

> Let it be published as widely as possible so that it is read extensively ··· this is what will give me the greatest pleasure. I wish I could convene a great concert in Delhi which should be attended by the elite of the city, after dancing girls should dance in rhythm with the singing of this *Musaddas* (June, 1879).[6]

Azad read a great deal of Hali's works. He considered Hali's *Hayat-e-Sadi* as an outstanding literary work and defended his *Hayat-e-Jawed* against the criticism made of it on literary and religious grounds. In the period of social and intellectual degeneration of Muslim community, Hali gave a new vision. Hali was a poet who thought and felt deeply about his community, and to use T.S. Eliot's expression, wrote his time. On the need for social advancement of Muslims Azad absorbed the elements of Hali's thinking and transformed them. As a result of this influence of Hali, Azad criticised the old notion of lauding literary works and emphasized the need for using modern canons of literary criticism in reviewing books.

There is an interesting account of Azad's first meeting with Hali. By 1904, when he was about sixteen years old, Azad had established his reputation as the editor of *Lisan al-Sidq* widely known for its high literary standard. As a mark of recognition for his contribution to journalism the 'Anjumene-Himayat-e-Islam' Lahore invited him to address the conference at the end of March, 1905. Azad addressed the conference on 1 April, 1905 when his theme was 'Tablig-e-Islam Ka Tariqai-e-Kar'. While introducing him to Hali, Wahid-ud-Din Panipati requested the latter to make a guess about Azad's age. Being reticent by nature and a man of few words, Hali avoided answering this query. But on Wahid-ud-Din's insistence Hali correctly guessed Azad's age which was about seventeen. Hali could scarcely believe that the beardless youth was the editor of a reputed journal like *Lisan al-Sidq*. He was simply astounded to find Azad so young.

Douglas writes that Shibli's influence on Azad's political and religious thinking 'is much less certain'.[7] He thinks that Azad was too independent-minded to be influenced by any individual, and that in no case should Shibli be considered his intellectual guide. The editors of

Douglas' study, Gail Minault and Christian W. Troll, while hinting at Shibli's literary and religious influence on Azad, suggest that the relationship between the two and the possible influence of the older man on the younger deserve further research.[8]

Shibli Numani (1857-1914), an outstanding scholar of Urdu, Persian and Arabic, besides being a poet, historian, biographer, critic and theologian had a profound influence on Azad's intellectual development. Azad met Shibli first in Bombay in 1905, though they had been in correspondence with each other for about five years earlier. Shibli served as Director of Education and Arts from 1901-1905 in Nizam's Government at Hyderabad. Azad was well-acquainted with Shibli's writings. Shibli was about thrice Azad's age. When they met Shibli was greatly impressed by Azad's extraordinary intellect and he said to Azad "Your brain is a wonder of the age and I think that it should be exhibited as a museum piece.' Azad was then about sixteen and Shibli forty-eight. Mrs. Hannah More, a great literary figure and social reformer had also encountered a similar experience in England when she was flabbergasted to see the young Macaulay's precocity. Shibli recognised the genius of this youth before any one else had done. Because of Shibli's recommendation, Azad's *Lisan al-Sidq* became a literary organ of Anjuman-e-Taraqqi-e-Urdu. Azad's association with Shibli ripened into one of the most famous literary friendships.

In a recent study Shibli's attachment to Azad has been explained in terms of the former's narcissistic temper.[9] This study has misrepresented S.M. Ikram and Wahid Qureshi.[10] Narcissism is self-love but some writers in Pakistan have suggested a homosexual relationship between Shibli and Azad. It is not possible to express an opinion on this obscure issue in view of the paucity of contemporary material and information on the subject.

Shibli invited Azad in 1905 to assist him in the editing of *al-Nadwa*, a journal of the Nadwat ul-Ulama, a theological academy in Lucknow. Nadwat ul-Ulama, an association of Ulama was founded in 1893 with the object of bridging the gulf between the old and new ideas. The Nadwa *madrassa* Dar ul-Ulum was established in 1858 to provide instruction in Islamic studies and Western learning (including English and Mathematics) and to create a new type of modernized Ulama who besides Islam and its history, should be acquainted with trends of contemporary thought. Shibli was the moving spirit behind the Nadwa as its Director.

Azad joined the editorial staff of *al-Nadwa* at Lucknow as sub-editor and remained there in that capacity from October 1905 to March 1906. Entrusting Azad with the responsibility of editing a standard journal like *al-Nadwa* at such a young age was Shibli's recognition of his scholarship and literary standing. Later Azad remained constantly in touch with Shibli through correspondence. Despite their difference in age Shibli and Azad had many views in common on fundamental matters. About his close association with Shibli during the period of his stay in Lucknow, Azad wrote :

> I used to be with the Maulana constantly. He was an early riser and I too was like this from childhood. It was the time for tea. We used to discuss various literary subjects. At these times he would recite Persian verses in his chamber in his unique style. Then he would explain these verses. In the evening we would go for a walk in the Qaisar Bagh and some other places and spend the whole time in learned and literary discussions.
>
> In truth I will never be able to forget the delightful moments that I spent in his company. I derived great benefit from that companionship. When the Maulana died, many virtues and lovely things were buried with him, but the greatest was his companionship that I have never experienced anywhere in the world. His passion for knowledge, broad and comprehensive, also disappeared with him.[11]

In a moving letter addressed to his friend Nawab Sadar Yar Jung Maulana Habibur Rahman Khan Sherwani dated 27 October, 1940, Azad recalled with nostalgic feelings his close associations with Shibli.[12] Azad felt at that moment that the horizon instead of stretching out as it did in the earlier days was closing in upon him with advancing age. New acquaintances could not take the place of those close friends who were removed by death or otherwise got separated. To be with Shibli was a literary adventure, a voyage of discovery. Azad's association with Shibli for about six months in Lucknow had acted on him as a great intellectual stimulus and widened his range of interests.[13]

When Rashid Rida, editor of Cairo's periodical *al-Manar*, was to address the assembly of Nadwat ul-Ulama on 16 April, 1912 Shibli called Azad from Calcutta to translate his Arabic speech into Urdu. For this task he had preferred Azad to his own pupil Sulaiman Nadwi, a reputed Arabic scholar. Azad translated Rida's speech. Nadwi records that the magic of Azad's oratory on the occasion cast a spell on the audience.[14] Malihabadi narrates that Azad heard Rida only for a short while and then he went out. He appeared only when the time for translation came. Azad explained to Nadwi with a laugh later that he only needed to hear Rida in the beginning because he could anticipate what was to come.[15] Azad had been reading Rida's works including *al-Manar* for a number of years and understood his viewpoint on social and political problems. That is why he could translate Rida's speech without hearing it in full.

Shibli was engaged in writing the life of the Prophet. A few days before his death he started feeling desperate about completing this work. He sent a telegram to Azad to come and take up this work. When Shibli was involved in a dispute in Nadwa which led to his resignation in July 1913 Azad firmly and consistently defended Shibli in the pages of *al-Hilal* by what Nadwi calls his 'fire-emitting pen."[16] In *al-Hilal* Azad published a number of Shibli's articles and poems.[17]

Shibli and Azad held identical views on the reform of the Ulama through the diffusion of new ideas among them and on the use of critical methods in history like Ranke's. Both of them wanted to vindicate and rehabilitate the true spirit of Islam but they firmly believed in reconciling the old with the new. Shibli was anxious to bring out his co-religionists from their narrow shells and adjust them to modern times which also became an article of faith with Azad. Influenced by the *Mutazlites*, Shibli was a rationalist gifted with artistic sensibility and a marvellous power of expression.[18] Azad too set high value on rationality for understanding literature, religion and society. Shibli used Urdu as a vehicle for his scholarly contributions. Azad too followed the same course. Shibli's influence is closely reflected in Azad's animated prose style characterized by high speed and a quick succession of concentrated images.[19]

In politics Shibli was a Pan-Islamist, anti-Muslim League and pro-Congress. Azad too adopted the same attitude. In the pages of *al-Hilal* Azad enthusiastically propagated Pan-Islamism, ridiculed the League and admired the Indian National Congress. Both rejected Sayyid Ahmad Khan's policy of subservience to the British. Besides Shibli, other writers who interested Azad were Muhammed Husain Azad (1835-1914), a well-known biographer and author of *Abe-e-Hayat*, Nazir Ahmad (1831-1912), a novelist and translator of Legal Tradition and Abdul Halim Sharar (1860-1912), a creator of historical fiction and writer of chaste Urdu prose.

Because of his intellectual background, cultivated literary taste and flair for writing, nothing could suit Azad's genius more than journalism. Malihabadi has been given in his book *Zikr* a list of articles written by Azad before he was eighteen.[20] These articles deal with literary, religious, social, legal and scientific themes, but their main focus remains Islam and its history.

From early age Azad appears to have had a longing for poetry. He took to writing poetry at eleven and adopted Azad as his 'takhallas' (a pen-name meaning free and open-minded) which he was to retain throughout his life. Abdul Wahid Sehsrami aroused Azad's interest in poetry. He used to visit his sister Amani Bi, a maid-servant in Azad's household.[21] This brought him close to Azad. Azad's first Urdu poem appeared in *Armaghan-e-Farakh*, an anthology published from Bombay in 1899 by Hakim Farakh, formerly editor of *Azad Panch*.[23] He also launched his first poetical anthology *Narang-e-Alam* with Abdul Wahid's help from Calcutta in 1899. This book is not available.[24] He produced a quatrain on the accession of King Edward VII to English throne. It appears that Azad's total poetical output came to about 320 verses. He sought guidance on his poetic compositions from the renowned poets – Dag, Amir Minai, Maulana Muhammad Zafar and Ahesan Shauk Naimvi. His poems appeared in *Khadang-e-Nazr* of Lucknow in 1897.[25] It cannot be said with certainty whether the poems attributed to Azad were composed entirely by him or were a joint venture produced with the help of his guides. There are instances when even small lads turn into poets. As a child Pope had 'lisped in numbers.'

Recalling his early interest in poetry in his letter to Ghulam Rusul Mihr dated 3 December, 1936, Azad wrote how one day Ghalib's pupil, Nadir Shah Khan Shauq Rampuri in order to test his poetic ability asked him to compose a few verses on the model of *'Yad Na ho shad na ho'* (May not remember, do not be happy).[26] Azad, then a lad of about twelve years, took up the challenge in good humour and produced verses on the spot. Shaukhi was amazed at this performance and said, "The chap looks to be twelve but by God, one can't believe what he has performed."[27]

Azad's oft-quoted verse shows his uncommon promise as a young poet:

*Azad be-khudi ke nasheb-o-faraz dekh*
*puchhi zamin ki to kahi Asman ki*

(Azad, see the rise and fall of self, You asked about the earth, we told you about the sky).

From his poetical composition it appears that Azad wrote them in a conventional form. His diction was pedestrian and themes romantic. Much of it was just sentimental stuff. One could not have expected much by way of poetry-writing from a youth of twelve or thirteen. Azad himself regarded his early poetical exercises as 'entirely childish'. Poetry with him was merely a juvenile pastime, not an occupation of serious thought. That is why his interest in poetry waned but he had felt elated to see his name in print. His brother was a better poet and showed real technical skill in his compositions.

From a very early period Azad took journalism as his vocation in a most serious and solemn spirit. This reflected the natural bent of his mind, drawing sustenance from the deeper layers of his personality. He launched his first literary journal *al-Misbah*, modelled on the Egyptian *Misbah-Al-Sharq*, towards the end of 1901, when he was about 13 years old.[28] The first article published by him was on *Id* festival. A page of this journal was reserved for literary topics. Azad wrote on a variety of subjects, drawing upon his miscellaneous reading. The journal contained pieces on 'Imam-al-Ghazali,' 'Newton and the law of Gravity,' and 'Khakani Sherwani.'[29] The journal lasted three months or so.

After the closure of *al-Misbah* Azad associated himself with *Ahsan-al-Akhbar*, a weekly edited and published probably in 1901 by Maulvi Ahmad Husain of Fatehpuri and Abdul Guffar, a bookseller and owner of a press. Azad produced a provocative article on 'Islam and Muharram' which raised a storm among the local Shias because of the scathing criticism it made of some of the rituals connected with the festival.[30] The Shias were outraged and held out a threat to Azad's life. The journal lasted only two to three months.[31] In exchange for this journal, the office of *Ahsan-al-Akbar* received Egyptian and Arab journals and newspapers including the Cairo periodical, *al-Hilal, al-Maqtataf*, and Rashid Ridas' *al-Manar*. It was then that Azad had the opportunity of reading the famous *al-Hilal* and *al-Minar*. Azad also contributed pieces to *Tufa-e-Ahmadiya* published and edited by Maulvi Ahmad Husain Fatehpuri from Calcutta. Earlier it had appeared as *Tuhfa-e-Muhammadiya* from Kanpur. This journal mostly contained religious articles.

Azad also wrote for *Makhzan*, one of the leading Urdu literary magazines of the day edited by Shaikh Abdul Qadir and published from Lahore.[32] Azad contributed to it in May, 1902 an interesting article on the 'Art of Newspaper Writing' in which he discussed the utility of newspapers as an instrument of moulding public opinion. He showed how the newspapers in Europe and U.S.A. had brought about a change in social thinking. His contributions included a ten-page piece on the life and poetry of Hakim Khakani Sherwani.[33] It appears from this article that his object was to produce an anthology of the lives of some famous Persian poets by discarding old techniques and adopting the autobiographical mode of delineation.

On the accession of King Edward VII to the English throne, Azad wrote a short article in *al-Punch* published on 4 October, 1902 which shows his appreciation for the royalty.[34] Azad had some association with *Edward Gazette* published from Shahjahanpur, which was probably the first paper to be completely edited by him.[35] *Maraqq-e-Alam* was edited by Hakim Muhammad Ali from Hardoi. Azad wrote an article in it on 'Modern Knowledge and Islam' in January 1902. He suggested to the editor the desirability of improving the contents of the articles on scientific themes. Azad worked as editor of the prose section of *Khadang-e-Nazr* which was edited and published by Munshi Naubat Rai Nazr from Lucknow. Some of the leading writers like Iqbal, Abdul Halim Sharar and Munshi Ahmad Ali Kakorwi contributed articles to this journal.[37] Azad wrote an informative piece for it in two instalments on 'Zamanay-e-Qadim main Kabutron-ki-dak' (Postal service through pigeons in Ancient times). His other contributions included 'Punctuation' (October, 1903), 'Rulers of the Past' (February, 1903) and 'X-Ray' in two instalments (April-May, 1903).

Azad launched his journal *Lisan al-Sidq* (Voice of Truth) when he was only fifteen. This journal established him as a writer and editor and brought him fame. It seems that Khan Bahadur Muhammad Yusuf Jafri gave him some financial aid to undertake this enterprise.[38] The first issue of the paper appeared on 20 November, 1903 and the last one in April-May, 1905. It was supposed to be a sixteen-page weekly but its pages increased sometimes running to forty-eight and sixty. In all it had thirteen issues. It was first published from Harrison Road, Calcutta and later from Agra and Bombay. It was priced at Rs.1.6. It had in all thirteen issues but the issues relating to June-July, 1904, August-September, 1904 and April-May, 1905 were combined. With Shibli's recommendations, *Lisan al-Sidq* became an organ of the Anjuman-e-Taraqqi-e-Urdu (Society for the Advancement of Urdu) with the result that within three issues it had about 700 paid subscribers. Its contributors included celebrities like Shibli, Maulvi Muhammad Zakaullah (1832-1910), Persian and Arabic scholar and historian, and Abdul Halim Sharar. This journal was published irregularly due to Azad's indifferent health, his disturbing family circumstances and the financial strains that he encountered in its publication. Sometimes two or three issues of the journal appeared jointly which came out after an interval of two or three months.

The *Lisan al-Sidq* was a literary journal with politics left out. It also excluded poetry. In its issue of August-September, 1904 Azad set out clearly the aims of the journal which were to (1) promote social reforms by discarding social abuses; (2) popularise literary criticism through reviews of books for improving the quality of literature; and (3) cultivate taste for literature among the reading public, particularly in Bengal. These were laudable aims intended to arouse social conscience, to refine literary taste and to stimulate thought among the educated classes. Azad's object was not to entertain or delight but to instruct and generate ideas. He also promised to bring out articles on scientific themes. His readers demanded the inclusion of religious themes in the journal but that was not to be as the journal soon ran out of funds.[39]

At this stage of life when Azad was only fifteen the issues of *Lisan al-Sidq* show clearly that he was deeply committed to the cause of reforming Muslim community. He thought that the Muslims were intellectually and socially backward because of their poverty, lack of education and social practices involving wasteful expenditure beyond their means on marriage and religious ceremonies. He stressed in the journal that such wasteful expenditure leads to the ruination of a large number of families.

In *Lisan al-Sidq* Azad pleaded for the promotion of education among Muslims which he regarded as a key to all improvements. According to Azad, education awakened the mind through diffusion of knowledge. Like Bacon he believed that knowledge is power. Books being a storehouse of knowledge, he made a distinction between good and bad books and wanted proper books to be made available to the public. He wanted to promote those books which contained modern knowledge and were free from puerile fables and idle fancies. He protested against the publication by the Anjuman-e-Taraqqi-e-Urdu of books dealing with trite themes. He noted that only one book published out of five hundred by the Anjuman was worth studying while the rest were useless.[40]

Azad deplored that even a standard literary biography like *Hayat-e-Jawed* could not be sold out. This only showed lack of interest for literature among the public. He asserted that Urdu and Turkish literatures stood no comparison in the richness of their content with Arabic literature because the latter had enjoyed for long the advantage of having European works translated into it. Azad felt that Urdu literature was deprived of this advantage.[41] Azad did not regard Urdu as a classical language but its glory, he thought, lay in the poetry of Ghalib and Anis.[42] He believed that Urdu would be the language of the people of India. He pleaded for the absorption into Urdu of English words like 'ticket', 'rail', 'engine.' He was opposed to a sectarian approach in acquisition of knowledge. He wrote, 'I will never say, banish English words from our language.'[43]

It is amazing that the youth who was nourished on religious education under strict parental authority should possess such a fervent passion for modern knowledge. This is the true spirit of Rousseau. Azad wanted the translation of scientific and philosophical works into Urdu so that the reading public could emancipate itself from outmoded thinking and social abuses. He conceived of philosophy as completely unified knowledge and religion as 'unknowable phenomenon.' He recalls how Jamalud Din al-Afghani (1839-97) had aroused in his pupil Muhammed Abduh (1849-1905) love for modern knowledge.

Azad thought that human mind could no longer be satisfied with the sentimental poetry of Shelley and Tennyson but needed for a better comprehension of the world the inductive method of Francis Bacon and scientific laws of Newton and Darwin. In his famous letter in 1823 to Lord Amherst, Governor-General of India, Ram Mohun Roy had also shown admiration for Bacon's rationality. Azad recalls Abduh's meeting with the British philosopher Herbert Spencer (1820-1903) and their discussion of sociological and political questions of the day.

In *Lisan al-Sidq* Azad shows his firm faith in the liberating role of education. He deplores the common tendency of adopting a passive attitude towards the acquisition of knowledge. He represents a true Renaissance spirit by his emphasis on science, modernity and dignity of man. However, although he lauds Bacon and Newton in *Lisan al-Sidq*, there is no clear evidence to show that he had a proper grasp of the experimental method of investigation. In his mode of thinking he was more Socratic than Baconian. He elaborates on the type of themes that his journal should like to deal with : 'what is knowledge, what is science and its range and branches,' 'what is virtue' and 'how to explore the universe.'[44]

Azad realized that for improving the quality and content of knowledge, criticism of books published was absolutely necessary. Criticism, he thought, was not flattery or adulation, but a critical and dispassionate evaluation of books uninfluenced by personal biases. Azad joined issues with Abdul Qadir and Nawab Sadar Yar Jung Ḥabibur Rahman Khan Sherwani on their criticism of Hali's *Hayat-e-Jawed* in *Makhzan* and *Aligarh Institute Gazette*.[45] Azad defended Hali and Sayyid Ahmed Khan.[46] He also cites the example of Ghalib's criticism of Sayyid Ahmad's *Ain-e-Akbari* which had offended the latter. Azad regarded Ghalib's review as a just estimate of Sayyid Ahmad Khan's work.

Azad pays a compliment to Sayyid Ahmad for showing to the Muslims a way to their future, but criticises him for concentrating on Aligarh to the exclusion of Bombay and Gujarat from his sphere of social and educational reforms.[47] To him, Sayyid Ahmed's interpretation of Quran was candid "uninfluenced by any personal bias."[48] He agreed at that point of time with Sayyid Ahmad's contention that the Congress was a Hindu organisation because the majority of the Muslims had kept themselves out of it.[49] Interestingly, he wrote a few months later favourably that the President of Congress session for the year was Ferozeshah Mehta, a Parsi.[50] He disagreed with Sayyid Ahmad on giving an exaggerated importance to English education to the neglect of Oriental studies. According to Azad, it was Shibli who did the greatest service to the cause of Indian education by bringing the content of European knowledge to the Muslim thought through translation of standard European works. He ridicules the Hindus for glorifying their past more than any people in the world.[51]

Azad comes out of his *Lisan al-Sidq* as a forward-looking youth seized with the passion of reforming his countrymen through education which he regarded as a powerful means for the regeneration of Muslim society. He tried to assume the role of a regenerator of his times at a young age. It is true that he did not work out the details of his programme for the uplift of his coreligionists. We expect of youth only a fragmentary view of life but the view of society which Azad projected appealed to large sections of the Muslim community in India. His mind was bubbling with ideas which he shared with his readers. He wanted to refine literature through the use of literary criticism. Above all, he encouraged the cultivation of scientific temper which he thought necessary for the social and educational advancement of Muslim society.

Azad was greatly influenced by Sayyid Ahmad's social, religious and educational ideas, but he was not Sayyid Ahmad's blind follower. Nor was he merely Shibli's echo. In a letter to Professor Al Ahmad Saroor, dated 18 April, 1918, Abdul Majid Daryabadi wrote, 'It is a strange irony that Azad being so near and close to Shibli remained so far from him.'[52] Sayyid Ahmad Khan's prose was pedestrian but *Lisan al-Sidq* is written in a simple, direct and unadorned style closer to Hali. However, on literary and educational themes Shibli set a standard for Azad which he was to develop and extend later by wide reading and firm grasp of human experience. In *Lisan al-Sidq* there is nothing narrow about Azad. He promotes an enlightened social outlook in literature.

After the closure of *Lisan al-Sidq* due to shortage of funds, at the invitation of Shibli, Azad joined *al-Nadwa*, the literary organ of Nadwat ul-Ulama, a paper of Islamic theology. Azad worked for *al-Nadwa* from October, 1905 to March 1906 although he may also have had a hand in some of its earlier issues in 1904.[53] Usually Azad is mentioned as sub-editor of *al-Nadwa* but the fact is that his name did not figure in the editorial board consisting of Shibli and Habibur Rehman Sherwani.

To associate Azad, a youth of about seventeen, with a scholarly journal like the *al-Nadwa* was indeed a notable recognition by Shibli accorded to him as an accomplished writer. During his association with *al-Nadwa*, Azad contributed several articles to it. He wrote an article on 'The Muslims', 'Treasure of Knowledge' and the 'Guardianship of Europe.' The article appeared in two parts. In the first part, Azad showed how the European interest in Arabic language and literature arose and in the second, he provided a list of works dealing with this theme.[54] A regular feature of *al-Nadwa* was 'Scientific News' under which Azad published an article illustrating the efforts made in Europe to evolve a common language known as Esperanto.[55] Under it there were also announcements made of reports on the works of al-Ghazali, Ibn Taimiya and Imam Shafi.

Azad produced the entire issue of *al-Nadwa* including the material on 'The Judiciary in Islam' which dealt with the administration of justice in Islamic history.[56] The article is divided in three parts dealing with the (1) duties of the plaintiff and defendant in the court of law; (2) method of prosecution; and (3) the principles of evidence. In this elaborate article Azad emphasised the need for the maintenance of

لا تهنوا ولا تحزنوا وانتم الاعلون ان كنتم مؤمنين — القرآن الحکیم

# الھلال

قیمت سالانہ ـ ۸ روپیہ — ایک ہفتہ وار مصور رسالہ — ششماہی ـ ٤ ـ ۱۲ آنہ

جلد ۱ — کلکتہ : ۱۳ جولائی ۱۹۱۲ — نمبر ۱

فہرس



قیمت فی ... ـ ۴ آ[illegible]

The front page of *al-Hilal*, 13 July, 1912: Jamaluddin al-Afghani's photograph

# البلاغ

ایک ہفتہ وار مصوّر رسالہ

نمبر - ۱ | کلکتہ : جمعہ - ۴ محرم سنہ ۱۳۳۴ ہجری | جلد ۱

Calcutta : Friday 12 November, 1915.

## نوا را تلخ تر می زن چو ذوق نغمہ کم یابی ! !

محل ایسا کیا تعمیر عرفی کے تخیل نے
تصدق جس پہ حیرت خانۂ سینا و فارابی
فضاء عشق پر تحریر کی اس نے نوا ایسی
میسر جس سے آنکھوں کو ہے ابتک اشک عنابی

* * *

مرے دل نے یہ اکدن اسکی تربت سے شکایت کی
نہیں ہنگامۂ عالم میں اب سامان بیتابی
تغیر آگیا ایسا مزاج اہل عالم میں
کہ رخصت ہوگئی دنیا سے کیفیت وہ سیمابی
فغان نیم شب شاعر کی بار گوش ہوتی ہے
نہ ہو جب چشم محفل آشنائے لطف بے خوابی
کسی کا شعلۂ فریاد ہو ظلمت ربا کیونکر
گراں ہے شب پرستوں پر سحر کی آسمان تابی

* * *

صدا تربت سے آئی : شکوۂ اہل جہاں کم کن
نوا را تلخ تر می زن چو ذوق نغمہ کم یابی
حدی را تیز تر میخواں چو محمل را گراں بینی

[ اقبال ]

( استدراک ) صفحہ ( ۱۱ ) مذاکرۂ علمیہ کے مضمون میں جا بجا
" کرومیٹوفیل " کا لفظ آیا ہے - اسکا انگریزی املاء یہ ہے : Chromatophil

The front page of *al-Balagh*, 12 November, 1915: Iqbal's poem in Persian

# الہلال پریس کے ضمانت کی ضبطی

بنگال گورنمنٹ نے ۱۶ - نومبر سنہ ۱۹۱۴ع کو الہلال پریس کی دو ہزار کی پہلی ضمانت ضبط کرلی ' اور الہلال کے دو نمبر مورخہ ۱۴ و ۲۱ - اکتوبر سنہ ۱۹۱۴ع بھی جو ڈبل نمبر کی صورت میں ایک ساتھہ شائع ہوے تھے ' ضبطی میں آے ' بنگال گورنمنٹ نے جن مضامین کو قابل اعتراض قرار دیا ہے وہ " حدیث الجنود " اور " سقوط انٹورپ " ہیں - ایک بلجیین تصویر بھی قابل اعتراض قرار دی گئی ہے جسکے نیچے قرآن حکیم کی یہ آیت درج ہے:
و ما ظلمہم اللہ و لکن کانوا انفسہم یظلمون

سوء اتفاق سے مولانا اسوقت دورے میں تھے اور اون کی عدم موجودگی میں ضبطی و خانہ تلاشی کا وارنٹ آیا - دفتر کی طرف سے اونکو اس واقعہ کی اطلاع دیگئی تو اونھوں نے بذریعہ تار کے ہدایت فرمائی کہ " جو نمبر چھپ رہا ہے اوسکو فوراً شائع کردو ' اور ایک مختصر نوٹ میں ضبطی کی اطلاع کے ساتھہ یہ اعلان کردو کہ ہم اپنی ذات سے آخر وقت تک " الہلال " کو جاری رکھنا چاہتے ہیں اور انشاء اللہ العزیز رکھینگے - اسلیے ہم حسب ہدایت اس پرچہ کو شائع کردیتے ہیں ' اور " الہلال " کی آیندہ زندگی کی قارئین کرام کو کامل توقع دلاتے ہیں - و من یقنط من رحمۃ ربہ الا الضالون ( ۵۶ : ۱۵ )

[ سب ایڈیٹر ]

Notice in *al-Hilal* of 18 November, 1914 on the Government action of confiscating the double number, 16-17 (14-21 Oct., 1914)

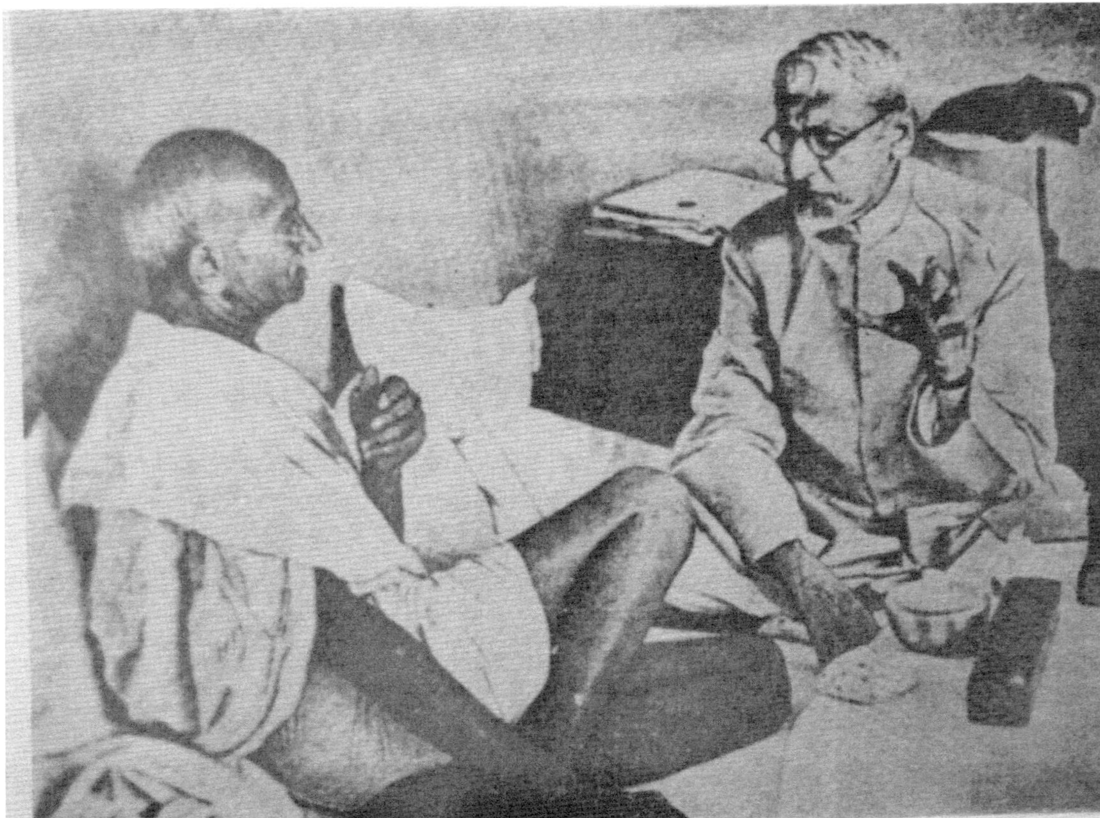

Azad with Gandhi

Azad with Nehru, 16 May, 1949

# انتساب

غالباً دسمبر ۱۹۱۸ء کا واقعہ ہے کہ میں رانچی میں نظر بند تھا۔ عشا کی نماز سے فارغ ہو کر مسجد سے نکلا، تو مجھے محسوس ہوا، کوئی شخص پیچھے آ رہا ہے۔ مڑ کے دیکھا تو ایک شخص کمبل اوڑھے کھڑا تھا:

"آپ مجھ سے کچھ کہنا چاہتے ہیں؟"

"ہاں جناب، میں بہت دور سے آیا ہوں"

"کہاں سے؟"

"سرحد پار سے"

"یہاں کب پہنچے؟"

"آج شام کو پہنچا۔ میں بہت غریب آدمی ہوں۔ قندھار سے پیدل چل کر کوئٹہ پہنچا۔ وہاں چند ہم وطن سوداگر مل گئے تھے۔ انہوں نے نوکر رکھ لیا، اور آگرہ پہنچا دیا۔ آگرہ سے یہاں تک پیدل چل کر آیا ہوں"

"افسوس، تم نے اتنی مصیبت کیوں برداشت کی؟"

"اس لیے کہ آپ سے قرآن مجید کے بعض مقامات سمجھ لوں۔ میں نے الہلال اور البلاغ کا ایک ایک حرف پڑھا ہے"۔

یہ شخص چند دنوں تک ٹھہرا، اور پھر یکایک واپس چلا گیا۔ وہ چلتے وقت اس لیے نہیں ملا کہ اُسے اندیشہ تھا، میں اُسے واپسی کے مصارف کے لیے روپیہ دوں گا، اور وہ نہیں چاہتا تھا کہ اس کا بار مجھ پر ڈالے۔ اُس نے یقیناً واپسی میں بھی مسافت کا بڑا حصہ پیدل طے کیا ہوگا۔

مجھے اُس کا نام یاد نہیں۔ مجھے یہ بھی نہیں معلوم کہ وہ زندہ ہے یا نہیں۔ لیکن اگر میرے حافظہ نے کوتاہی نہ کی ہوتی، تو میں یہ کتاب اُس کے نام سے منسوب کرتا۔

۱۳ ستمبر ۱۹۳۱ء

کلکتہ

ابوالکلام

A page from Azad's manuscript of *Tarjuman al-Quran* in which Azad wrote that he would have dedicated the Tarjuman to his destitute and self-respecting admirer who had come on foot all the way from Qandhar to Ranchi (where Azad was interned ) to seek his help in understanding Quran. This man had stayed with Azad for a few days and left him suddenly fearing that Azad might give him some material help for his return journey which he did not wish to accept. Azad did not remember his name or his whereabouts equality before law, the judge's impartiality and his accessibility to the public and complete ban on corrupt practices. According to Azad, Islam provides sound guidelines for the legislators and judges. He wrote:

> The materialistic law of the universe has no hold on the heart or the conscience of the judge to ensure that he follows its dictation. Religion does with its spiritual and divine power what materialistic law can never do ··· Islam gives to the judge the benefits of rules and with its spiritual premises, tends to sway his heart to do right.[57]

In another article Azad throws light on the advances made in the education of the dumb.[58] He also pleaded in a short note for the establishment of a big library for philosophical and historical books in the Nadwat ul-Ulama.

Azad's association with *al-Nadwa* at seventeen deepened his understanding of Islamic history and theology and widened his interest in European learning and sciences. Shibli was an institution by himself, and Azad's close association with him for about six months was bound to vitalize his thinking. This association was to be of great benefit to Azad for his future work. The *al-Nadwa* was not a journal for the multitude but for the learned elite and Azad's association with it served to build up his image as a sound authority on theological issues.

When Azad was working for *al-Nadwa*, he received a message from Shaikh Ghulam Muhammad, the proprietor of the newspaper *Wakil* to take over the editorship of the paper. Hamid Ali Siddiqi, the former editor of the paper, had left it to rejoin his official assignment.[59] Azad had first met Ghulam Muhammad when he had gone to attend the meeting of the Anjuman-e-Himayat-e-Islam at Lahore in 1904. The proposal that Azad should work for *Wakil* had been mooted at that time too. The editorship of this prestigious paper attracted Azad. The *al-Nadwa* was meant exclusively for the Ulama whereas *Wakil* had a wider coverage and had the largest circulation among Urdu papers except the *Oudh Akhbar*. The *Wakil* dealt with serious matters of national and international importance. Sensitive issues like Aligarh politics, the Turkish-Egyptian problem and Hejaz Railway controversy had figured in the paper. Azad took over the editorship of *Wakil*. He expanded the editorial from two to four columns and increased the number of articles on literary and historical themes. Within a few months the circulation of the paper increased to over one and half times of what it was at the time of his taking over as editor.

At the end of 1906 Azad had to return to Calcutta due to his brother's death. His father pressed him to settle in Calcutta. Azad started the weekly *Dar-al-Sultanat* in the middle of January, 1907. As he did not like the policy of the paper to be determined by the opinions of the proprietor of the paper, he quitted *Dar-al-Saltanat* and rejoined *Wakil*. He made *Wakil* a bi-weekly from a tri-weekly. A point, however, soon came when he could no longer agree with Shaikh Ghulam Muhammad on policy matters due to a radical change in his own political outlook. On this account he left *Wakil* in July, 1908, went first to Bhopal and then to Poona. When he was at Poona he received a telegram about his father's serious illness. He rushed to Calcutta to find his father dead. That was in August, 1908.

In his study of Azad, Dr. Manzur Ahmad regards Azad's essay on 'Sarmad' published on 5 July, 1910 as a sort of prelude to *al-Hilal*.[60] This essay written with stupendous force at the request of Hasan Nizami was a culmination of Azad's earlier efforts to attain excellence in his literary compositions. The martyrdom of Sarmad at the hands of Aurangzeb and his cohorts symbolized for Azad a flagrant abuse of justice which strikes down simple individuals who live and die for the love of God and truth.[61] Azad stressed that without suffering for love attainment of real spiritual strength was not possible. In this composition Azad attains a lucid and liquid melody in his style and mood that also reflects an idealistic romantic fervour. The anguish of Azad's heart over human suffering expresses itself in this moving composition. The same note was to find its echoes later with added grandeur through the fiery pages of *al-Hilal* and *al-Balagh*.

It is now widely recognised that the pages of *al-Hilal* and *al-Balagh* are saturated with the ideas and revolutionary fervour of Shaikh Jamaluddin al-Afghani (1837-97), a revolutionary leader who was determined to free Muslim land from Western domination and of Shaikh Muhammad Abduh (1849-1905), an apostle of Pan-Islamism and a great reformer of Muslim society.

After his father's death in 1908, Azad's journey to Islamic countries including Iraq, Syria, Egypt and Turkey and also to France had a profound influence on his political thinking.[61] He found a new world astir with ideas of liberty, progress and revolutionary Islam. During the tour he met the Iranian revolutionaries fighting against the Qajar autocracy and the followers of Abduh and Saeed Pasha and the supporters of Mustafa Kemal Pasha. He held discussions with the

'Young Turks' and learnt of their revolutionary programme. These Arabic, Turkish, Irani and Afghani revolutionaries had developed a strong anti-Imperialist attitude and they lamented over the indifference towards the freedom of their country which they noticed among the Indian Muslims. This made a great impression on Azad. Sayyid Sulaiman Nadwi has raised some doubts about Azad's visit to the Middle East but his authority is questionable as he nursed bitterness against Azad. There is no reason to doubt the account of this visit given by Humayun Kabir.[62] Azad had earlier read a great deal of Egyptian and Turkish literature including the writings of Abduh and Rashid Rida of *al-Minar*. He held Afghani in great esteem as a writer and thinker.

It would be naive to think that it was the Middle East experience alone that inspired Azad to take a plunge into the journalistic venture of *al-Hilal* and *al-Balagh*. That would be an over-simplification of a complex issue. As noted earlier, the episode relating to his rejected love described in a metaphorical and allusive manner in *Tazkira* had opened to him a new vision of his mission in life – the service of his community. The bitter experience of frustration in love made Azad employ a relatively mature defence mechanism – sublimation. He began to experience henceforth a genuine satisfaction in the cause of his community and his personal ambitions found an appropriate expression through this sublimating channel of social service.

Azad felt chagrined by the piteous spectacle of the Muslim community in India which he thought had 'no religion' and 'no politics.' The Muslim League had been founded in 1906 to represent and safeguard the interests of the Muslims. But he regarded the League as a completely servile creature of the British Government in India. He was disturbed by the revocation of the Partition of Bengal in 1911. He found Muslim politics at a low ebb. The Montagu-Chelmsfort Report noted later that throughout the troubled years, 1907-1910, 'the Muhammadans, with a few unimportant exceptions, held successfully aloof from the revolutionary movement and retained their traditional attitude of sturdy loyalty.'[63] But Azad was greatly impressed by the social and educational advancement of the Hindus. He wanted a similar spirit to be generated among the Muslims. On the international scene Italy had conquered the province of Tripoli in 1911. The Balkan states were determined to dismember Turkey. The background of these happenings on the international plane lent a new urgency to the cry of 'Regeneration of Muslim community.'[64] Even the Muslim League had started voicing this problem. It became a major theme of the Presidential address of Ameer Ali at the Muslim League Conference in 1910.[65] Some of the prominent Muslim leaders were talking about reforms in Muslim society. A solution that could work according to many Muslim thinkers was Pan-Islamism.[66] Azad experienced a similar impulse at this particular juncture of his rich political career. It was the impact of the plight of Muslim countries and the degrading condition of Muslims in India that moved Azad to launch *al-Hilal* and *al-Balagh*.

Jamaluddin al-Afghani had acquired fame in the Muslim world by his propagation of Islam and his staunch opposition to Western Imperialism. The Muslim countries were oppressed by European domination. In 1878 the Ottomon Empire had been humbled by Russia. The Calaphite was shorn of its territory. Egypt was losing its independence. The British Government in India was advancing up to Afghanistan under General Roberts. The British were extending their influence in Iran and the Persian Gulf. This dismal picture of the Muslim world stung Afghani into activity to rally the Muslims to fight European encroachments on the Middle Eastern countries.

As a semi-voluntary exile in Europe Afghani had struggled fiercely to unite the Muslims and inspire them to undertake liberal reforms. He considered unity among Muslims absolutely necessary for their dignified existence. With the assistance of his disciple Abduh he published a journal in Arabic *al-Urwat al-Wuthqa* (The Indissoluble Bond) from Paris to arouse the Muslims to unite themselves for fighting the forces of Western aggression and exploitation.[67] In his *Refutations of the Materialists* (1880) he showed that the modernization of Egyptians is not only compatible with but also contingent upon the retention of the rightly interpreted ancestral faith.[68] He firmly believed that religion was the only foundation on which nations could build the citadels of their happiness.[69] He visited India several times and denounced the British rule in this country. He also assailed Sayyid Ahmad Khan's pro-British leanings and his 'materialist' religious preachings.

Muhammad Abduh whom H.A. Gibbs regards as one of the greatest of reformers of Islam, the chief Mufti in Egypt, was a Pan-Islamist and anti-Imperialist. Like Afghani, he sought the freedom of Muslim lands from European domination. He wanted Islam to be understood in its original simplicity which also became a passion with Azad.

Abduh exercised a great influence on the thinking of some of the leading intellectuals in Egypt on religious and cultural issues. An inveterate foe of blind adherence to tradition, he considered asceticism a grave impediment to cultural progress. Both Afghan and Abduh used Islam as a force to foster nationalism among their coreligionists. Azad too made this his mission in *al-Hilal* and *al-Balagh*. Both Afghani and Abduh considered religion and politics inseparable from each other and Azad too adopted this as his principle. It is from Islam that Afghani and Abduh had derived ideas and inspiration to formulate their line of action for the regeneration of Muslim society which, according to them, was backward because of poverty, ignorance and the moral decay it had suffered over the years. Islam for them was the greatest progressive force in history that could provide the only adequate solution of modern social and political problems. Under the impact of their writings, Muhammad Rashid Rida (1866-1935), started *al-Manar* in 1897. This journal carried the ideas of Afghani and Abduh and influenced a segment of Muslim intelligentsia in India. A comparison of *al-Hilal* and *al-Balagh* with the writings and thoughts of these religious, social and political thinkers would show how great the influence exercised by them on the religious and political thinking of Azad was. There is a close similarity in their ideas on the fundamental issues of religion and politics.

Azad launched *al-Hilal* (the Crescent) on 12 July, 1912 from 13-14 Macleod Road, Calcutta, and from its very inception it took the Muslim community by storm. This paper continued till 18 November, 1914.[70] Azad was then twenty-four. The paper appeared from Calcutta with the editor's name as Ahmad Al Mikni Babi ul Kalam al Dehlwi. Azad's object was not to delight or entertain his readers. It was for him a serious business of preparing his community for waging a battle against injustice and oppression. He was not animated by commercial interests as there were other openings for him to exploit for such mundane purposes. The *al-Hilal* was entirely the product of Azad's own efforts and it bears the stamp of his personality. Azad may have raised some funds for *al-Hilal* with the help of his father's disciples but there is no clear evidence to support this view. He never bothered to obtain donations for the paper as he thought that their acceptance would jeopardize the independent character of the paper which he jealously wished to safeguard. Nor did he seek any advertisements to increase the financial resources of the paper for its security and consolidation.

Azad considered two things absolutely necessary for the Muslim community: first, recovery of the lost faith in the pure spirit of Islam and second, the diffusion of Western learning and sciences among them. Quite a number of newspapers and journals were published in North India but he found them unsatisfactory both in terms of their contents and the quality of their production. Being a regular reader of Egyptian papers he had acquired technical knowledge necessary for production of good journals. The first two issues of his own paper appeared in Turkish type. He had seen Jarji Zaidans' *al-Hilal* published from Cairo. He borrowed this name for his paper but in contents and approach it represented an altogether different viewpoint.

The Egyptian *al-Hilal* reproduced extracts from Western thinkers while Azad's paper included original writings and maintained its independent character. Its approach was national and it covered religion, political and literary themes in a broader perspective. Azad's *al-Hilal* was priced Rs. 8 for six months and Rs. 4.12 *annas* for four months. For the students Azad fixed the annual concessional rate at Rs. 4.12 *annas*. For maintaining a high standard in journalism, he was ably assisted by scholars like Sulaiman Nadwi, Hamid Ali Siddiqui, Abdul Wahid Nadwi, Maulana Abdullah-ul-Amadi, Maulana Hadi, Abdul Salam Nadwi and Ruknuddin Sehsrami. They produced quite a number of features for *al-Hilal* but none of them stuck to him for more than four to five months.[71] On events connected with contemporary European developments Mirza Muhammad Askari rendered a valuable service. By and large, Azad maintained anonymity with regard to the articles published. This caused acrimony among the contributors who wished to see their own names in print. He discouraged publishing signed articles.

For Azad *al-Hilal* was a labour of love. He worked hard for it. He took great pains for publishing it in typescript and not lithograph which he condemned as obsolete. He also reproduced illustrations to make it attractive. He was also its proof reader. The British Government was perturbed over *al-Hilal*'s virulent anti-British propaganda and demanded a security deposit of Rs. 2000 on 18 September 1913 which he paid instantaneously. The British paper *Pioneer* from Allahabad was highly critical of Azad's sensational articles on the European war front which it branded as anti-British and even seditious. The Government forfeited the deposit and demanded a fresh security of Rs. 10,000 on 17 November, 1914. Azad closed the paper. He started another paper *al-Balagh* on 12 November, 1915, which he continued till 13 March 1916. Azad had to stop *al-Balagh* also when the Government externed him from Calcutta. He made another attempt at a later stage to renew the publication of *al-Hilal* and in this second attempt it continued from 10 June, 1927 to 9 December, 1927. But at that stage Azad was so much steeped in the activities of the national movement that his intensive and highly crowded political activities hardly left him any time to indulge in journalistic ventures.

It is important to note that Azad did not publish his weekly from North India – Lucknow, Delhi, Agra or Lahore where Urdu was a popular language but from Calcutta where readership of Urdu papers was somewhat limited. In the guise of teaching the basic tenets of Islam, Azad ingeniously hid the meanings of liberty which he expounded in an oratorical style heavily loaded with Arabic and Persian diction and enriched by glittering similies and metaphors. He thought that the Government would not understand the import of his articles. Through his discussion of the plight of Turkey and the portraits of the prominent Egyptian, Turkish and Afghan personalities, he propagated the revolutionary idea of liberty. What is clear beyond doubt is his scathing criticism of the European powers and their treatment of Muslims who were being subjected to oppressive measures.

Azad was convinced that the only way to regenerate Muslim society, which was socially, economically and politically backward, was through the message of Islam which, according to him, was a panacea for all ills. He believed that it was Islam that would strengthen the moral fibre of Muslim community and rally it for a common mission to fight injustice and shape its future destiny. But how could the message be conveyed? How could the demoralized Muslim community be rejuvenated? How could the Muslims be enthused to take up the challenge of the times and stand on their own feet? These were the questions that agitated Azad's mind. Azad regarded the press as a strong weapon for the diffusion of ideas and he gave the message of Islam through the pages of *al-Hilal* as a means for the regeneration of Muslims. For him Islam was a complete system in itself which governed every aspect of life.

In the launching of *al-Hilal* Azad had in mind a distinct mission, a crusade, a battle for reform and regeneration of Muslim community. It was time for him to do plain speaking and he did it without fear. He wrote that *al-Hilal* was a sort of a 'whip for the dead hearts', to integrate the *millat* through the message of Islam. But Islam meant to him something very different from what it would mean generally to people. It was for him pure and simple Islam as laid down by the Quran originally and not as interpreted by the medieval interpreters.

For building up their self-confidence Azad did not wish to offer

Muslims any new philosophy. He had no magic wand to stir the Muslim community. The foundation, he believed, had already been laid. It was the philosophy of Islam, which his countrymen had unfortunately forgotten and which he thought, could alone bring about their moral and spiritual uplift. Azad looked further than the reforms he had envisaged. Once the Muslim community built up its moral character, he saw no reason why it should suffer any longer from the degrading political servitude. That is why both *al-Hilal* and *al-Balagh* are thick-sown with Quranic verses. In fact Quran provides the substance and structure of these two weeklies.

It is clear from the study of *al-Hilal* and *al-Balagh* that Azad did not wish to cater to the taste of the general reader. The religious and scholastic content of these two weeklies was of a standard that would elude the grasp of the common reader. Being a profound scholar of Islamic history he knew the force and influence of the Ulama in Muslim society. So he thought that it was the educated, the Ulama, that had first to be educated in the real sense so that they could later exercise the right kind of influence on a wide segment of Muslim society through the propagation of their ideas. In other words, through the pages of *al-Hilal* and *al-Balagh*, Azad wanted to build up a strong constituency of a dedicated set of Ulama to carry the message of Islam to the wider public.[72] The conception of *Hizbullah* (Party of God) which fascinated Azad was a projection of a similar idea which he wanted to organise. Azad also had in mind the Western educated Indian Muslims who in their blind adulation of Western civilization were forgetting their cultural roots. He firmly believed that a servile imitation of the West would hamper the moral and spiritual growth of these individuals. He thought that Islam could save them from losing their cultural moorings. His audience, thus, constituted the Ulama and the Western educated Muslims for whom he intended *al-Hilal* and *al-Balagh* to carry a special message.

About these two classes, the Ulama and the Western educated, Azad wrote as follows :

> It drives me mad to see the deplorable sight that today among the Muslims there are only two kinds of leaders, first the traditionalists that are the Ulama and the modernist group, the western-educated intellectuals. Both are ignorant of religion and both are paralysed limbs of the community. They have no idea of their destination ··· the one is unable to set a boat. The other too can't find the shore.

> The first group beset by religious superstitions or prejudices is stagnating while the other is caught up in atheism, imitation of the West and love of power and position.[73]

In the pages of *al-Hilal* and *al-Balagh* Azad tells us repeatedly that his object in these weeklies is to propagate the true message of Islam among his co-religionists because he firmly believes that by imbibing the spirit of Islam they could raise themselves in the scale of human civilization. Azad thinks that the greatest thing for a Muslim was to build up his character and the Islamic framework could be used by him to liberate himself from the present state of degradation.

Islam is thus the guiding star of Azad's thought in *al-Hilal* and *al-Balagh.* There is no issue of these papers papers which does not elaborate on, interpret or highlight the noble sacrifices of the martyrs who had laid down their lives without fear in the cause of Islam. His work in *al-Hilal* was nothing, if not eloquent, and his pages are replete with Quranic citations which he supported with wide-ranging examples from the fields of history and literature. Azad does not move an inch without bringing in Islam in these weeklies. Almost every social and political issue is discussed in them from the Islamic angle. He regards Islam as one of the greatest social and intellectual movements which possessed the power of transforming society. He firmly believes that Islam alone can produce a change in the Muslim mind which is entangled in mundane interests behind a cloak of religious pretensions.[74]

For Azad contact with Islam was contact with Truth. According to Azad, Islam exalts the dignity of the individual and sets high moral and spiritual values for the guidance of its followers.[75] Azad shifted the emphasis in religious thought from the outward observances and rituals to the inner life of faith and to a loving reverence for the person of Muhammad. Islam to him was not a dogma but a living system which brought people closer to the springs of the highest virtues. Using a poetical image Azad describes Islam as a 'caravan of fragrance and a breath of many fresh breezes.'[76]

By citing Quranic verses in *al-Hilal* and *al-Balagh* Azad emphasized that Islam stood upon the moral ground of the dignity of the individual, social action, self-sacrifice, mutual affection and common brotherhood. Through these weeklies he propagated that Islam was the real panacea for the social and moral regeneration of society.[77] But he was convinced that all reform must begin with a return to the oldest and most original truth of Islam intelligible to the laymen.

It is in Quran that the authority of Islam is grounded and for this reason it is Quran which becomes the focus of Azad's attention in *al-Hilal* and *al-Balagh*. It has definitive authority for Muslims and offers a guiding standard for their conduct. That is why he wanted to make the Quran a living code of everyday life among his coreligionists who because of their abysmal ignorance and apathy had discarded this glorious heritage.[78] He warned the Muslims that their real salvation lay in submitting themselves to the commands of Quran. He wrote, 'I need only Islam's book, the Quran.'[79] Azad had great faith in the future of Muslims because he thought that they were meant for *Haq* (truth) but he warned them that their future could be safe only if they were truly religious in spirit and feared God.[80] That is why he repeatedly exhorts them to be 'true Muslims.'[81]

It is not merely the Muslims of his own country that Azad thinks about but Muslims of the entire world. He sheds tears over the sufferings of the Muslims in Egypt, Turkey, South Africa and China. He emerges in *al-Hilal* and *al-Balagh* as a firm and convinced Pan-Islamist who conceives the idea of the brotherhood of Muslims all over the world bound by common faith, beliefs and traditions. He tells us that the loud cry of *Allah o Akbar* would unite Muslims everywhere in the world, as would the image of Cardovo mosque which inspired Iqbal to compose a great poem.

The view of Islam as the source of power and goodness is stamped on the pages of *al-Hilal* and *al-Balagh*, but to characterize these weeklies as strictly religious in the conventional sense would be unjust. To Azad religion and politics were inseparable because Islam governs all aspects of life. He wrote that the 'Mosque is the real place of religion and politics'.[82] For Azad Islam 'opens the key to politics'.[83] Politics, according to him, becomes in its turn chilly and spiritless when stripped of Islam. Politics meant to him wielding power.[84] He thinks that because Muslims forgot the message of Islam and its heritage, they lost their glory in India and elsewhere. Thus in his calculations he reduces political order to Islamic order. For political mobilization of Muslims he regarded Islam as a potential force. He was convinced that nothing could unite the Muslims more effectively than Islam. That is why he exhorted the Muslims not to depend for their future on the Government but on Islam.[85] By citing historical examples he emphasised that Islam rejected all types of slavery and stood for liberty and democracy. He wrote, 'Islam taught us to love freedom and not to accept slavery.'[86]

A correspondent asked Azad about the nature of politics he would recommend for Muslims — whether it should be on the model of the British, i.e., constitutional or liberal, moderate or extremist as manifest during the Swadeshi movement or of the militant nationalists. Azad replied that the Muslims should in no case emulate the Hindus or the British in politics but depend wholly on Islam.[87] He wrote, 'Come to the book (Quran). That is the answer.' Azad wanted his coreligionists to follow the straight path of the Quran which lays down the following basic principles for guidance :

1. The Unity of God.
2. Muslims are the 'blessed' of all the communities.
3. God has given justice (*adal*) to the Muslims.
4. Muslims stand for peace.
5. The Quran opposes autocracy and arbitrary government.
6. Muslims should endeavour to establish a parliamentary system of Government.

The point to be emphasised is that Azad wanted to base politics on the message of the Quran.

The five six-monthly volumes of *al-Hilal* and one of *al-Balagh* open with the *fatiha* editorials which, according to Azad, reveal the real significance of his papers.[88] In fact they confirm his commitment to Islam and the Quran which is evident from the following prayer which he repeats in every volume:

> O, Lord, in this journey which I had begun, take me to a better place ··· Though I am weak thou by thy favour and persistence in the conflict between the truth and falsehood, grant me victory.[89]

In *al-Hilal* and *al-Balagh* Azad repeats the Quranic injunction of enjoining the good and forbidding the evil (Amr Bil Ruf WA Nahy An Al-Munkar).[90] By digging up examples from history Azad shows how this injunction of enjoining the good and forbidding the evil has been flagrantly violated by the Ummayyids and later by the Ulama on whom the Turks depended for their guidance at the time of Turkish invasion.[91] The Fatwa editorials discuss the meaning and significance of Jihad and fix the responsibility of the chosen few for accomplishing 'God's purpose.' Further they exhort the Muslims, the 'friends of God,' to oppose the 'friends of the Satan,' meaning thereby the British and other ruling powers that misuse power and abuse authority. With utmost modesty Azad writes that the genius that blazed in *al-Hilal* is by no means his own creation, but the 'divine gift' bestowed on him to serve the cause of the Muslim community.

In *al-Hilal* Azad emerges as a staunch champion of the cause of liberty. In the first issue of *al-Hilal*, he published the photographs of Jamaluddin al-Afghani, Muhammad Abduh and Rashid Rida captioned with high-sounding titles and highlighting their persistent struggles for freedom, justice and equality in the Muslim world.[92] Rida had visited Nadwa ul-Ulama, Lucknow in 1912 at Shibli's invitation. On that occasion Azad had translated his Arabic speech into Urdu. Inspired by this visit Azad published a series of articles in the first three issues of *al-Hilal* on Rida entitled. 'A Great Reformer and Wise Leader,' extolling his passion for liberty and reform.[93]

In these articles Azad surveyed the reform movements initiated by Afghani and sustained by Abduh. Azad tells us how Abduh had opposed vehemently the stern orthodoxy of the Ulama who had misled the people by misinterpreting the Quran. Azad then takes up for discussion the salient features of Rida's personality and his achievements.[94] He evokes the nostalgic memory of the past by reminding his readers how al-Beruni in the fourth century and Ibn Batuta in the eighth century had visited India to witness the glory of Muslim rule, but now when Rida comes he finds India groaning under foreign yoke where the Muslims are forgetting the richness of their cultural heritage including Islam and the Arabic language. Azad shows how Rida's father had been tortured by the agents of Sultan Abdul Hamid II of Turkey and how Rida himself was harassed by the Ulama in Egypt especially the teachers at al-Azhar whom he had assailed for preaching false doctrines. Azad goes on to comment that due to the strong support from the Khedive and Lord Cromer, British Comptroller General in Egypt from 1883 to 1907, Rida managed to survive and started later another Dar ul-Ulum. Azad's object in writing these articles was to inspire his readers with the ideas of these three revolutionaries so that they should emulate them in propagating Islam and fighting for freedom, equality and justice.

Azad came closely in touch with the thoughts of religious leaders in the Arab world, who were stirred into political action to agitate for the political independence of their countries. Azad welcomed this manifestation of ardent nationalism which he regarded as a great force for gaining political independence. Azad declared that the history of thirteen centuries of Islamic heritage showed that Islam and nationalism were not incompatible. It is against political servitude that his strictures are directed in *al-Hilal* and it is to liberty that his views are firmly dedicated. In the light of his historical analysis Azad saw the certainty of the triumph of liberty. He declared: 'No country can remain a slave any longer in the twentieth century.[95] In saying this he anticipated the future course of history.

Azad went further ahead than most of his contemporaries in his firm commitment to the liberation of his country from foreign rule. Attacking the Muslim League's policy of abject servility to the ruling power, Azad wanted a clear declaration for 'self-government under England.'[96] He thought it necessary to enforce unity among his coreligionists by the propagation of Islam which alone could save them from political servitude.

Azad differed violently with Sir Sayyid Ahmed Khan on quite a number of vital issues concerning the Muslim communities' attitude towards the British Government in India. Sayyid Ahmad had professed loyalty to the British. He firmly believed that the salvation of the Muslims lay in collaborating with the ruling authority for the protection of their rights. Anglo-Muslim entente was the corner-stone of Sayyid Ahmad's policy. He felt that if the Muslims did not win the confidence of the Government, they would fall behind the Hindus in education and public employment. So he exhorted the Muslims not to embroil themselves in politics. This, according to him, would be an unwise course and would hit their interests. He was bitterly opposed to the Muslims joining the Congress or carrying on any other type of agitation for gaining political privileges. He regarded Hindus and Muslims as two separate nations. He also vehemently opposed the introduction of the parliamentary system of government in India because he feared that the Hindu majority in representative institutions would jeopardise the possibility of any fair deal to Muslims as a minority community. Sayyid Ahmad had deprecated in 1887 the system of representative institutions, even in the local self-government, being opposed to the principle of election in local bodies like the Municipal Committee and District Boards.

While recognising the valuable service rendered by Sayyid Ahmad Khan to the Muslim community, Azad criticized his policy of subservience to the British.[97] He believed that such a servile attitude was undignified and unworthy of a self-respecting people or community. Whenever he came by any opportunity, he did not fail to attack the notion of collaboration with the *Raj*. Azad became a grave digger to Sayyid Ahmad's notion of subservience to the British. He took the view that by the crafty policy of 'Divide and Rule' the British had made Hindus and Muslims antagonistic to each other as though they were bitter rivals competing for petty loaves and fishes while the right course for both the communities was to fight the British to prevent them from bringing ruination to their country.[98] By quoting verses from the Quran, Azad shows in the pages of *al-Hilal* that Islam stands for liberty and rejects every type of servitude. Thus he emerges from *al-Hilal* as a champion of liberty. It was difficult to give a call for liberty in those days but Azad had the courage to do so in his paper.

Azad exhorts his coreligionists to come out openly and join politics. He pleads with them, cajoles and tickles them, expostulates with them, warns them, thunders at them and evokes the memory of the past to stir them to action. His writings on liberty and the servitude of Muslims under foreign rule possess an extraordinary evocative power and made a tremendous appeal to the emotions of his coreligionists. The following is a typical passage in *al-Hilal* in which Azad makes a stirring appeal to his coreligionists.

> Whatever is destined for a nation cannot be averted. Surely a day will come when India's political revolution will dawn. The chains of slavery which she had tied on her feet will vanish all at once with the touch of the sword of liberty in the twentieth century. Suppose at that moment the history of the progressive stages of India's national life is to be written, then do you know, what will be written about seven crore Muslims?
>
> It will be written then that when India was fighting for freedom, the Hindus sacrificed themselves, bravely for the cause of liberty, but the poor Muslims chose to hide themselves in caves. It is a fact that the Hindus battled for freedom and in no case did they remain silent spectators. Swayed by noble passion they declared themselves as rebels in the cause of liberty…
>
> The future historian will write that law of determination operates in history. No country can remain a slave any longer in the twentieth century. But the world will remember unfortunately that all these revolutionary changes came about without any contribution made by the Muslims of India. How will the Muslims take that verdict?[99]

The pages of *al-Hilal* are also replete with strong criticism of the Muslim League, its way of functioning and its feudal leadership which always fawned on the British and did hardly anything for the welfare of Muslims. Hasan Nizami, a famous Urdu writer, who differed with Azad on many political matters, records that in 1908 at the residence of Zahid Suhrawardy, while talking of politics, Azad scribbled on a piece of paper, 'Everything acceptable except the Muslim League.'[100] In fact, Azad had developed a strong aversion for the League from its very inception and decided not to have any truck with it. Azad did not want the 'ill-fated' Muslim community to serve as a plaything of the 'covetous rulers'. He shared Shibli's hostility to the League and the British. Shibli whose political attitude lay between the Deoband Ulama and Sayyid Ahmad Khan had noted:

> The object of the Simla Deputation was, and it was frankly expressed to get a share for the Muslims in the political rights obtained by the Hindus. Day and night its refrain was that the Muslims were given safeguards. We do not understand the importance of the Simla deputation. It was the biggest show of the communal stage.[101]

Azad published quite a number of Shibli's poems in *al-Hilal* which ridiculed the programme and activities of the Muslim League in his characteristic style of using images and symbols. He was completely disenchanted with the Muslim League leadership which for its self-aggrandizement had thrown itself at the mercy of British ruler.[102] He firmly believed that Muslim League leaders were not worth mentioning as leaders since they never had the courage to demand self-government from the British. He repudiated the leadership of the aristocratic Agha Khan (1875-1958), leader of the Ismailies who had led the Simla delegation. According to Azad, Agha Khan 'does not belong to the people'.[103] Through the pages of *al-Hilal* by using an admixture of wit and sarcasm. Azad exposes the motivation and mechinations of what he calls the 'self-styled' leaders of the Muslim community.[104] The targets of his criticism included Nawab Sir Salimullah Khan (1884-1915), Muhammad Shafi, the landed magnate in Punjab, Raja of Mahmudabad (1879-1931) and Altaf Ahmed Khan (1867-1930). He was firmly convinced that the Muslim League had been instrumental in giving a wrong turning to the future of Muslim community.[105]

Azad wrote that due to the British policy of 'Divide and Rule', the Muslims had broken off their relations with the Hindus who 'were the real active group in the country.'[106] The British machinations had also succeeded in dissuading the Muslims from joining the Congress. Azad explains the strategy which the British adopted to create a rift between the Hindus and Muslims. He wrote:

> The British foresaw that if no toy were given to the Muslims, they could not be kept away from the national political movement. So they impressed the Muslims with the supreme importance of Western education. It worked perfectly. Other leaders were drunk with patriotism while we were drunk with the wine of education. Our neighbours were in the sun of liberty and we were lapping our dewdrops of education. In this way we spent our forty years.[107]

About the genesis of the Muslim League, Azad made the following sarcastic comments:

> Since no one could sleep for ever, the British realized that the Muslims might wake up and join the Congress which represented the vigilant people of India. To avoid this danger, we were given a new toy - the Muslim League.[108]

About the subtle British policy evolved to win the loyality of the Muslims, Azad wrote in a language interspersed with lively images as follows:

> As a matter of fact the act of the Muslims in joining the Muslim League was not the result of any political consciousness but the door of the political garden opened before them and they were shown in. If you are pushed into a garden you smell the flowers just in the same way as you would have done if you had come in of your own with free will. The basic thing is to enter the garden. If at this juncture the Muslim leaders had left us alone the puppets would have learnt to stand on their own legs to move forward. But we were told that the reasons for which we had been kept away from politics were still valid. We were warned that Hindus constituted a majority and if we joined them they would crush us. The advice given to us was that we should have our rights recognised by the Hindus. That was a new drug. The result was that the govern-

> ment which should have been the target for the Muslims saved itself and their own neighbours became their spear's mark instead. Thus even after the Muslims had entered politics, the government had nothing to be afraid of.[109]

To Azad Muslims League was not a political party that grew naturally as a result of the fulfilment of Muslim aspirations but an artificial product created by the British for the gratification of their vested interests. He wrote in clear terms that the 'Muslim League has betrayed the people.'[110] Addressing the League in *al-Hilal*, in 1912, he said, 'you have insulted Indian politics during the last six years.'[111] According to Azad, the greatest mistake that the League committed was that its politics was 'rooted in Aligarh – the tree was already there, but its roots had dried up.'[112]

On racial discrimination in South Africa Azad wrote that because of Gandhi 'fire burns in the hearts of all Indians in South Africa.'[113] He exposed the atrocities committed on Indians in South Africa. He wrote that the cruelties perpetrated on Indians 'are beyond limits.' The British courts in South Africa threatened the workers 'not to resort to strike, otherwise, they will be starved.' Azad also expressed his admiration for G.K. Gokhale and Lajpat Rai.

It is clear from the pages of *al-Hilal* that Azad supported cooperation between the Hindus and the Muslims in the cause of political agitation against the British. Afghani and Abduh whose writings had profoundly influenced his thinking had preached harmony between the followers of different faiths for fighting political battles. Azad had realised by 1914 that Hindu-Muslim unity was absolutely necessary for any political struggle in India. Though in the initial stages he did not elaborate on the theme of Hindu-Muslim unity which became a ruling passion of his in later life, it is clear from what he wrote that he could never conceive of any political struggle waged in India without cooperating with the Hindus.

Azad extols the secular outlook of Ganga Prasad Varma, the editor of *Hindustan* in Lucknow for about thirty years, whose mission was to forge Hindu-Muslim unity.[114] Azad described Ganga Prasad Varma as 'among the great men of India' whose every action has been animated by a spirit of service and pure dedication to the country. Azad mentions about his meeting with Varma who asked him to prepare a plan for Hindu-Muslim unity in Bengal. On Varma's death he suggested the setting up of a memorial fund to perpetuate his memory. He hoped that the Hindus and Muslims would contribute generously to it and promote thereby friendly feelings between both the communities. In view of Azad's thinking about the Congress, his attitude towards Gandhi and the position taken by him on Hindu-Muslim unity, it is difficult to accept Douglas' contention that 'Hindu-Muslim unity was not in itself, an integral part of his first appeal to the Muslims.'[115]

Admonishing the Muslim community for having committed a political suicide by its complete indifference to active politics, Azad cited the example of Madan Lal Dhingra, a Hindu youth, who inspired by the burning passion of patriotism had sacrificed himself for the liberation of his country.[116] Azad wrote that by his act Dhingra had 'shown the path to others.'[117] Dhingra had assassinated Sir William Curzon Wyllie, Aide-de-Camp to the Secretary of State for India in London on 1 July, 1909.[118] By eulogising Dhingra's action, Azad justified the use of force in political struggle.

According to Azad, Islam stands for peace but it also sanctions the use of force as a defensive measure in any armed conflict. Azad used the word *Jihad* in terms of its religious as well as political connotations. *Jihad* means in common parlance a struggle for the faith, either a struggle against the enemies of the faith (holy war) or the struggle against one's baser instincts. For Azad *Jihad* is of three types – (1) *Jihad* of property, the giving of goods; (2) *Jihad* of the voice; and (3) *Jihad* of life which justifies war.[119] Azad was a peace-loving man who promoted goodwill and amity among people but for the political liberation of a country from foreign rule, he thought it a religious duty to use force wherever necessary. Azad praises in *al-Hilal* the gallantry of Muslim soldiers during the Tripolitan war which he described as a glorious example of *Jihad*. He also pleads for the boycott of British goods and the use of Swadeshi in India as a justifiable act against the British rule in India.

Dealing specifically with the question of Muslim politics *vis-a-vis* Hindus, Azad asserts that the fear which the Muslims entertain about their being swamped by the Hindu majority because they are small in number was gratuitous.[120] He urges that in politics sheer numbers should not matter. He recalls how in the past the Muslims who were in small numbers by their unswerving faith in Islam had stood up like tigers to assert their independence.[121]

Azad took up in *al-Hilal* a number of sensitive issues which aroused the passions of the Muslims against the British. The Kanpur mosque issue in 1913 enraged the Muslim community. In order to widen the road, the Kanpur municipality decided to demolish a corner of the courtyard of the Macchli Bazar mosque and a part of the Hindu temple. The Hindu protest against the proposal saved the temple but the mosque was demolished. The trustees of the mosque were satisfied with the municipality's offer to build a new structure in place of the material removed but this did not satisfy the Muslim community which regarded the demolition of the mosque as a calculated move on the Government's part to disregard their sentiments. Muhammad Ali and Raja of Mahmudabad approached the Government to reverse their decision but in vain.

A Muslim mob marched towards the mosque on 3 August 1913 with the intention of restoring the structure that had been destroyed. The mob turned violent and the *Kotwal*, a Muslim, accompanied by a few policemen was stoned by the infuriated mob. The police resorted to firing, killing 14 or 15 people. The shooting inflamed the Muslims against the Government and there were protests all over the country against this high-handed act. Ultimately the Viceroy, Lord Hardinge went down to Kanpur and in consultation with Mazharul Haq of the Bankipur Bar and Raja of Mahmudabad brought about a compromise and thereby mollified the Muslim sentiments.

Azad gave a wide coverage to the Kanpur mosque incident in *al-Hilal* and whipped up the Muslim feelings against the Government. The first article on the subject appeared in *al-Hilal* on 11 June, 1913. The article 'The site of Martyrdom' had a subtitle, 'The painful sight of Edrine (Adrianpolis) in Kanpaur.' In this piece Azad compared the sorrows of Kanpur Muslims with the atrocities suffered by the Turks at the hand of hostile Christians on the fall of Edrine. Azad went personally to Kanpur to soothe the lacerated feelings of his coreligionists. He also raised the Kanpur Relief Fund for the families of those killed in the incident. Sulaiman Nadwi wrote that Azad emerged as the most popular leader among the Muslims due to the bold stand that he took on the Kanpur mosque against the Government.[122]

In a series of five articles published in *al-Hilal* Azad presented a scheme of founding Hizbullah (Party of God). He may have adopted the idea of establishing Hizbullah from Hizb ul-Ummah which had been founded by Abduh's followers in 1907. He mentioned it for the first time in the issue of *al-Hilal* dated 9-16 April 1913 but he made the actual announcement of Hizbullah in *al-Hilal* on 23 April, 1913. A week later he informed his readers that in response to his proposal 800 names had been received for the membership of Hizbullah. Azad regarded Hizbullah as the next logical step to the publication of *al-Hilal*, a fruitful realization of his dreams of creating a permanent organisation for the revival of the true spirit of Islam.

Azad's main idea was to create a new type of Muslim leadership imbued with the informing zeal of transforming society in accordance with the teaching of Islam. In the third article of the series he laid down the aims of Hizbullah. In the fourth instalment of the articles, Azad wrote :

> A burning flame possesses you but a whiff of air will lighten a thousand lamps. You have now the power to change Muslim society, to make the devout Muslims submit to God and to recover the lost morality, knowledge and the forgotten spirit of Islam. We have the Quran, why do we seek a new God? Why should we go after new fancies? We have experimented with innovations enough – we are entirely fed up with them. Leave us alone so that we should sacrifice the entire new world of loves for the trifle of old flames.[123]

Azad presented four-page constitution of Hizlbullah in the *al-Hilal* of 3 December, 1913. In this article he refers to the eight attributes which he would like the members of Hizbullah to possess and which he regards as absolutely necessary conditions for the membership of Hizbullah. These qualities are:

1. Those who offer repentance to God;
2. Those who serve God;
3. Those who praise God;
4. Those who fast to God;
5. Those who submit to God;
6. Those who fall prostrate in worship;
7. Those who abide by what is right and refrain from what is wrong;
8. Those who observe the limits set by God.

These qualifications are so broad and general that any one trying to adopt them may find them difficult of realization.

For the creation of a new type of Muslim leadership Azad decided to set up in 1914 the Madrassa Dar ul-Irshad, the headquarters of the Hizbullah. Some disciples of Azad's father donated a piece of land for this purpose. Azad prepared the courses of study for the entrants to the Madrassa and it was set down that they would be required to complete these courses within a year.

Separate classes were arranged for the English-knowing students. The main emphasis in the courses of study was on the teaching of Quran and its interpretation. Dar ul-Irshad began to function from October 1915. It was a residential institution and the students were accommodated in a double-storeyed house situated in the European locality in Calcutta. The course of study in Quran was in full swing, and the work on the publication and interpretation of Quran also commenced.[124]

Azad's aim in the creation of Hizbullah and Dar ul-Irshad was ethical. In Hizbullah he had the vision of what Arnold Toynbee calls a 'creative minority,' a cohesive group of individuals who would inaugurate Islamic Renaissance in the country and inspire his coreligionists to follow strictly the tenets of Islam. However, due to the shortage of funds and lack of proper organisation the Dar ul-Irshad experiment soon failed. Sulaiman Nadwi had expressed the view that "The work of Dar ul-Irshad will never move out of imagination into the realm of practical action."[125] This proved to be largely true. Hizbullah and Dar ul-Irshad had a false start and the whole scheme seemed to be so idealistically utopian that it seemed to be neither fish, flesh nor good herring.

As Editor of *al-Hilal* Azad was deeply concerned with maintaining the freedom of the press. Whenever the Government imposed restrictions on the press, Azad opposed it vehemently and expressed his strong resentment over it in *al-Hilal*. The *Urdu-e-Moola*, an Urdu weekly, founded by Hasrat Mohani, (1877-1951) had to be closed in May,1913 because the Government demanded a security of Rs. 3000 from its editor which he was made to pay. Hasrat Mohani, a versatile writer and poet had expressed strong pan-Islamist and anti-British views in *Urdu-e-Moola*. A great admirer of Tilak, he was also a bitter critic of the machinations of the British rulers in India, which he tried to expose in his inimitable prose. He took a leading part in the Kanpur mosque agitation and assailed the British Government for its calculated policy of hurting Muslim sentiments. His weekly became extremely popular among the Aligarh students in the first decade of the twentieth century. For publishing his articles on 'The Educational Policy of the English in Egypt' Mohani was sentenced to imprisonment for two years which was later reduced to one year.

When *Urdu-e-Moola* was closed, Azad produced a long article in *al-Hilal*, protesting against the British action. In his article in *al-Hilal* on 21st May, 1913 Azad drew the attention of his readers to the privations which Mohani and his family had to suffer at the hands of the Government. Azad wrote:

> The Government ordered Hasrat Mohani to pay a security of Rs. 3000 but he was not in a position to pay even Rs 3.. The Government is using the Press Act to throttle the weekly. The more our freedom is curbed, the more shall we feel inspired to assert it.

Azad warned the Government that they might gag the newspaper but they would never be able to suppress the voice of nine crore Muslims. Describing Mohani as a 'Faqir-e-Millat' and paying him rich tributes for his patriotism, love of freedom and nobility of character, Azad wrote about the miserable plight of Mohani's family who were on the verge of starvation because of lack of means of subsistence.[126] Mohani's son was trying to make his living by grinding two máunds of wheat. The police ransacked Mohani's house and reduced to ashes his manuscripts and books. Azad describes these tragic events in a moving narrative and asserts with confidence that the sacrifices of men like Mohani in the cause of freedom would never go in vain.

The *Urdu-e-Moolas*' was not a solitary case. *Tauhid* had also its security confiscated.[127] The *Comrade* was forced to deposit security in August 1913 and the *Muslim Gazette* was also suppressed. A security of Rs. 2000 under Section 3(1) of the Indian Press Act of 1910 was demanded from *al-Hilal* on 19 September, 1913 which Azad deposited on 23 September, 1913.[128] Azad filed a petition against it to the High Court, Calcutta.[129]

In his article Azad criticized the Government action in demanding a security from him and declared that this attack on his paper amounted to an attack on Islam.[130] He declared with a passionate conviction, 'All politics which is not derived from Quran is false.' Pointing out that whatever politics his paper was preaching was based on the tenets of Islam, Azad asked, 'If the Government believes that he was preaching sedition, then the logical corollary is that Islam is seditious'.

Azad attacked the Press Act on which the Government was relying for the suppression of newspapers. He prepared a scheme for the setting up of Indian Press Association and in this connection, a meeting was held in Indian Press Association Hall on 20 October, 1913 with

Surendranath Banerjee in the Chair. A Sub-Committee for drafting the Constitution was constituted with Surendranath Banerjee and Lal Mohan Ghosh, the editors of *Amrita Bazar Patrika*, Maulvi Mujibur-Rehman, editor, *Musulaman* and Maulana Azad as its members. Another meeting of the Association was fixed for November 19, 1913. The *al-Halal's* security of Rs. 2000 was forfeited on 16 November 1914, and both of its issues of 14 and 21 October, 1914 were confiscated. The last issue of *al-Hilal* of the first phase appeared on 18 November, 1914. The *Comrade* and *Hamdard* were also banned in May 1915. Zafar Ali Khan's *Zamindar* of Lahore, which had considerable influence in Western U.P. was suppressed. The Ali brothers and Hasrat Mohani were interned in 1916. Azad too was waiting for his turn.

Azad expressed his differences with Sayyid Ahmad on education in the pages of *al-Hilal*. Sayyid Ahmad had tried to model his Aligarh Anglo-Oriental College on Oxford and Cambridge and criticised the Government for making the Universities of Punjab and Allahabad as seminaries of Oriental languages. Azad was also deeply interested in the diffusion of Western learning and sciences in India, but through Oriental languages. He was firmly convinced that English could never become the *lingua franca* of India. But Sayyid Ahmad, though a patron of Urdu language, laid greater emphasis on English as a means for educating the people of India.

Azad was undoubtedly a great votary of modern knowledge. In February 1913 he started a column in *al-Hilal* on 'Scientific News' (Muzakira-e-Ilmiya) which included articles on 'Radium', 'Scott's expedition to the South Pole,' Dr. Montessori's educational experiments, J.C. Bose's botanical investigations and Darwin's contributions, etc. This column evoked an extraordinary amount of interest among the readers. In *Lisan al-Sidq* Azad had pleaded for the diffusion of scientific knowledge in India. He valued education not as a means for obtaining jobs, but as an instrument for creating a genuine religious, humanistic and scientific outlook. He condemned the popular craze for collecting degrees. He complained that those who had managed to obtain degrees did not make any efforts to produce creative work. He found no incompatibility between the true spirit of Islam and modern scientific knowledge. His stand on education was similar that of Ram Mohun Roy who had demanded not only western learning and sciences, but also the revival of the study of *Vedanta* or Divine knowledge.

In addition to articles on theological themes, *al-Hilal* included a number of articles on topics of literary and historical interest. It published the poems of Shibli, Akbar Allahabadi, Hasrat Mohani and Niaz Fatehpuri. There appeared in *al-Hilal* extracts from Shibli's great life of Prophet, *Sirat-al-Nabi* and a challenging reply to Iqbal's famous 'Shikwa' (a complaint) composed by Mustaffa Khan Shirhi.[131] Other features included reviews on the life and poems of Omar Khyayyam and Khawaja Farid-ud-Din Ganj Shakar, on *Id*, *Roza*, *Hajj* and on Fatehpur Sikri and some Muslim buildings in India and abroad. The *al-Hilal* also carried pieces on themes like the biographical sketches of Alexander the Great, Fredrick the Great, Lord Nelson, extracts from the French Paper, *Le Figaro* and the love story of Charles Stuart Parnell, an Irish Protestant who personified the spirit of intense nationalism of the nineteenth century.

A lively discussion ensued in the pages of *al-Hilal* on the use of words like *haz* for pleasure and *karb* for pain which Abdul Majid Daryabadi had used. But Azad preferred *lazzat* and *alam* to these words.[132] Even Akbar Allahabadi got involved into this literary controversy which sparked off wit and sarcasm. However, there was not even a trace of acrimony in this entire otherwise polemical discussion.

When Rabindranath Tagore was awarded the Nobel prize, Azad reproduced his photograph in *al-Hilal*. Azad wrote three articles on the 'Art of Oratory' in which he discussed the eloquence of Marcus Tullius Cicero (106 B.C.-45 B.C.) and Demosthenes (385-322 B.C.). He tells us how Demosthenes thundered against Phillip of Macedonia in his orations and endeavoured to inspire among his fellow-citizens the hatred against Phillip that animated his own bosom.

Azad brought to light in *al-Hilal* the hitherto unpublished poems of Ghalib which throw light on the poet's attitude towards the British Government.[133] Azad showed that Ghalib was obsessively concerned about his pension. Ghalib petitioned the Lieutenant-Governor of the Western Provinces, Sir Donald Frell McLeod in 1881 and assured him of his unstinted loyalty to the British. He wrote a panegyric (*qasida*) in honour of Queen Victoria, the Empress of India and also Lord Canning, the Viceroy. Complaining about British apathy towards his material interests, Ghalib wrote :

*Number raha na nazr, na khilat ka intzam*

Tr. (Neither sat in the Durbar, gift nor robe were given to me)

Ghalib thus appears in *al-Hilal* as a pathetic figure compelled by straitened circumstances to make overtures to the British. During the traumatic events of 1857 he did not stir out of his Ballimaran house in Delhi and maintained a discreet silence over the earth-shaking public events. However, Ghalib's servility to the ruling powers does not diminish Azad's admiration for his poetry.

Clearly, besides the theological interests which *al-Hilal* promoted, it also presented a highly developed concern for literary issues. The heterogeneity of material in *al-Hilal* naturally induced a variety of thought and feeling. One doubts whether any other journal could rival it in the seriousness of its themes, the power of its eloquence, and the force of its style.

Turkey's involvement in the Balkan wars became a subject of wide interest in Indian journalism. The Italian invasion of Tripoli in October 1913 also agitated the Muslim mind in India. Montenegro, Serbia, Greece and Bulgaria attacked Turkey in the first Balkan war. Turkey was wiped out from the map of Europe except for a few miles round Constantinople and the great fortress of Adrianpole. Azad took up in the pages of *al-Hilal* the oppression of Turkey at the hands of European powers who were determined to drive her out from Europe. In the *al-Hilal* of 27 May, 1914 Azad announced that out of each annual subscription of rupees eight and fifty paise of his paper, rupees seven and fifty paise would be sent in aid of Turkish fund. Azad applied this condition to 4,000 subscriptions. He also made a personal contribution to the Turkish fund. He addressed a meeting in support of Turkey in Calcutta on 2 February 1913 and collected Rs. 30,000.[134] M.A. Ansari (1880-1936) had led the Medical mission in December 1912 to Turkey to provide medical aid to the fighting Turkish army in Balkan war. Azad lauded this effort in *al-Hilal*.

Azad provides a blow-by-blow account of the ravages of war suffered by Turkey. His long article on 'Tripoli' presents an illuminating analysis of various war fronts.[135] He was able to procure information about the Balkan wars from various English newspapers like *The Times*, *Telegraph*, *Pall-Mall*, and *Globe*. He gives a wide coverage to the heroism displayed by Turkey in fighting Italy despite shortage of men and material.[136] A number of photographs of Egyptian and Turkish military generals were published in *al-Hilal* to highlight their gallantry against heavy odds. Azad's sympathies remained with Turkey throughout and he sounded a warning note to his countrymen that the fall of Turkey would mean the fall of Islam. He was highly critical of Agha Khan's support for the British he had expressed on the Turkish issue in his open letter to the Muslims in *Times of India*.[137] Agha Khan had advised Turkey to vacate her possessions in Europe.

Azad reproduced Mazharul Haq's virulent attack on Agha Khan in *al-Hilal* and condemned him for his audacious step to jeopardise Muslim interests in Turkey.[138] Azad was deeply perturbed over Turkey's defeat and was interested in probing the reasons that were responsible for it. He happened to meet Usmani Nizami Pasha, a well-known publicist from Turkey at Carlton Hotel, Lucknow and he explained to him how Turkey's defeat had come about.[139] By using Nizami Pasha's arguments, Azad shows that Turkey was defeated mainly for two reasons, firstly, her shortage in men and material and poor means of communication, and secondly, Britain's mischievous policy of misleading Turkey, and giving her the impression that she would not be attacked by any power and advising her not to make any preparation for war. On the Turkish defeat of Adrianpole Azad wrote a fiery piece :

> If to-day on the battlefields of Balkan, the followers of Islam with the Quran in their hands are being torn to pieces, then we, as Muslims, are accountable to God and the Prophet . . . if a Turk feels the pain of a thorn on his foot, by God, we have no right to be called Muslims if we do not feel the rankling thorn's pain in our hearts because Muslim community is one and wherever there are Muslims, they are part of it.[140]

By highlighting in *al-Hilal* Turkey's misfortunes inflicted on her by the aggressive policies of European powers and the brave resistance put up by her to save her independence, Azad aroused great sympathy in the Muslim mind for Turkey and strong resentment against the European powers, particularly Great Britain. In his treatment of Turkey, Azad comes out in *al-Hilal* as a staunch pan-Islamist and anti-British.

The European war broke out on 1st August, 1914. Azad gives in *al-Hilal*, a vigorous, lucid and racy account of the personalities and events connected with the war. The main focus of *al-Hilal* is to show the emergence of Germany as a great military power on the world's stage. Azad's account of the personality of Bismarck is candid. He regards him as a political genius of the highest order who accomplished a glorious piece of work in raising Germany's status as a big power.[141] While tracing the rise of Bismarck – a natural result of his sagacity and will power – Azad explains the causes and consequences of the Franco-Prussian war which marked a turning point in the diplomatic history of Europe. Azad offers details even on the Ems telegram which reflected Bismarck's insight and ingenuity evident in the way he put France in the wrong.[142]

The *al-Hilal* issues of August-September dilate on Germany's military and political strength. Azad makes a comparative evaluation of the moral power of England and Germany. He discusses the British adoption of the Dreadnought type of battleships and the defensively designed Tirptiz's German navy. The *al-Hilal* presents brief character-sketches of Moltke, Chief of the General German Staff, the Kaiser William II, Emperor Francis Joseph of Austro-Hungary and Francis Ferdinand of Austria. These sketches show his wide reading and the skill of a literary jack of all trades, as well as his gifts as a journalist. It is extraordinary that Azad could manage to offer such details on the war. His main sources for this information, as we have pointed out earlier, were newspapers like *The Times*, *Globe*, *Morning Post*, *Daily Telegraph* and *Times of India*.

The general impression created on the readers' mind by *al-Hilal* was that of the invincibility of German power.[143] The harsh treatment accorded to Turkey had embittered Azad and he had turned into a bitter critic of the British Government in India. The breaking of the war gave him the opportunity he was waiting for to pour out his wrath against the British victories and ridicule the feebleness of British resistance.[144] In his article of 14 October, 1914 published in *al-Hilal*, Azad wrote :

> Germany will also occupy Calais very soon. With the fall of Calais the chapter in the history of the war which refers to the subjects of Belgium and the coast of English channel will be closed.[145]

Azad makes the point that the Germans succeeded in fighting in other countries while the British were contained in their own land. He winks at the German troops' advance towards Paris.[146] He is out to make rather hasty judgements on issues of war. He elucidates the features of German character which he admires for its thoroughness, industry, discipline and inventive ability but regards the English a 'nation of shopkeepers.'[147]

The issues of *al-Hilal* from August 1914 onwards show unmistakably Azad's pronounced bias in favour of German strength and his sneer at the British. The Government forfeited the security of Rs. 2000 and confiscated the combined issue of *al-Hilal* dated 14 and 21 October, 1914. The Government objected to the articles, entitled 'Hadith-e-al-Jaunud aur Saqoot-e-Antwerp' (Military News and the Fall of Antwerp). On the fall of Antwerp, Azad published a photograph of Belgian soldiers under a tree enjoying those moments when the war is on. Under the picture appeared the Quranic verse : 'God is not cruel to them but they are cruel to themselves.' Azad wanted to show how the Belgian soldiery, the 'natives of the luckless nation' wasted away its time while the Germans were fighting with tremendous force of discipline and concentration.

The Government of India took a serious view of the anti-British, pro-Turkish and pro-German views of *al-Hilal* and demanded another security of Rs. 10,000. Azad closed the press. Since the beginning of the war, particularly because of Turkey's involvement in it, *al-Hilal* was becoming very popular; for example, its sale doubled in Hyderabad, and in Bengal the numbers of subscribers reached 4300.[148] The Government took action against it on the initiative of the *Pioneer* (Allahabad) which wrote an editorial on 1 November, 1914 entitled, 'Pro-Germanism in Calcutta.' This article warned the Government about the mischievous propaganda carried out by *al-Hilal* against the British. The *Pioneer* wrote :

> *Al-Hilal* is a weekly illustrated newspaper published in the Urdu language in Calcutta and is edited by a Delhi Musalman named Abul Kalam. It has a large circulation among Musalmans in these provinces, and probably in other parts of India. Ever since the war broke out, its attitude has been so strikingly pro-German that it must be a matter of amazement to all who read the paper that the Government has managed to tolerate its writings. Probably this may be accounted for by the fact that the paper attracts little or no attention in Calcutta itself owing to its being published in Urdu; and there can be little doubt that this was one of the main causes which led the editor to choose Calcutta as the place of publication. Another reason may be the style of the most mischievous sarcasms and innuendoes, most of which lose their effect when translated into English, and it is most unlikely that many European officials read the paper in the original.[149]

The *Pioneer* cited *al-Hilal* as writing that the fall of Paris was a certainty and the German troops were close to Paris but did not mention the Austrian retreats and the victories of Russia and the British navy.

The *Pioneer* quotes *al-Hilal* as writing that 'not an inch of German territory has passed into the occupation of their enemies.' The Government's attention was particularly drawn by the *Pioneer* to the photograph of Belgian troops whom Azad ridiculed for their apathy to the war which he regarded as a serious business of sacrificing one's life. The *Pioneer* asked the Government to take action against the paper that was preaching sedition. The *Pioneer* concluded :

> We may say that a government at such a time as the present allow a British subject to publish unchecked such malicious insinuations against the British soldiers at any rate may long claim to the position of a most un-Germanic spirit of toleration.

The Government of India took the initiative of dealing with *al-Hilal* on the recommendation of the Director of Criminal Intelligence, Sir Charles Cleveland. The Bengal Government, however, was reluctant to move in the matter. Instead it used the services of Nawab Syed Shams-ul-Huda, a member of the Bengal Legislative Council to intervene and bring round Azad.[150] The Government of India wrote :

> The scandalous article in *al-Hilal* (referring to the Military news) has attracted no attention from the Government of Bengal. The Bengal Government must be requested to take legal action and proceed against *al-Hilal*.[151]

The Government of India could not wait any longer. In the Intelligence reports Azad was described as an extremely able and dangerous man.[152] About the circumstances leading to the Government action, the sub-editor of *al-Hilal* wrote in its issue of 18 November, 1914 as follows :

> The Bengal Government forefeited the first security of Rs. 2000 from *al-Hilal* on 16 November, 1914 and confiscated both the combined numbers of *al-Hilal* dated 14-21 February, 1914, in which the articles objected to were 'Hadith-al-Janud and Saqoot-e-Antwerp' (Military News and Fall of Antwerp) under which the caption was 'God is not cruel to them but they are cruel to themselves'. It so

> happened that Maulana Azad was on tour and the warrants for the forfeiture of security and house search were issued in his absence and he was informed about them. He instructed the office telegraphically "Publish the issue of *al-Hilal* immediately which is under print and while informing the readers about the forfeiture of security, add a short note saying 'we wish to continue *al-Hilal* till the last and God willing will do so.' We are therefore, publishing this issue and assure that we will not relent."[153]

The Government demanded another security of Rs. 10,000 which Azad did not pay. Hence the closure of *al-Hilal*.

A year after the closure of *al-Hilal* Azad started another paper *al-Balagh*, (the message) from a different address, Ripon Lane, Calcutta. Its first issue appeared on 12 November, 1915 and the last one with triple numbers 15-17 for 17-31 March, 1916. The name of the editor figures in the second issue. The paper existed for about five months. Azad was assisted by M.I. Zakarya in the running of *al-Balagh*. Seventeen issues were published as far as numbers are concerned but in reality they were combined into eleven.

The first issue of *al-Balagh* opened with Iqbal's poem in Urdu which was reproduced under the title 'Adbiyat (Literary pieces). This was the only poem of Iqbal published in *al-Hilal* and *al-Balagh*. The opening poem in Persian reads as follows :

*Nawa ra talkh tar mi zan cho zauk-e-naghma kam yabi*

Tr. (Sharpen your voice when you find lack of passion in music).

The *al-Balagh* contained many *fatihas* in Arabic running into two issues with quotations from the Quran and *Hadith*. The *al-Balagh* was not different in spirit and thought from *al-Hilal*. *Al-Balagh* was in fact a continuation of *al-Hilal*, a variation on the same theme – the recovery of lost faith in Islam.

Azad made it clear that he would publish in *al-Balagh* two types of articles: one for the learned and the other for the laymen. The *al-Hilal* was meant for the learned but in *al-Balagh* Azad had the general public in mind. That is why he published in *al-Balagh* features of general interest like 'Muslim Architecture' in Bijapur, Ahmedabad, Golkanda, etc. Special articles appeared in *al-Balagh* on 'Islam and Socialism,' 'Greek influence on Islam' and the 'Impact of War on Morality.' Azad also reproduced in the paper poems composed by well-known poets like Zauq, Ghalib and Hasrat Mohani. Azad wrote an illuminating estimate of Shibli on 12 November, 1915 whom he described as 'Fiqir-e-baynwaz' (a self-abnegating soul). He also made a strong plea for the study of Western historical method. But the framework within which Azad arranged his historical and religious material was Islam.

Azad had realised after the closure of *al-Hilal* that his political views as embodied in the paper had led to the Government's action against him. So now after a year he was careful enough and he did not wish to get trapped again by attacking the Government the way he had done in *al-Hilal*. The preaching of the gospel of Quran in every issue of *al-Balagh* was to build up the character and morale of the Muslim community so that it should possess sufficient strength and self-confidence to assert its political rights. *Al-Balagh* was a fortnightly largely with direct politics left out. But what was strikingly common in both *al-Hilal* and *al-Balagh* was the entire reliance on the authority of Quran as a source of religion and philosophy for the uplift of the Muslims all over the world.

It would be a facile generalisation to say that *al-Balagh* was old wine poured into new bottles. While *al-Hilal* called for positive direct action on the part of Muslim community against the Government, *al-Balagh* pleaded with the Muslims for self-education, self-examination, and self-sacrifice. *Al-Hilal* enjoined upon the Muslims to do or die, but *al-Balagh* said softly, 'Extinguish thyself for the love of Islam.'

Niaz Fatehpuri, a well-known Urdu critic and editor of *Nigar*, Lucknow has compared *al-Hilal* and *al-Balagh*. He calls *al-Hilal* a leaping flame, but *al-Balagh* a 'spiritual introspection and reform,' *al-Hilal* a forthright challenge and *al-Balagh* God's message touching the heart.[154] In fact, *al-Hilal* was the stormy sea and *al-Balagh* the stillness of night, *al-Hilal* a pricking nettle but *al-Balagh*, a cool balm. *Al-Hilal* was more concerned with the present but *al-Balagh* looked far ahead for the future destiny of Muslims. Azad stressed in *al-Balagh* the spiritual values that make a nation. He emphasized that *al-Hilal* was thunder, a call for *Jihad* but *al-Balagh* was spiritual ecstasy. *al-Hilal* was concrete, a blowing trumpet but *al-Balagh*, the message of love that touches the strings of the heart.

Azad was ordered on 28 March, 1916 under Defence of India Regulations to leave Bengal within two days but this period was extended to eight days. Earlier his entry had been banned in Delhi, Punjab, U.P., and Bombay. The only place he could go to was Bihar and he went to Ranchi. He hoped that he would manage to publish *al-Balagh* from there, but he could not do so. He was interned in Ranchi on 18 July, 1916.

The question is why did the Government intern him when it did not find anything incriminating in *al-Balagh*? The Government had seen how Azad had magnified events in Balkans into a crusade of Christians against Muslims and by his virulent attack on the British in *al-Hilal* had fomented strong pan-Islamic and anti-British sentiments.[155] The Government had reasons to believe that his papers were being subsidised by the Committee of Union and Progress dominated by Turkish and Egyptian nationalists formed at Constantionple with a view to inflaming the Muslim mind in India against the British.[156] Azad was branded as a Turkish and German spy. Sir Charles Cleveland, Director of Criminal Intelligence of India, wrote about Azad in his note dated 15 May, 1916 :

> I look upon Abul Kalam Azad as probably the most responsible figure in the Mohammadan world. I do not think there is any other personality that could arouse the same personal sympathy and fanaticism in the general Muslim society.[151]

It is clear from the Intelligence reports that through his writings and speeches Azad had exercised considerable influence on the formation of anti-British opinion in India during the war. The Government of India kept a close watch on his association with the Ali brothers and Ajmal Khan. Azad was also in touch with Mazhar-ul Haq whom he visited in Bankipur and these meetings the Government suspected to be a sort of mutual consultation for conspiring against it. Of course, the Government of India could not forget his tirade and hostility against the U.P. Government in the Kanpur mosque episode.

It is clear from the study of Intelligence reports that Azad was involved in the Silk Letter Conspiracy case and was 'listed in the Army of God' as the 'Lieutenant-Colonel in company with such active workers on Trans-frontier Mullas and prominent encouragers of the conspiracy.'[158] Later three letters written on length of yellow silk and sewn into the lining of messengers' coats fell into the hands of the Government of India in August, 1916. This led to the curbing of the Silk Letter Conspiracy. It is also stated in the Intelligence reports that a German emissary had been in touch with the friends of the Editor of *al-Hilal*.[159] It was therefore not for the publication of his articles in *al-Balagh* that Azad was interned in Ranchi but for his active participation in politics which made him appear in the Government view an extremely dangerous man.

Azad's *al-Hilal* and *al-Balagh* can be said to have played an epoch-making role in Indian journalism. These journals were unique in many ways and had neither precursors nor successors. Azad has explicitly claimed that in the running of these journals he had no commercial motive and he considered even a tinge of commercialism so intolerable in this regard that he would rather die than give any countenance to it.[160] Azad was about twenty-four when he started *al-Hilal* and the total period during which these journals ran was about three and a quarter years. The venture proved to be a remarkable success. Within a few months of *al-Hilal*'s publication, its circulation had reached about 25,000.[161]

It appears from hints to be found in his papers that Azad was really satisfied with their performance.[162] He felt as though the mission of his life had been fulfilled.[163] A sense of failure in his mission would, however, sometimes seize him and he would feel discomfited about the whole arduous enterprise.[164] When moments of despair were on him he did not know what to do and where to go: He found himself utterly helpless and like Jean Valjean of *Les Miserables*, a character for whose sorrows he had great admiration, he would pour out the anguish of his own heart in the pages of his journals. He wrote:

> I want the eyes that weep. I wept and made people weep. I salute those who shed tears and whose hearts are bruised because shedding tears brings in the flood of love.[165]

Tears signify here the woe-befallen state of the Muslim community and love its cure through the message of Islam.

The *al-Hilal* and *al-Balagh* were not the work of a mere specialist but soul-stirring appeals of an inspired individual who knew how to touch the deeper chords of the Muslim community to do its duty. They were a crusade, a mission and a movement which Azad launched to uplift the Muslims by inculcating in them the true message of Islam. His ardent convictions for the purity of his mission was so firm that using Faiz Ahmad Faiz's expression, one could say that he had soaked his fingers into the blood of his heart for the toil and tears of his coreligionists.

Azad comes out of these journals as a religious divine, a preceptor and a political leader who wanted to awaken the Muslims to the responsibility of turning themselves into true followers of their faith and liberating their country from foreign rule. Azad stuck to the religious idiom because he thought it to be the only way to rally the Muslims and to embroil them in the whrilwind of politics. Thus Azad made Sayyid Ahmads' politics obsolete. Recalling the glory of his *al-Hilal* days before the Jamiat-ul-Ulama-e-Hind on 18-21 November, 1921 six years later, Azad said in his presidential address:

> It is this anguish (for the suffering of the Muslims) with which I had coloured the pages of my *al-Hilal* with my tears of blood and on whose theme and words I had spread my heart and mind. Since 1911 till today this has been the goal of my aspiration and passion of my soul without which existence is futile. Not a morning has dawned when my heart has not been filled with this passion and not an evening has set in when in its longing have I not felt the torment of my soil. I have scarificed for its love my entire life and for its agony of separation I have spent four long years.[165]

Azad,s notion of religion was not narrow or exclusive. That is why Azad enjoined upon the Muslims to co-operate with the Hindus in the liberation of their country. His journalism gave a message of political freedom in unequivocal terms. One of the means he suggested was to boycott the use of English goods in India. He was in a sense precursor of Gandhi in politics and he did for Muslims in 1912-16 what Gandhi was to do on a bigger scale in 1919-1921.

Maulana Muhammad Ali said that he learnt the art of leadership from the prose of Azad and the poetry of Iqbal. When Maulana Sayyid Ahmad Akbarabadi complained that Azad's *al-Hilal* contains photographs, Shaikh al-Hind Maulana Mahmudul Hasan, the Principal of Deobond (1851-1920) and one of the leading Muslim theologians, and scholars and an interpid freedom fighter of his time who was exiled to Malta, said 'Why should I not read *al-Hilal* ? This periodical has taught us the lesson of *Jihad* which was our duty and which we had sadly forgotten.'[166] Sayyid Sulaiman Nadwi, Azad's bitter critic, wrote in the same vein :

> I must in all fairness say one thing. This was the time when Maulana Abul Kalam Azad was bringing out *al-Hilal*, and Muslims

> were set on fire by his passionate words. He sounded loudly and fiercely the trumpet of *Jihad*, whose name people were afraid to mention, so that the forgotten lesson was on the tongues of people again.[167]

The resurgent spirit of Islam found its expression in *al-Hilal* and *al-Balagh* which gave to the Muslim community a sense of dignity and self-confidence. It fostered among them a spirit of unity and solidarity. It brought religion and politics closer to them. Both these journals drew men out of their scholastic cloisters and pushed them into politics. Azad did for Muslims which Sayyid Ahmad had not been able to do. His journals had a dynamite underneath them designed to explode the supine Muslim politics of mendicancy and give a rude shock to the citadel of foreign rule. Here is a typical trumpet call to the Muslims whose refrain reverbates through the pages of *al-Hilal* and *al-Balagh* :

> Whence to obtain the bugle to awaken the nine crore of Muslims who are sleeping . . . where are the eyes which claim to shed tears for the Muslim brethren, where the hearts which are proud of the wounds of the fallen community; the enemy is breaking open the doors of the town and the inmates are weeping over their lot . . . the dacoits are lost in deep slumber. . . . But oh : those who consider weeping a courageous act and despondency, a vitality of life, listen: your house is on fire . . . . The storm is raging and the fierce flames are leaping but there is none, none whatsoever among you to fetch water. If you are waiting for this time, then surely the time is come. If you are waiting for the boat to sink, then also there is not much time left.[168]

In *al-Hilal* there are also a number of passages of ringing eloquence which reflect Azad's fervent devotion and reverence for God; for example, in the issue of *al-Balagh*, 24 December, 1915 Azad emphasizes that God's purpose is fulfilled when one extinguishes one's self, loves mankind and sheds one's tears for it, suffers for others, which is holy and even kisses the executioners' hand. There are also some lively features of speculative nature in the journals raising fundamental questions like 'Who am I ? or Where lies our salvation ? '

Because of his virulent attack on the Muslim League and Aligarh party in *al-Hilal*, Azad courted much unpopularity among an influential segment of Muslim society. He also received threatening letters from some of his readers which he published in *al-Hilal.*[169] Sometimes one suspects Azad himself composed some of the letters to counter the opposite point of view. A few of these letters were couched in vulgar language. Azad was dubbed a 'dog and an out-of-date *Maulvi*' who was misleading the gullible and simple Muslims by his journalistic acrobatics. His critics argued that religion as preached by Azad's pen was a thing of the past and that for any progress it was vital not to cling to the past but to look forward.

Azad, it is true, used the religious idiom as did Gandhi later, but then there was no other choice for the leaders of opinion at the time but to follow this course in view of the conditioning circumstances in which the country was placed. The question was how to rally people for a cause and the use of religion was considered by far the easiest and most effective weapon for uniting people and making them fight against foreign rule. The religious idiom was a legacy of the nineteenth century Indian Renaissance, a consequence of the historical process which could not be reversed. An egg once scrambled cannot be unscrambled!

The tone of al-Hilal's religious peity was loud, harsh and shrill. It had the echo, authority and majesty of Quran. That is why Sayyid Ansari, a promising writer who died young wrote: 'It is my conviction that if Quran had not been a revelation, then it would have been rendered either in the prose of Azad or the poetry of Iqbal.'[170] What Wordsworth said of Milton is applicable to Azad's performance in *al-Hilal* and *al-Balagh.*

Thou hadst a voice whose sound was like the sea!

It seems as though Azad was addressing his coreligionists from a lofty tower through the pages of *al-Hilal* and *al-Balagh*. The narrative in these journals is stately and the prose being heavily loaded with Arabic constructions is, at times, beyond the comprehension of an average reader. Azad chose words like *mudir* for editor, *jarid* for *akhbar*, *Dar-ul-Akhbar* for reading room etc.

Azad's rhetoric consists of vigorous buffy-snuffy epigrams and torrential images. He demonstrates in these journals a remarkable gift for phrase-making. The evocation of metaphors is a great gift of creative art and Azad derived his metaphors from flowers and thorns, dawn and darkness, storm and tide, flame and moth, water and desert, love and separation, etc. Sometimes he produces an electrifying effect on his readers by the powerful effect of his eloquence. By evoking the memory of men of the past who suffered in the cause of truth, he moved his readers to tears. But behind whatever he wrote there was the force and strength of his restless and curious spirit, writhing over the sorrows of others. In both of these journals there were articles which one could read with the least effort solely for their literary merit.

We have seen how *al-Hilal* and *al-Balagh* occupy a unique place in the religious and intellectual development of Azad. Azad's interest in journalism never flagged. After his release from Ranchi in 1919 he was trying to get a paper under way but he was able to produce nothing but fragments. Azad started a weekly – *Paigham* in Urdu on 23 September, 1921 from Calcutta which continued till 16 December, 1921. With his arrest on 10 December, 1921 the paper stopped. *Paigham* had only thirteen issues containing a hundred and ninety-two pages. Its weekly circulation reached 10,000. Its price per issue was two annas but was sold at rupees two.

Azad plunged into active politics in 1920 which left him little time for journalism. Until his arrest at the end of 1921 he was constantly busy touring the country and drumming up public fury in support of the Khilafat and Non-cooperation movements. How could he find time to edit *Paigham* in such circumstances? He left the entire management of the paper to his friend and later his fellow-prisoner Abdur Razzaq Malihabadi.

The *Paigham* propagated the ideas and programme of the Khilafat and Non-cooperation movements. Though in some articles it expounded the tenets of Islam, its main focus remained on contemporary Indian politics. By quoting the Quran, it exhorted the Muslim soldiery to resign from army service as any support to the British was un-Islamic when the country was involved in Khilafat agitation.[171] The paper protested against the arrest of the Ali-brothers and Dr. Saif-ud-din Kitchlew.

The *Paigham* also contained articles of general interests on the French Revolution, the National Assembly and a biographical sketch of George Washington. Some special features which figured in the paper included those on Islamic history; a piece on Ibn Taimiya whom Azad regarded as a saviour during the Mongol invasion, and short notes on the importance of Imam and the role of the Ulama in Muslim society. Azad also expressed his anguish over not being arrested when his colleagues were languishing in jail in the cause of India's freedom. Azad comes out in *Paigham* as a nationalist leader fighting for Khilafat and Non-cooperation movements, but his dedication to Islam which he regards as a complete faith is as firm as it was in *al-Hilal* and *al-Balagh*. The style of *Paigham* is simple and easy and free from the heavy and turgid embellishments of *al-Hilal*. One really misses in *Paigham* Azad's masterly touch.

After his release from jail, Azad launched a fortnightly *al-Jamia* in Arabic on 1st April, 1923 which continued till March, 1924. The main object of this paper was to acquaint the Arabic world with the political developments in India and to foster the spirit of pan-Islamism. The paper was edited by Malihabadi though Azad kept a general supervision over it. The paper contained in all 394 pages. *Al-Jamia* lasted for about six months. In its first issue the paper criticised the cooperation of the Sharif of the Mecca with the British Government.[172]

Azad was frightfully busy with his political activities but he kept an eye on the material compiled for *al-Jamia*. In his letter to Malihabadi dated 19 April, 1923 Azad advised him not to publish Rashid Rida's article as it had criticized the 'Young Turks' which, he thought, could produce an adverse effect on the Turkish Government.[173] Azad deprecated the idea of publishing extracts from Iqbal's 'Israr-e-Bekhudi' as it was composed in Persian but he permitted the reproduction of his 'Tarana-e-Milli' in the paper. With the abolition of the Caliphate in 1924, Azad stopped the publication of *al-Jamia*.[174]

Azad made another attempt to renew *al-Hilal* which he started publishing from Delhi with Malihabadi as its editor. This journal lasted from 10 July to 9 December, 1927, approximately for about six months. Twenty issues of the paper appeared. This paper deals with the political and intellectual life of the Muslim community. Serious intellectual articles as well as those of general interest appeared in this journal.

Azad wrote a series of articles on 'Islam and Nationalism' in which he raised the question as to what constitutes 'Nationality.'[175] He also presented the translations of *Surah Fathiah*. He published an article on 'French Revolution' showing that it had failed to solve the problem of human rights.[176] He reproduced in the paper extracts from the Communist Manifesto.[177] He criticised the Marxist interpretation of history saying that economics alone does not solve the complex problems of political life.[178] He explained the distinction between the State and Government.[179] The *al-Hilal* reproduces a comprehensive statistical data compiled from the writings of James Mill, Lord Elphinstone, William Digby and John Fredrick Shore to expose the economic exploitation of India by the British.

Articles of general interest on Napoleon, Byron, Victor Hugo, Darwin and Mustafa Kemal Pasha also appeared in *al-Hilal*. Azad raised the question whether Napoleon turned into a Muslim.[180] C.R. Das's death in 1925 was a great blow to Azad as he had been associated with him for a long time. Azad wrote a brilliant estimate of Das in *al-Hilal*, highlighting his statesmanship, clarity of thought and integrity of character.[181] A book entitled *Rangila Rasool* by Mahasha Rajpal from Lahore had appeared on the life of the Prophet which aroused great indignation in the Muslim community. In a cool and dignified manner Azad wrote a piece in *al-Hilal* to mollify the injured feelings of the Muslims saying that Islam is a great religion and its greatness is not by any means affected by a scurrilous publication. He pleaded with his coreligionists to ignore the book.[182] The *al-Hilal* of 1927 was a paper largely of a general nature lacking any scholastic or literary flavour. Azad himself wrote little for it, though his ideas got through it under his general guidance of editorial policy.

It would be seen from the foregoing analysis that Azad's commitment to journalism was firm and passionate. In the pre-*al-Hilal* period it was a period of experimentation with him but in *al-Hilal* and *al-Balagh* he was at the zenith of his journalistic powers and he elevated journalism to the excellence of a literary art. After his plunge into active politics in 1920 he could not find sufficient time to sustain his interest in journalism. What journalism lost by his involvement in politics was made up by his remarkable contribution to our national movement. The loss to journalism was a gain to the freedom struggle.

## REFERENCES

1. J. Natarajan, *History of Indian Journalism*, pp. 204-05.
2. Christian W. Troll, *Syed Ahmad Khan*, p. 14.
3. *Ibid.*
4. Muhammed Sadiq, *A History of Urdu Literature*, p. 346.
5. Braham Nath Datta, '*Hali Aik Azim Insan*' pp. 20-35, in S.Y. Qureshi (ed.), *Hali* (1837-1914); see also pp. 20-35.
6. Malik Ram, *Hali*, p. 57.
7. Douglas, *op. cit.*, pp. 74-75.
8. *Ibid.*
9. Syed Shahbuddin Dasnawi, *Shibli*, pp. 83-97, 100.
10. S.M. Ikram is the author of *Yadgar-e-Shibli* and Qureshi, *Shible ki Hayat-e-Muashka*. Both the books were published from Pakistan.

11. *Zikr*, pp. 293-94.
12. Abul Kalam Azad, *Karwan e-Khyal*, pp. 92-95.
13. Sayyid Sulaiman Nadwi, *Hayat-e-Shibli*, Part I, pp. 443-44.
14. Sayyid Sulaiman Nadwi, *Makatib-e-Shibli*, I, p. 637.
15. *Zikr*, pp. 19-20.
16. *al-Hilal*, 17 April, 1913, 30 April, 1913 and 17 May, 1913, see Sayyid Sulaiman Nadwi, *Hayat-e-Shibli*, p. 656.
17. See *al-Hilal*, 19 Jan. 1913, 5 and 12 Feb., 1913.
18. Mutazilite, the name given to a group of thinkers in the eighth century A.D. who were mainly responsible for the growth of speculative thinking in Islam on the basis of Greek philosophical concepts.
19. Mohammad Zia-ud-Din, 'Maulana Shibli, Maulana Azad key Taulkat Par Aeyk Nazar' in *Ajkal*, Azad number, Nov. 1988.
20. *Zikr*, p. 281.
21. *Kahani*, p. 215, see 'Abul Kalam Azad, Ba Haisiyat Sahafi' in Khaliq Anjam, *Abul Kalam Azad*, ed., p. 489.
22. Ghulam Rasul Mihr, *Naqsh e-Azad*, p. 107.
23. Malik Ram, 'Maulana Azad Ba Haisiyat Sahafi' in *Ajkal* Maulana Azad Number, Nov., 1988, p. 87.
24. *Ibid*, pp. 81-87.
25. Abu Suleman Shahjahanpuri in *Urdu ki Tariqqi main Maulana Azad ka Hissa*, p. 9.
26. Ghulam Rasul Mihr, *op. cit.*, pp. 106-07.
27. *Ibid.*, p. 108.
28. Maulana Imdad Sabri, *Imam ul-Hind Maulana Azad*, p. 38.
29. *Kahani*, p. 253.
30. *Ibid.*, pp. 259-76.
31. *Aiwan-e-Urdu*, Dec., 1988, p. 44.
32. *Kahani*, p. 253.
33. Abdul Qavi Dasnawi in 'Azad Vadi-e-Sahafit Main' in *Aiwan-e-Urdu*, December 1988, p. 44.
34. *Ibid.*, pp. 44-45.
35. *Ibid.*
36. Abdul Qavi Dasnawi, *op.cit.*, p. 45.
37. Malik Ram, *'Maulana Azad Ba Haisiyat Sahafi'* in *Ajkal*, op. cit., pp. 81-87.
38. *Kahani*, op. cit., p. 280.
39. This section on *Lisan al-Sidq* is based on the files of the journal in the Indian Council of Cultural Relations and on Abdul Qavi Desnawi (ed.), *Mazamin-e-Lisan al-Sidq*.
40 *Lisan al-Sidq*, Jan. 1905.
41. *Ibid.*, Aug.-Sept., 1904.
42. *Ibid.*
43. *Ibid.*, Jan., 1905.
44. *Ibid.*, April-May, 1905, pp. 41-42.
45. *Kahani, op. cit.*, p. 293.
46. *Ibid.*, pp. 283-84; *Lisan al-Sidq*, 4 Feb., 1904.
47. *Lisan al-Sidq*, Jan., 1904.
48. *Ibid.*, Aug.-Sept., 1904.

49. *Ibid.*, Jan., 1904.
50. *Ibid.*, May, 1904.
51. *Ibid.*, Jan., 1904.
52. Maulana Abdul Majid Daryabadi (ed.), *Khatootat-e-Majidi*, p. 245.
53. *Kahani*, pp. 128, 190-91 and 287-90.
54. *al-Nadwa*, pp. 2, 8 (October 1905).
55. *Ibid.*, pp. 2, 11 (Jan., 1906).
56. *Ibid.*, pp. 2, 12 (Feb., 1906).
57. *Ibid.*
58. *Ibid.*, pp. 1, 3 (March, 1906).
59. *Kahani*, p. 292; Maulana Imdad Sabri, *Imamul Hind Maulana Azad*, p. 58.
60. Malikzada Manzur Ahmad, *Maulana Abul Kalam Azad*, pp. 21, 23-25.
61. Abul Kalam Azad, *Rubbayat-e-Sarmad*, pp. 5-29; *IWF*, pp. 7-8. See also Abdul Majid Daryabadi, *Maktub-at-e-Sulaimani*, Vol. I, pp. 9-10.
62. Generally it is believed that Azad visited the Middle Eastern countries twice, first in 1905 and then in 1908. After examining the issue of his foreign visits, Ghulam Rasul Mihr has come to the conclusion that Azad went to the Middle East in 1908. See Ghulam Rasul Mihr to Riazur Rehman Sherwani, 3 Jan. 1963, in *Jamia* May 1988, No. 2, Vol. 85, p. 3.
63. Parliamentary Papers, *Report on Indian Constitutional Reforms*, Vol. VIII, Command No. 9109, p. 14.
64. Francis Robinson, *Separatism among Indian Muslims*, p. 174.
65. *Ibid.*, p. 197.
66. *Ibid.*
67. Zaine N. Zeine, *The Emergence of Arab Nationalism*, p. 69.
68. G.E. Grunebaum, *Islam*, p. 188; See Syed Ahtsham Ahmad Nadwi, 'Jamalud-Afghani aur Abul Kalam Azad' in *Ajkal*, Nov., 1988, pp. 64-68.
69. *Ibid.*
70. This section relating to *al-Hilal* (1912-1914) is based on a survey of its material from the reprint in five volumes published by the Al-Hilal Academy, Lahore, (Pakistan) in 1981 and compiled by Abdur Rashid Arshad. Some of the original files of *al-Hilal* and *al-Balagh*, though brittle, are available at the library of Indian Council of Cultural Relations, New Delhi. Malik Ram also possesses the original copy of *al-Balagh* files.
71. Abdulla ul-Amadi had been associated with *al-Nadwa* and *Wakil*, and Sulaiman Nadwi with *al-Nadwa*.
72. *al-Hilal*, 14 July, 1914.
73. *Ibid.*, August 4, 1912, p. 4.
74. *Ibid.*, 9 Oct., 1912, p. 5.
75. *Ibid.*, 8 Sept., 1912.
76. *Ibid.*, 18 Aug., 1912, p. 8.
77. *Ibid.*
78. *Ibid.*, 8 Sept., 1912.
79. *Ibid.*, 10 Dec., 1912, p. 315.
80. *Ibid.*, 13 and 20 May, 1914, p. 372.
81. *Ibid.*, 19 Sept., 1912, p. 8.
82. *Ibid.*, 14-21 Sept., 1914.
83. *Ibid.*, 23 Oct., 1912.

84. *Ibid.*, 8 Sept., 1912.
85. *Ibid.*
86. *Ibid.*
87. *Ibid.*, 10 Dec., 1912
88. Douglas, *op. cit.*, pp. 110-14.
89. *Ibid.*, p. 100.
90. *al-Hilal*, 18 Jan., 1913, 15 Jan., and 22 Jan., 1913.
91. *Ibid.*, p. 111.
92. *Ibid.*, 13 July, 1912.
93. *Ibid.*, 13 July, 21 July and 28 July, 1912.
94. Douglas in his biography of Azad has pointed out some inaccuracies in Azad's articles on Rida. See Douglas, *op. cit.*, pp. 109-10.
95. *al-Hilal*, 18 Dec., 1912, p. 7.
96. *Ibid.*, pp. 5-6.
97. *al-Hilal*, 1 Aug., 1912, pp. 3-7; 18 Aug., 1912, pp. 6-7.
98. In his article on 'Maulana Azad aur Sir Sayyid Key Asrat,' Khaliq Ahmad Nizami takes the position that Sayyid and Azad were not antagonistic to each other in their outlook but were complimentary to each other; they represented two different stages in the evolution of Indian politics. The dissimilarities in these two leaders' approach to politics, education and liberty, are, however, overlooked. See *Ajkal*, Maulana's Azad Number, Nov., 1988, pp. 57-63.
99. *al-Hilal*, 18 Dec., 1912.
100. Dr. Riazur Rahman Qureshi, 'Mir-e-Karwan, Abdul Kalam Azad,' p. 62, in Khan Abdul Wadood Khan (ed.), *Tehrik-e-Azadi wa Yakjehti*, p. 5.
101. B.N. Pande, 'Trends in Muslim politics, The Role of Aligarh Deoband', 1857-1918; in '*A Centenary History of the Indian National Congress*, 1885-1985, Vol. I, B.N. Pande, (ed.), p. 306.
102. *al-Hilal*, 18 August, 1912, p. 327; July 1912.
103. *Ibid.*, 18 Dec., 1912.
104. *Ibid.*, 7 Jan., 1914.
105. *Ibid.*, 1 August, 1912.
106. *Ibid.*, 1 Sept., 1912.
107. *Ibid.*
108. *Ibid.*
109. *Ibid.*, 4 August, 1912.
110. *Ibid.*, 18 Dec., 1912.
111. *Ibid.*, 18 Dec., 1912.
112. *Ibid.*
113. Ibid., 26 Nov., 1913, 4 Feb., 1914, 14-21 July, 1914.
114. *Ibid.*, 8 July, 1914.
115. Douglas, *op. cit.*, p. 147.
116. *al-Hilal*, 1 Aug., 1912.
117. *Ibid.*
118. See for details, V.N. Datta, *Madan Lal Dhingra and the Revolutionary Movement.*
119. *al-Hilal*, 13-20 May, 1914.
120. *Ibid.*, 7-14 Jan., 1914.
121. *Ibid.*, 1 Sept., 1913.

122. Sulaiman Nadwi, *Hayat-e-Shibli*, p. 607.
123. *al-Hilal*, 30 July, 1913.
124. *al-Balagh*, 3 Nov., 1915.
125. Sulaiman Nadwi to Abdul Majid Daryabadi, 26 Jan., 1915 in *Maktubat-e-Sulaimani*, Vol. I, p. 37.
126. Douglas translates 'Faqir' as a holy man, See *op. cit.*, Glossary, p. 307. 'Faqir' is a self-abnegating individual, indifferent to things worldly.
127. Francis Robinson, *op. cit.*, p. 216.
128. Home Pol., A. Jan., 1914, No. 11.
129. *Ibid.*, B. April 1914, 70-72.
130. *al-Hilal*, 1 Oct., 1913.
131. *Ibid.*, 22 Jan., 1913, 5 Feb., 12 Feb., and 26 Feb., 1913.
132. *Ibid.*, 15 June, 25 June, 20 Aug., 17 Sept., 1913.
133. *Ibid.*, 17 June, 1914 and 18 Nov., 1914.
134. *Ibid.*, 5 Feb., 1913.
135. *Ibid.*, 13 July, 1912.
136. *Ibid.*
137. *Ibid.*, 13 July 1912, 26 July, 1913.
138. *Ibid.*, 17 Feb., 1913.
139. *Ibid.*
140. *Ibid.*, 6 Nov., 1912.
141. *Ibid.*, 5 Aug., 1914.
142. *Ibid.*, 9 Sept., 1914.
143. *Ibid.*, 13 Sept., 1914, 21 Sept., 1914.
144. *Ibid.*, p. 14, Oct., 1914.
145. *Ibid.*
146. *Ibid.*, 29 July, 1914.
147. *Ibid.*, 5 Aug., 1915.
148. *Home pol.*, A. Feb. 1915, Nos. 178-204, K.W.
149. *The Pioneer* editorial is taken from the *Home, pol.* A. Feb., 1915, Nos. 178-204, K.W.
150. *Home pol.*, A, Feb. 1915, Nos. 178-204, K.W.
151. *Home pol.*, Deposit, Sept., 1913, Feb., No. 17.
152. *Home pol.*, A, May, 455, 456, 1916.
153. *al-Hilal*, 18 Nov., 1914.
154. See Niaz Fatehpuri's views on Maulana Azad in Imdad Sabri, *Imam ul Hind Maulana Azad*, op.cit., p. 123.
155. *Home pol.*, Sept., 1913, File No. 17.
156. *Ibid.*, 1915, B., Sept., 582-85.
157. *Ibid.*, A, May, 1916, 455-56.
158. *Ibid.*, A, June, 1919, 517-25.
159. *Ibid.*, A, Feb., 1915, 178-204, K.W.
160. *al-Hilal*, 3-10, July, 1912, 7-14 Jan., 1914.
161. *Ibid.*, 14-21 July, 1914.
162. *Ibid.*, 13-20 May, 1914.
163. *Ibid.*, 29 July, 1914.
164. *Ibid.*, 30 Sept., 1914.
165. Abul Kalam Azad, *Khutbat-e-Azad*, p. 114.

166. Malik Ram, *Kutch Maulana Azad Kay Barey Main*, 1989, p. 96. See for Azad's tribute to Mahmudul Hasan, Azad, *Khutbat-e-Azad*, pp. 93-94.
167. Quoted in Douglas, *op. cit.*, p. 100
168. *al-Hilal*, 16 June, 1913.
169. *Ibid.*, 8 Sept., 1912 and 19 Oct., 1912.
170. Quoted in Manzur Ahmad, *Maulana Abul Kalam Azad*, p. 223.
171. *Paigham*, 21 October 1921 and 11 Nov., 1921.
172. For details on *al-Jamia* see Abul Salam Shahjehanpuri on *al-Jamia*, Calcutta in *Ajkal*, Maulana Azad, Number Dec., 1988, pp. 88-94.
173. *Ibid.*, See, Abu Salman Shahjahanpuri, *Makatib-e-Abdul Kalam Azad*, p. 128.
174. Ibid., See on *al-Jamia* in *Ajkal, op.cit.*
175. *al-Hilal*, 17 July, 1927.
176. *Ibid.*, 8 July, 1927.
177. *Ibid.*
178. *Ibid.*
179. *Ibid.*, 16 Sept., 1927.
180. *Ibid.*, 28 July, 1927.
181. *Ibid.*, 24 June and 8 July, 1927.
182. *Ibid.*, 9 December, 1927.

# 3

# RANCHI DAYS : *TAZKIRA*

Azad's first experience of his three and a half years of internment at Moorabadi, a village outside Ranchi, forced him to live on his own in solitude. With his introspective nature, he found in this a good opportunity to involve himself in his literary pursuits and make full use of his creative faculties. He took upon his cherished dream of *Tarjuman al-Quran*. He also wrote *Sirat Imam Hanbal*, lives of *Shah Waliullah* and *Shaykh Mujaddid alf-i-Thani*, *Ibn Taimiya* and *Sirat-e-Ashiab*.[1] He would also address his coreligionists in the local Jama Masjid and expound the teachings of Islam. He built a mosque, a madrassa and set up the Anjuman-e-Islamia for the propagation of Islam. When Sulaiman Nadwi visited Ranchi in 1918 he was greatly impressed by Azad's devotion to Islam and the unique service he was rendering for its advancement. He goes to the extent of saying that Azad's earnest endeavours succeeded in giving a new impetus to recovery of faith in Islam among people at Ranchi.[2] Abdul Majid Daryabadi also testified in his letter of 1 April, 1919 that a great revolution had taken place in Azad and he had greatly reformed himself by 1918.[3]

By 1916 when he was about twenty-eight Azad had become a prominent public figure in the literary and political circles of the country. The banning of his weeklies and his internment had aroused widespread sympathy for him among people. M.K. Gandhi had come to see him at Ranchi but was not permitted to do so by the Government. People were naturally curious to know about Azad, the former editor of *al-Hilal* and *al-Balagh* who was now interned at Ranchi. Cut off from the outside world Azad found during this period much time to read, write, think and meditate.

Azad's friend, Fazluddin Ahmad Khan suggested to him the idea of writing his autobiography. Azad had known Fazluddin since 1902. Fazluddin was educated in Japan and he later settled in Calcutta. He had acted as the Manager in *al-Hilal* and *al-Balagh*.[4] Being of a shy and reserved nature Azad was not inclined to write his autobiography which seemed to him a 'ridiculous venture.' But Fazluddin's persuasion worked on him and he started writing his autobiography known as *Tazkira* in June and completed it by 17 October 1916, within a short period of five months. The text of the book came to 317 printed pages and was published from *al-Balagh* Press, Calcutta in the middle of September, 1919.[5] The first part of the Ms. of *Tazkira* contained an account of Azad's ancestor Shaikh Jamaluddin which formed its first chapter. Azad dealt with the life of Jamaluddin's son, Shaikh Mohammad and with Azad's father's maternal grandfather, Maulana Munawwaruddin in the second and third chapters. However, manuscripts of the second and third chapters were lost and could never be recovered. So the first chapter along with a twenty page brief account of Azad's early life was published as *Tazkira*.[6]

One difficulty that Azad experienced while writing *Tazkira* was with regard to his procuring books for his study. He had no library facilities available to him nor could he use his family records which were stored in Calcutta. He had to depend largely on his phenomenal memory, although at a later stage he did manage to obtain *Nuskah-e-Mushif, Tazkirat-ul-Wasliin, Akhbar-ul-Akhyar, Tabqat-e-Akbari* and *Muntkhib-ul-Twarikh*.[7] He was also getting some journals like *Maarif* regularly and had with him a few other books.[8]

The arrangement between Azad and Fazluddin for the writing of *Tazkira* was that Azad would write ten to twelve pages every day and give them to Fazluddin. Then he would engage himself in some other scholarly work. Next day Azad would start writing again while keeping a mental note of what he had written previously or what he had put on a piece of paper for his recollections. On certain themes in the text he would write by way of clarification footnotes running into twenty and thirty pages making the material clumsy for the reader. Fazluddin took the liberty of reducing these footnotes. When Azad had written about 500 pages, Fazluddin found to his discomfiture that the account contained hardly anything about Azad's own life. He posed fifteen questions to Azad and asking him to answer them, but Azad refused to be so bridled. Eventually he dismissed the account of his entire early life in just twenty pages.

Fazluddin went ahead with the publication of *Tazkira*. Azad learnt of its publication from a press note that appeared in newspapers. About 204 pages of the text had already been printed. Azad wanted to withdraw the book but it was too late. When the book appeared Azad was unhappy about it, which is evident from his later reactions. Azad wrote : "Everything connected with *Tazkira* has caused me pain."[9] He wanted to have at least a second look at the manuscript but Fazluddin knew what the 'second look' would mean. Azad's notion of scholarship was high and he never wanted it to fall below classical standards.

What material did Azad include in *Tazkira* ? An autobiography is a document of personal experience of an individual. However, Azad says little about himself in *Tazkira* except in the last twenty pages. Azad wrote in *Tazkira* about his ancestors and some famous religious leaders. Ostensibly Azad presents character-sketches of some of the leading religious thinkers and leaders of India and abroad. There is an underlying message in Azad's intellectual exercise. At the end of *Tazkira*, Azad wrote : "These pages are the reflections of my disturbing and scattered thoughts."[10] Let us see how Azad goes about his work and what matters he actually covered there.

As an autobiographer Azad started writing on his family lineage in *Tazkira*. In his account he gave prime importance to Shaikh Jamaluddin, his ancestor on the parental side. Jamaluddin was a profound scholar, religious divine and distinguished authority on *Hadith*. Azad pays an eloquent tribute to him for his integrity of character and high sense of honour. He described Jamaluddin as a self-abnegating individual devoid of any trace of ambition and worldly possessions.[11] He would not even care to build a house for himself. He said, "I fear to build a house for myself because that would make my heart a desert."[12] Before closing his *Tazkira* with a brief account of his early life, Azad returns to his ancestor Jamaluddin. Abd-ul-Qadir Al Badauni's appreciation of Jamaluddin in *Muntakhab-ul-Twarikh* aroused Azad's enthusiam. Badauni had written :

> He (Jamaluddin) is very learned in the traditional saying of the prophet. Having associated with men who are devoted to the life of poverty and self-effacement he has now for some time past recognised the delights of such a life and grace of God helping him, has set himself to follow it for good, and has no longer any dealings with the worldly, but is busied in teaching and instructing his pupils.[13]

Azad also reproduces an extract about Jamaluddin from Abdul Haq 'Muhadith' Dihlawi (1551-1642) who praised Jamaluddin's erudition, religious fervour and uprightness.[14]

Azad tells us that Jamaluddin had the courage to defy Emperor Akbar when he refused to sign the Infallibility decree which had assigned to the latter the prerogative of an absolute *Mujtahid.* While many others lurched and stumbled to win favours with the royal authority, Jamaluddin remained firm in his convictions and refused to flinch from his principles. Jamaluddin expressed great admiration for Sayyid Mohammad of Jaunpur who had claimed to be a Mahdi. This had caused great resentment among the Muslim orthodoxy. Sayyid Mohammad had a large following and found an ardent adherent in Sultan Mahmud (1458-1511). Jamaluddin refused to accept Sayyid Muhammad as a Mahdi but held him in high esteem for his religious fervour and saintliness.

Azad says that whatever might have been the specific reasons, whether it was Jamaluddin's refusal to sign the Infallibility decree or his admiration for Sayyid Muhammad, Jamaluddin began to be distrusted by the ruling authority. This changed things for Jamaluddin and he found the atmosphere quite rough for him. As a man of independent character he left the country in disgust and settled in Mecca for about thirteen years until his disciple Aziz Koka, Akbar's foster-brother, persuaded him to return to India where he began to devote himself entirely to the pursuit of learning and teaching the young.[15]

Azad makes interesting observations on both the issues, the status of the Mughal emperor and the claims to the Mahdi status of Sayyid Muhammad Jaunpuri. Azad thinks that Akbar's decree was perfectly in order. He had power to back the authority of the Ulama. The misfortune, however, was that Akbar abused this power because of his ignorance of Islamic doctrines. Azad wrote :

> In fact, the Khalifa of the time, those vested with authority as well as the members of Council had the right of *lijtihad* in every age and its denial has been the cause of all the disasters in Muslim history.

Azad justifies Sayyid Muhammad's claim to be a Mahdi on the ground that the degrading conditions in which the country was placed provided sufficient validity for it but he makes it clear at the same time that his claim to be *Mahdi-e-akhir al zaman* (the final arbiter till the end) had no justification.[17]

The readers of *Tazkira* would have expected that while dealing with Jamaluddin, Azad would also write on his other ancestors such as Shaikh Muhammad Mohsin and Shaikh Muhammad Afzal but he did not do so. Instead he presented a character-sketch of Sayyid Muhammad Jaunpuri highlighting his profound religious nature and nobility of character. He quotes Shaikh Abul Haq who wrote about Sayyid Muhammad : "He was a true *alim* and close to God."[18]

Thereafter Azad gives moving accounts of Shaikh Abdulah Niyazi and Shaikh Alai who were suspected of entertaining Mahdvi beliefs.[19] Sticking to his convictions, Shaikh Alai had refused to bow to the royal authority of Islam Shah of Gujarat (1545-1554) wrongly written in historial works as Salim Shah. Mukhdum al Malk Mullah Abdulah of Sultanpur Shaikh-e-Islam (the principal *alim* of the State) advised Islam Shah to inflict the severest punishment on Alai and he was whipped, tortured and executed and his body was trampled under the feet of an elephant. Similarly Azad describes the tortures inflicted on Niyazi by the ruling authority. After reading the accounts on Alai and Nayazi which cover more than a hundred pages the reader realizes that Azad's purpose in writing *Tazkira* was very different from what Fazluddin had originally envisaged.

The Ulama as a social and religious force have always occupied a pivotal position in Muslim society. But Azad shows extraordinary courage when he tells us how the time-serving Ulama, being subservient to the ruling authority and swayed by their innate prejudices against anything new, have generally subjected men of piety and profoundly religious nature to grave injustice and torture and have been instrumental in their executions. He cites many instances in the pages of *Tazkira* to show how the narrow-minded, selfish and power-drunk Ulama, in the total disregard of the injunctions of Islam, have wrought misfortune on men of truly religious nature. He has called the time-serving Ulama *sagan-e-dunya*, (dog of the world) who in the name of religion have sacrificed truth and perpetuated ignorance and fanaticism.[20] Azad firmly believes that such men do great harm to humanity. They pride themselves on being custodians of religion and repositories of wisdom but in reality they are narrow-minded and short-sighted hypocrites who twist the injunctions to serve their own purpose or adopt devious means to dodge or evade the highly important spiritual issues confronting them in their own time. They think it politic to say "times are out of joint. Let us wait." The besetting sins of the Ulama, according to Azad, are intellectual arrogance and excessive presumption.[21] Azad is firmly convinced that, unless accompanied by charity, religion becomes a scourge to mankind.

Azad's mind was seething with ideas while he was writing *Tazkira*. His pen flowed incessantly and he did not know how to stop. Things crowded in his mind. Surveying the pages of Islamic history he tells us how Ibn Hanbal (780-855) and Ibn Taimiya (1262-1328), a distinguished Syrian theologian, bore with equanimity the oppression and calumnies inflicted on them by their adversaries.[22] Azad also cites the example of Shaikh Ahmad Sirhindi, a man of profound religious faith, who had aroused the wrath of Emperor Jahangir who put him into prison at Gwalior.

The one person to whom Azad returns time and again in *Tazkira* is Ibn Taimiya for whom he expresses great regard and reverence. Azad does not discuss his doctrines but he gives the reader some idea of his positive, powerful and unique personality.[23] Azad portrays him as a perfect man, a true *mumin*, great in word and deed and unrivalled in spiritual strength and religious knowledge.[24] Azad thinks that the most apt expression that could describe him was *An-e-dared* meaning that he possesses the royal splendour. People were so dazzled by the force of his personality that they dared not face him.[25] Azad was deeply moved by his personality. He lamented that people in India knew so little of him. He pleads that Indians should emulate his example for solving their manifold problems.

Azad does not stop at the contributions of these fearless and bold men of profound religious faith who faced untold suffering in their own times. He tries to trace the source of their indomitable strength. Whence did this power of fighting injustice and living for truth come? What is it that made them so bold and strong and impelled them to stand up against the ruling powers and remain steadfast in their convictions? Azad emphasises that it is Islam that gives them moral and spiritual power to fight for truth and justice. This is not a new formulation that Azad has offered only in *Tazkira*. He had said the same thing repeatedly in *al-Hilal* and *al-Balagh*. Azad wrote in *Tazkira* : "It is God and the book (the Quran) that really matter."[26] It is a pity, Azad argues, that the U'ama did not understand and interpret the true spirit of the book but by their misinterpretations misled people into forming wrong notions about Islam.

Azad gives a moving account of the life of the prophet. He does not discuss his teachings or his arduous struggles against his adversaries. He is interested in writing the biography of the Prophet. He raised certain lively questions which are exciting for any biographer of Muhammad. The questions he wanted to answer in the Prophet's biography were : Who brought up the Prophet ? What period did he live in ? Who were his friends and foes ? What was the state of his people ? What did he do with the world and what did the world do to him ? What was the nature of his external and domestic life ? How did he spend his days and nights? What did he talk about in ordinary conversation ? How did he live? What were the major events that occurred in his life and in what state did he leave his people behind ?[27] Azad treats the Prophet as a most fascinating personality who loved his people. Azad repeats the suggestion he had earlier made to Shibli that it would be a highly rewarding experience for a biographer of the Prophet to write his life from the Quran.[28] He expressed the view that Quran is Divine knowledge and the Prophet its expression in action.[29]

There are brilliant passages in *Tazkira* on the system of education in Egypt. He also takes up the issue of the old and new knowledge.[30] He thinks that there is no antagonism between Islam and new knowledge. According to him, the advance of scientific knowledge in no way affects the fundamentals of Islam which offer to mankind a philosophy of life nor does the Islamic way of life hamper in any way the advancement of scientific knowledge. However, he assails the obsession of the Western-educated class with the materialistic view of life on account of which it tends to neglect the fountain of spiritual inheritance.

Azad raises the conflict between the time-serving Ulama and the religiously dedicated individuals to the level of a perpetual struggle waged between the forces of good and evil which operate inexorably in human affairs. Like George Bernard Shaw he believed that it is dangerous to be too good but he was firmly convinced that ultimately truth triumphs. For resolving the conflict between the rigid theologians and religious leaders, Azad quotes Ibn Taimiya's views :

> The right path is to seek truth tempered by justice. In fact they are identical. It is necessary to balance them. One is to follow the *Quran* and *Sharia* and the other is to love and and rever the profoundly religious men who have forsaken everything for love of God. When a balance is not struck between these two views, then misfortune follows which has led to strife. While one group believes that the slightest deviations from the prescribed religious practices which a religious man makes should be enough to condemn as an apostate, the other group thinks that reverence to the religious leaders should mean the subordination of religious injunctions to their dictates.[31]

Both these attitudes, Azad regards as extravagant hocus-pocus by which people have been easily duped. Azad has also attacked in *Tazkira* the Israelite view of Islam which is juristic to the neglect of ideal life which Quran has recommended.

The message of *Tazkira* is that Quran is the real panacea for the ills of society. According to Azad, Quran insists on the purity of conduct and it is the word of God and the example of Prophet which show the way to it.[32] The road to self-perfection lies through love of God and man. Love is the glory of earth which forms a theme of the concluding part of *Tazkira*.[33] Azad wrote that "his despondency in love led to the understanding of Reality."[34] It is the divine part of love, a priceless possession, namely, reverence, beliefs and trust, which works for true happiness of man. On the subject of love Azad has given us some verses which sharpen our appreciation of his broad humanity.

*Qisa-e-Sikander o Dara na khanda aim*
*Az ma Bajuz hikayat-e-mehr-o-wafa, mapurs*

We have not learnt the story of Alexander or Darius
Do not ask us anything but the story of love.

*Har gaz namirad ankey dilish zinda shud baishq*
*Sabt ast bar jarida-e-alam dwam-e-ma*

Nobody dies whose heart is illumined with love.
This truth is inscribed on the tablet of the world for all time to come.

It would be clear from the foregoing account that *Tazkira* is the *al-Hilal* and *al-Balagh* stripped of their political character. *Tazkira* is a prelude to the *Tarjuman al-Quran*, Azad's masterpiece. It is also close to the spirit of his composition on 'Sarmad' in which he had drawn the profile of a truly self-abnegating man who was a lover of God and man and courageous enough to bear his suffering with supreme indifference. It is an epitome of the spirit of Islam as reflected in the lives of some of the profoundly religious men who have suffered for the defence of truth. It takes us into many bypaths of Islamic history that throw light on the capricious vicissitudes of fortune. The most outstanding feature of the entire work is its vitality. *Tazkira* also contains a veiled criticism of the past, particularly the hypocrisy and humbug we often find there.

In fact *Tazkira* is an expression of the anguish of a man's search for reality. It is the outpouring of a soul that scorned narrow dogma. It is the saga of a heroic spirit which is neither baffled by adversity, nor defeated by irreversible fate and accepts any situation in the firm conviction of righteousness of the cause to which it has dedicated itself. *Tazkira* cannot be regarded as an autobiography in the conventional sense of the term since it tells us very little of Azad's life. It is an experiment in introspection, a quest for self-discovery and a search for the meaning of life. Azad is distressed inwardly but outwardly he shows philosophical repose. Mujeeb has some interesting comments to make on *Tazkira* :

> The *Tadkirah* can be read as an essay in modern religious thought. But it is much more than a book, it is a symbol, it is a personality. It is fire and passion, great sorrow of a great heart, the funeral music of a tragedy and a jubilant song of victory. It is an autobiography that becomes an ideal, an idea that transformed itself into flesh and blood.[35]

Azad saw around him social and cultural decay and a threat of worse to come. In *Tazkira* he is concerned with a society that has vanished from our minds. His own inner struggles and tensions pervade the entire work. He regards himself as an heir to the rich religious and cultural tradition of Islam which he considers to be a true guide for his moral and intellectual development. He makes a strong plea in the work for the regeneration of man and society through suffering and self-abnegation and complete surrender to the true spirit of Islam as embodied in *Quran* and the example of the Prophet.

The *Tazkira* is not meant for the general reader but for the learned who are steeped in Islam and Islamic history. This work reflects Azad's wide range of Islamic scholarship which is embodied in the very idiom of his thought and is backed by a massive force of character. The plenitude of Azad's erudition seems at times to burst the receptacle in which he has poured out his material. Some of the passages in *Tazkira*, heavily loaded with Arabic constructions and enriched with Arabic and Persian verses, are really strenuous reading. The question of anyone trying to emulate *Tazkira* does not arise at all. It is like a fiery wine that gets into the head and leads to uneasiness. Some parts of *Tazkira* point to a strain of quasi-metaphysical imagination and reveal a melancholy which at times stirs deepest thoughts.

The *Tazkira* might appear a disjointed work, somewhat fragmented and incomplete but underlying it there is a unity of theme and purpose which must not be lost sight of. Behind the character-sketches of religious leaders there persists a message of Divine knowledge. The *Tazkira* is a foretaste of the *Tarjuman* which followed. It shows the state of crisis Azad was in at that particular point of time. He was assailed by doubts about his future course of action. He did not know what to do. He was torn by the conflicts between the scholarly pursuits and political responsibility – the predicament of an intellectual who finds himself drawn into politics. In the midst of his scholarly pursuits, Islam remained at the centre of his attention. He was so much overwhelmed by religion that his political perspective got somewhat blurred.

At this stage of his life Azad was solitary in Nietzche's sense of the word, a self-poised mind, stern-eyed, standing entirely on his own strength. At the end of *Tazkira*, Azad wrote : "The caravan of my hopes is seeing now the signs of a new goal."[36] In an intuitive flash Azad saw his future destiny!

## REFERENCES

1. Dr. Safia Muzzamil, *Abul Kalam Azad, Islam and Humanity*, p. 53.
2. Sulaiman Nadwi, *Maktubat-e-Sulaimani*, pp. 9, 13, 33.
3. Ghulam Rasool Mihr, *Tabarrakat-e-Azad*, p. 98.
4. Malik Ram, *Kuch Abul Kalam Azad Kay Barey Main*, pp. 3, 363.
5. *Tazkira* (1981), Fazluddin's Introduction, p. 18.
6. *Ibid.*, pp. 308-09.
7. *Ibid.*, p. 337; See Ghulam Rasool Mihr, 'Maulana Abul Kalam Azad' Aug., 1958, p.75; See *Tazkira*, Malik Ram's *Foreward*, pp. 9-10.
8. *Tazkira*, pp. 243, 246.
9. *Ibid.*, p. 14.
10. *Ibid.*, p. 337.
11. *Ibid.*, pp. 31-42.
12. *Ibid.*, pp. 11 and 37.
13. Al-Badauni, *Muntakhab-ul-Twarikh*, Vol. III, p. 167; *Tazkira*, p. 302.
14. *Tazkira*, p. 303.
15. *Ibid.*, p. 37.
16. *Ibid.*, p. 41.
17. *Ibid.*, p. 40.
18. *Ibid.*, p. 61.

19. *Ibid.*, pp. 60, 63-83.
20. *Ibid.*, pp. 149 & 256.
21. *Ibid.*, p. 73.
22. *Ibid.*, pp. 141-149.
23. *Ibid.*, pp. 159 & 174.
24. *Ibid.*, p. 246.
25. *Ibid.*, pp. 142, 162-64 & 170.
26. *Ibid.*, p. 57.
27. *Ibid.*, p. 201.
28. *Ibid.*, pp. 205-06.
29. *Ibid.*
30. *Ibid.*, pp. 235-37.
31. *Ibid.*, p. 55.
32. *Ibid.*, p. 28.
33. *Ibid.*, pp. 318-28.
34. *Ibid.*, p. 323.
35. M. Mujeeb, 'The Tadkirah, a Biography in Symbols', p. 134; in *Maulana Abul Kalam Azad*, Humayun Kabir (ed.), *op.cit.*
36. *Tazkira*, p. 335.

# 4

# INTO POLITICS

What was Azad's politics? Why was he impelled to join it? What are the factors that made him do so? When did Azad start taking active interest in politics? These are some of the questions we have to answer in order to understand his role in Indian politics. During the Swadeshi movement (1905-1908) that started against Lord Curzon's Partition of Bengal, Azad came in close touch with a staunch extremist Shyamsunder Chakrabarti and met other revolutionaries including the firebrand Aurobindo Ghose.[1] Chakrabarti was involved in organising railway strikes and was also connected with the famous daily *Bande Mataram* and *Bande Matram Bhikshu Samproday*, a fund-raising agency, for supporting subversive activities.[2]

The early revolutionaries tended to be 'aggressively Hindu' and entertained strong suspicions about the Muslims. The Muslim participation in the revolutionary activity was limited. Azad claims to have joined the revolutionaries.[3] He tried to dispel from the mind of the revolutionaries the general notion that the Muslims were opposed to the Swadeshi Movement.[4] Azad induced some of his Muslim associates to join the revolutionary movement and he succeeded in setting up secret societies in a few towns in Northern India.

On the basis of Intelligence Reports it has been shown that Azad was involved in subversive activities during the First World War.[5] The Intelligence Reports are often tendentious and grossly exaggerated. But it is true that Azad knew Sufi Amba Prasad and Ajit Singh, the revolutionaries and his association with them has been frowned upon by the British. During the war Azad had carried on a pan-Islamist and anti-British propaganda through *al-Hilal* and *al-Balagh*. He had championed the cause of the liberation of the country and even recommended *Jihad* for this purpose. Earlier he had been highly critical of Muslim league's policy of subservience to the British. Now as a member of the League he thought that even the League Resolution of 1914 favouring a 'suitable form of self-government' was rather mild. As noted already, Azad was involved in the Silk Letter Conspiracy.

According to Intelligence Reports, Azad turned the minds of many young students to revolutionary activity.[6] One report records that the 'fanatical school boys had been maddened by the subtle incitements of learned, eloquent but hypocritical priest Abul Kalam Azad.' These students were going to Turkey for training to wage *Jihad* against the British.[7] Azad was closely in touch with Obeidullah who had escaped to Afghanistan in 1915. He was engaged in doing spadework in India for intensifying revolutionary activity.[8] Obeidullah who was a Minister in the Provincial Government of India set up in Kabul was sending letters to Azad. In Intelligence Reports Azad is dubbed as an 'extremist' and 'a dangerous man.'[9] He was also consulted by Maulana Mahmudul Hasan on the desirability of going to the Middle Eastern countries.[10] Azad gave financial support to some of the conspirators because of the influence he wielded over the Muslim community in Calcutta.[11] He was expected to reach Kabul to assist Obeidullah in revolutionary activities.

It is evident from the Intelligence Reports that Azad was externed from Bengal not because of any incriminating article published in *al-Balagh* which was strictly a religious paper, but for his involvement in the Silk Conspiracy case and his close association with some of its leaders, and the Government of India considered his political activity dangerous. He was permitted to stay in Ranchi on the condition that he would stop all political activities, provide guarantees for his behaviour and give identity of his visitors and not leave Ranchi in any case until further orders.[12]

The terms 'moderate' and 'extremist' so often used to denote a particular type of political ideology are relative and their meaning can be understood only in the context of the times when they are used. Azad's political activity cannot be termed as 'Moderate' in the pre-1920 period. It is difficult to say what would have been Azad's politics had he not been arrested in 1916. Would he in that case have joined the Congress or actively worked for the Muslim League? These are hypothetical questions. But this much is certain that the politics of moderation whether of the Congress or the League variety could do longer appeal to him. Up to 1916 he was not sure of his political commitment, though his antipathy to the British rule was quite evident. However, when we come to 1920 we find that there is no confusion in his mind any longer. He saw his way clearly now. He had not become by then a professional politician. He had not met Mahatma Gandhi until January 18, 1920, although his father had remained in touch with him and Azad had received Gandhi's condolence telegram on his father's death. Azad's father had supported Gandhi when he was fighting against racial discrimination in South Africa. Gandhi wanted to see Azad at Ranchi but the Government disallowed him.

When Azad was released on 27 December, 1919, he found a new world and a new age in India. The country had been plunged into political turmoil in 1919 and it was politically astir as never before. During the period of his enforced seclusion and absence from the political scene the country had to witness the anti-Rowlatt Agitation, Satyagraha movement, Jallianwala Bagh massacre, Martial Law and its atrocities. A new spirit had been awakened in the country.[13] The 'Moderates' had lost their force and they looked like officers without troops. The year 1919 witnessed scenes of Hindu-Muslim unity when Hindus and Muslims drank water from the same glass. This manifestation of Hindu-Muslim unity disturbed the ruling authorities and they took it as a serious challenge to their existence. The confrontation between the people and Government during the agitations resulted in open clashes. Then came the tragic episode of the Jallianwala Bagh which marked a turning point in the political history of India. The Martial Law atrocities created terror among the people and they felt humiliated and outraged by high-handed acts like the Crawling Order and compulsory roll call of respectable lawyers at police stations.

People had gradually been driven to the point of exasperation and anger by the Government. Rabindranath Tagore renounced his knighthood in protest against the Jallianwala Bagh massacre. Gandhi returned his Kaiser-i-Hind Gold Medal and his Zulu War Medal. People were in a sullent and defiant mood. Muslim politics too ceased to be quiescent. Gandhi now emerged as a national leader. In his *Autobiography*, Jawaharlal Nehru called the 1919 Amritsar Congress as the first 'Gandhi Congress'.[14] When the Ali brothers appeared at the Amritsar Congress session they were received with a thunderous applause and became the 'darlings of the people.'

As noted earlier a major cause of unrest among the Muslims in India at this time was the humiliating treatment meted out to Turkey, the last great Islamic power. This enraged the Indian Muslims. The threatened dismemberment of the Turkish Empire, Greece claiming the whole of Thrace and Italy landing her forces in the gulf of Adalia, created serious apprehensions in the Muslim mind about the future of their holy places. The Muslims feared that the Sultan of Turkey would be deprived of the authority necessary for the discharge of duties going with his office as Caliph of spiritual head of Islam. Ever since Turkey had entered the war, the Muslims in India expressed their sympathy with that country and were preaching that the first duty of Muslims was allegiance to the Caliph. Turkey capitulated on 31 October, 1918. The Greeks demanded the coastal strip including Smyrna and the Arabs revolted against their sovereign and Caliph. The Indian Muslims led by Dr. M.A. Ansari demanded that all armed forces be withdrawn from the holy places, the Hijaz, Damascus, Baghdad, Najaf and Kerbela.

Azad had for long been deeply concerned about Turkey and her degraded position. Because of his pro-Turkish leanings his paper *al-Hilal* had been banned. When he came out of his internment he found that Turkey had been further humiliated. He also realized that the British Government had caused estrangement among his countrymen by inflicting on them wanton acts of cruelty. There could be no question for Azad of supporting the Government. Nor could 'Moderation' appeal to him. He felt attracted to the Khilafat movement and he plunged into it. How he could he keep away from it when the support for the Khilafat was matter for safeguarding the *Sharia*? And who else but Azad, an outstanding authority on the Quran, could be more capable of understanding the religious and political aspects of the problem!

Before 1920 Azad had defined the collective identity of the Muslim community in terms of Islam. But so far his had been an individual stand. Now with the emergence of Khilafat Movement he received institutional support for his own thinking. The die was cast and there was no turning back! It was during the Non-cooperation movement that he began to think of Hindus and Muslims forming 'Ummat-I-Wahidaa' (one nation). Thereafter he became a grand agitator and an ardent spokesman of the nationalist cause.[15]

Azad wrote that it was not he who sought politics but that politics sought him. He was swept off his feet by the tide of politics. It is necessary to understand Azad's role in the Khilafat agitation because this laid the foundations for his future development as a great political leader. The Khilafat issue agitated all strata of the Muslim community. Judith Brown who has made an intensive study of the political developments in India, 1915-1922, has divided the Khilafat movement into three distinct phases, the first phase lasting until 1919, the second from the release of the Ali brothers and Azad at the end of December up to early May 1919, and the third from mid-May to August, 1920 when the Khilafat was joined with the agitation of the Punjab into a single movement of Non-cooperation.[16] Initially Khilafat Committee was set up on 19 March 1919 at Bombay with Mian Mahammad Chotani, a rich timber merchant as its President. It was he who paid the travel expenses of the Khilafat delegation to England and extended a major part of the financial support for the agitation in Upper India. The All India Khilafat Conference took place at Lucknow on 21 September, 1919. The Khilafat Day was observed on 17 October to focus public attention on the Khilafat. Until November 1919 the Bombay Khilafat Committee controlled the entire campaign and on 23 November it changed its name to Central Khilafat Committee of India. According to Richard Gordon, a Cambridge historian, 'North India became the power house of the movement but Bombay was still the treasury.'[17]

From the very beginning Gandhi had expressed his sympathy for the Khilafat. At the Khilafat meeting on 23 November 1919 in Delhi he had mildly warned the Government that if the Muslim demands were not met he would launch a Non-cooperation movement. A subcommittee was formed to examine the whole question of Non-cooperation movement. The Bombay men did not wish to take any extreme measures and it was only when the Ali brothers and Azad came out of prison that the Khilafat movement in India got into full swing. Gandhi guided the deliberations of the Khilafat Conference presided over by Shaukat Ali at Amritsar in December, 1919. The conference decided to send a delegation to the Viceroy for presenting their case regarding the Khilafat and holy places and to obtain permission to go to England and America for projecting their viewpoint in those countries.

These developments confronted Azad when he was released. After his release from Ranchi he arrived in Calcutta on 13 January 1920. His followers gave him a big welcome. Profusely garlanded he was taken to Nakhuda mosque where he addressed the gathering on the Khilafat issue. The address was characterised by Azad's usual candour and force, although it lacked the Ali brothers' flamboyance of style and their fiery passion. He pointed out how in the pages of *al-Hilal* he had suggested a programme of paralysing the Government by refusing to pay taxes and boycotting institutions supported by the Government. This was a programme similar to the one Tolstoy had outlined in his writings. He urged the Ulama to give strength to the movement by their open participation. Their active involvement in this holy struggle, he felt, was of crucial importance for its success.

What concrete form of action did Azad propose for himself for the advancement of this movement which stirred him so deeply? He went to Delhi and attended the Khilafat Conference on 18 January, 1920. He met Gandhi there for the first time. Tilak and other Congress leaders were also present. Azad signed the deputationists ' petition which was to be presented to Lord Chemlsford, the Viceroy but he did not accompany the deputation to the Victory because he believed the matter had gone beyond memorandum and deputations. In their petition the deputation wanted recognition of the sovereignty of the Caliph and assurance of immunity of the holy places from war. They also asked for permission to go to England and Europe to present the Muslim viewpoint concerning Khilafat before the British Government and the Paris Peace Conference. Lord Chelmsford gave his permission to the deputation to go to England for the purpose mentioned in the petition and promised to provide facilities for their journey. Beyond this he declined to do anything.[18] He told the deputation that Khilafat was their own affair but he doubted whether the Allied powers would preserve the sovereignty and dominion of Turkey as it was before the war. He promised to write to the secretary of State to take into account the Muslim feelings in India. Muhammad Ali accompanied by Syed Hussain Ali, Sayyid Sulaiman Nadvi and Hasan Muhammad Hayat left India on 1 February 1920 to represent the Muslim viewpoint on the Khilafat to the Imperial Government.

In early 1920 the Khilafat agitation gained momentum. The Khilafat leaders, Muhammad Ali, Shaukat Ali, Abdul Bari and Azad toured the country, addressed meetings, raised funds and stressed the importance of Hindu support in fighting their cause.[19] Gandhi too was supporting the Khilafat movement. The third Khilafat Conference met in Bombay on 15-17 February, 1920. It produced two documents, the Khilafat Manifesto and the Constitution of All India Khilafat Committee. The conference laid down the Muslim demands and warned that dire consequences would follow if the Government did not leave the Ottoman Empire as it was before the war. But the conference did not suggest any specific action in case the Manifesto was ignored. A few days later when the Bengal Khilafat Conference was held on 28-29 February under the Presidentship of Azad, the atmosphere was surcharged with great excitement.[20] People were asking not for pious resolutions but a definite line of action to produce results. No poultice or palliatives. The meeting was preceded by a large procession led by Shaukat Ali, Abdul Bari and Azad and it passed through streets decorated with festoons and banners. Abdul Bari delivered a fiery speech which was almost a declaration of a *Jihad*. What he said at the meeting can be judged from the following report :

> They could sacrifice every Christian's life and property; they could burn them and even if they stole their property he would give them a *fatwa* in justification. He declared that had cannon and guns been at his disposal he would have declared war and would have burnt the Christians after saturating them with kerosine oil . . .[21]

This hard-hitting speech justifying the use of violent means for the realization of their object gives us an idea of the mood and temper in which the Khilafat was being conducted. Religion was being used to advance political ends. Bari was carried away by the torrent of emotion and had he not been restrained, he would have said much more. Curiously enough, Gandhi, the apostle of non-violence, was present and saw Abdul Bari's fury but did not consider it fit to make any adverse comments on the irrational stand taken by Bari.

Azad's Presidential Address at the conference was distinguished for its scholarship and mastery of historical literature on the institution of Khilafat. He quoted from the Quran and *Hadith* at length to support his thesis.[22] His performance was most impressive both in respect of the extent of knowledge he displayed and the grasp of the subject and its exposition. He traced the genesis and evolution of the Khilafat and explained the objectives behind this institution which included organising the Muslim community, administering justice and spreading God's message to the world. Azad stressed the temporal nature of the Khilafat without which he thought it was not possible to propagate the message of Islam. He regarded Khilafat as a symbol, with which to inspire Indian Muslims and rally them into an 'anti-British constituency.'

Azad built up the thesis that the Caliph was the spiritual head of the Muslim community to whom they must owe allegiance. Anyone who refused to do so had to be expelled from the community and the one who rebelled against his authority must be condemned. He further pointed out that in view of the Quranic principles there was no reason for Sunnis and Shias to disagree on this point. It was, he said, the Muslim's moral duty to defend the institution of the Caliph as it was a unifying force without which they would lose their sense of identity and cohesion. He urged the Muslims to defend the Khilafat by means of *Jihad*. According to Azad, *Jihad* meant not force but a struggle which could be undertaken not by violence but by peaceful means like delivering speeches and writing articles in order to mobilize strong public opinion. This struggle was absolutely necessary for preserving the Khilafat which was being threatened by the hateful European policy of capturing the holy places.

Azad regarded it a moral duty on the part of Muslims to defend the Khilafat and to save the holy places from falling into the hands of non-Muslims. He drew a distinction between non-Muslims like the British who were determined to destroy their religion and other non-Muslims like the Hindus who espoused the Turkish cause. Azad pleaded that in such circumstances Hindus ought to be treated as friends and the British as enemies.

While laying before the Muslims the programme for action, Azad thought that unity was the first condition without which Muslims would be like 'an unruly mob in a bazaar which could easily be dispersed.' On the other hand, with unity the Muslims could stand like a 'rock to face any eventuality.' He added that "with unity the Muslims would be like orderly rows of worshippers in the mosque on Friday, with hearts raised in one accord in prayer." About the present state of Muslims in the country, in his usual poetical vein he said that the Muslims "are now like drops of water, and not an ocean, pebbles not a mountain, links not a chain." He exhorted the Muslims to choose a learned and pious Muslim as their Imam, and act under his guidance.

Azad was deeply interested in the appointment of an Imam whom he considered absolutely necessary for the consolidation of Muslim community. He had ambition to be elevated to this position and to rally support for his candidature despatched Abdur Razzaq Malihabadi as his agent to Punjab, Sind and Bengal.[23] Maulana Mahmudul Hasan of Deoband had been sounded for this nomination but he declined. Instead he suggested Azad's name.[24] Mahmudul Hasan died in 1920 leaving the question open. Maulana Abdul Bari of Firangi Mahel, the first President of Jamiatul-Ulama-e-Hind in December, 1919 gave an evasive reply on Azad's candidature saying "I have no alternative but shall follow on this question the opinion of the public."[25] He said that he would accept Azad as Imam only if his candidature did not create any schism in the Muslim community. The Deoband Ulama opposed Azad's nomination on the ground that though he was an *alam* he did not strictly live the life of a devout Muslim to justify his appointment as Imam.[26] Realizing that there was opposition to his candidature, Azad withdrew from the scene to avoid any further controversy.[27] Thus Azad's ambition to lead his community as Imam was foiled.

Azad's suggestion about a super-*alim* as *Imam* was not taken up. However, the resolution passed by the Bengal Provincial Khilafat Conference could in no sense be regarded as of moderate nature.[28] The conference resolved that Muslims should abandon their loyalty to the British and support the Khilafat agitation if the pre-war sovereignty and dominion of the Caliph were not kept intact. The moderates of the Khilafat Committee were alarmed at the extreme position taken by the Bengal Conference. March 19 was proclaimed as another Khilafat day for special prayers, *hartal* and one last appeal to the Viceroy. Thereafter, the Muslims were to sever all connections with the Government, including the return of titles and resignations from the Legislative Council, and Civil and Military services.

As a matter of fact the Calcutta Conference recommended radical measures which reflected the spirit of Non-cooperation. The Hindus were called upon to support the Muslim cause, to boycott the British Government and to join the Muslims in their Non-cooperation struggle. The object was that if the Government did not do anything in the interest of the Muslims, then there was to be a complete breach with the Government for all times to come. In such a situation there would be no choice left for the Muslims but to launch Non-cooperation. The Bengal Khilafat Conference, it may be mentioned, took place before the Khilafat delegation met the members of the British Government in England.

Gandhi issued the Khilafat manifesto on 7 March 1920 in which he emphasised that there should be no violence and no boycott of British goods. He wanted the Khilafat leaders to go slow. He supported the idea of observing *hartal* on 19 March and warned that if the Khilafat demands were not conceded, there was no alternative left for him but to launch Non-cooperation. He had been trying to bridle the Khilafat leaders extremism but now that the things were going rather too far due to the intransigence of the British policies, he was compelled to adopt an agitational approach. The Central Khilafat Committee endorsed the Calcutta resolution to observe *hartal* on 19 March. It also accepted the idea of adopting Non-cooperation whenever necessary.

A *hartal* was observed on 19 March and there was suspension of business on a fairly wide scale. Largely attended meetings took place in sympathy with Turkey's plight.[29] Prayers were also held as a mark of expiation. In the meanwhile great disappointment was felt in India by the published account of the interview between the members of the Khilafat delegation and Llyod George, the British Prime Minister.

Llyod George declared that Turkey could not be given any special treatment and would have to be put on par with other Christian countries who had fought the Allied Powers.

On 22 March 1920 fifteen Muslim and ten Hindu leaders, besides Gandhi discussed the Non-cooperation plan in Delhi.[30] In *India Wins Freedom* there is confusion about the date of this Hindu-Muslim meeting which is mentioned as 20 January.[31] The meeting took place on 19 March. Among the leaders present were Gandhi, B.G. Tilak, M.M. Malaviya, Lajpat Rai, Dr. Ansari, Ajmal Khan, Azad, Abdul Bari and Shaukat Ali. Tilak did not support Gandhi's Non-cooperation, Malaviya expressed his reservations and Lajpat Rai supported only the *Swadeshi* part of the movement. Abdul Bari repudiated non-violence as a policy and Ajmal Khan was uncertain. A sub-committee was formed to examine the Central Committee's programme of Non-cooperation. Its members included Gandhi, Lajpat Rai, Ajmal Khan and Azad. Two days later Gandhi announced his plan of Non-cooperation at Meerut. He spelled out his Non-cooperation programme which was to renounce titles, resign from Government service and to stop paying tax. Gandhi warned that Non-cooperation would be implemented if the Turkish peace terms were not found favourable. Gandhi was strongly supported by Azad who said that his recent tour of Bihar had convinced him that the Muslims would respond to Non-cooperation enthusiastically. Gandhi also thought likewise. When challenged by Abdul Bari, Azad also supported Gandhi on the use of Non-violence.

Muslim feelings were being aroused all over the country. At the Meerut Khilafat Conference it was resolved to enlist the support of the *Ulama* for organising an All India agitation. The Ulama were religious leaders and Bari believed that if the Ulama issued a *fatwa*, the Muslim masses would have to fall in line with the Khilafat leaders to fight the British. A network of Khilafat committees came into existence in different parts of the country, particularly in U.P., Bihar, Bombay and Bengal provinces. Abdul Bari was the moving spirit behind the organisation of these committees. Some of the Khilafat leaders even advocated *Jihad*. On 12 May the Central Khilafat Committee decided to implement Non-cooperation programme in four stages and appointed a sub-committee to work out the plan. The members of this committee were M.M. Chotani, Shaukat Ali, Azad, Haji Ahmed Khatri and Mohamad Ali of Dharavi. The leading moderate Bombay leaders including Badruddin Abdullah Koor, Fazalbhoy Currimbhoy and Rahimtulla Chinoy were alarmed at the extremist politics and resigned in protest. In Chinoy's place Gandhi was elected to the Central Khilafat Committee.

On 14 May 1920 the Allied Peace Treaty of Savers with Turkey was published in India. The Arab countries were to become independent of the Ottoman Empire, and Syria, Palestine and Mesopotamia were placed under French and British mandates. Eastern Thrace and Smyrna were ceded to Greece and Deodacanese Island to Italy. Though Constantinople remained Turkish, the Straits were internationalised. The territories of the Ottoman Empire were considerably reduced and the holy places of Islam were removed from the Khalifa's control. Thus the Khalifa ceased to be the Warden of Muslim sanctuaries. These terms infuriated the Khilafat leaders. Gandhi termed this Treaty as a 'staggering blow to the Indian Mussalmans' and declared Non-cooperation as the only effective remedy left to right the wrong. He wanted an early joint meeting of Hindus and Muslims to consider the gravity of the situation created by the 'notorious' peace treaty.

The Central Khilafat Committee met in Bombay on 12 May, 1920 and decided in favour of Non-cooperation. This was largely Gandhi's doing. To ratify the Central Khilafat Committee's decision in All India Khilafat Conference took place on 1 to 3 June at Allahabad immediately after the All India Congress Committee meeting held at Benaras. Some of the Congress leaders had expressed their reservations about Gandhi's plan of Non-cooperation and they included Tilak, C.R. Das, Malaviya and Lajpat Rai. Thus the issue was postponed and the decision was left to the Calcutta Congress to be held in September. But the All India Khilafat Committee accepted Gandhi's leadership to work out Non-cooperation and a committee was constituted with Azad, Ahmad Hasan, Muhamed Ali of Dharavi, H.S. Khatri, Shaukat Ali, Kitchlew, Hasrat Mohani as members and Gandhi as its Chairman. Gandhi chose to describe this committee as Martial Law Committee of the Khilafat Committee.[32] The Khilafat leaders submitted themselves to Gandhi's control. The meeting resolved in favour of *Swadeshi* rather than a boycott of foreign goods. It also decided to establish a Khilafat volunteer corps and raise funds for the agitation. On 22 June the committee sent a memorandum to the Viceroy asking him to get the Turkish peace terms revised or to resign. They gave him time till 1 August to take action or to resign; otherwise Non-cooperation would be launched, they reiterated.

The Ulama began to exercise great influence on the Khilafat agitation and Non-cooperation movement. In November 1920 the Jamiat ul-Ulama-e-Hind persuaded by Abdul Bari made *Zakat* (to contribute two and a half per cent of their income) a religious duty. At the same session a *fatwa* was issued, the *muttaffiqa* fatwa signed by 500 Ulama, making Non-cooperation a religious obligation and declaring it lawful to join the Hindus in Non-cooperation and to follow Gandhi.[33] These directions from the Jamiat ul-Ulama-e-Hind were preached and carried to the countryside by the Ulama of Firangi Mahal, Nadwat ul-Ulama and Deoband.[34] Even the Shias joined the Sunni brethren in the Khilafat agitation. Thus the Khilafat brought the organised participation of Ulama into Indian politics to give a religious sanction for anti-Imperial struggle. The Non-cooperation had a large backing from the Muslim Ulama in the country.

The Ulama and *Sufis* were working enthusiastically for the Khilafat. They raised the slogan 'Islam in danger' and mobilized Muslim public opinion against the British by appealing to their religious sentiments. The Jamiat ul-Ulama-e-Hind issued a *fatwa* at Amritsar in 1921 which declared that if the British failed to do justice to the Sultan of Turkey, the Muslims should migrate to some Muslim country. Azad thought that the Muslims had no choice but to quit India and to migrate. He supported the *fatwa*.[35] About 1800 Muslims sold their property and resorted to *hijrat*. They started for the Afghan-border but had to retreat because of the ban on their entry into Afghanistan. Many of them died of heat and hunger on the way. This episode aroused further resentment in the Muslim mind. Azad wrote a pamphlet *Hijrat ka fatwa* (verdict in favour of migration) inviting those who were migrating to commune with him and receive directions.

Gandhi showed considerable sympathy for the Khilafat and decided to launch a Satyagraha on 1 August 1920. He had been finding it rather difficult to swing Congress in its favour. He had a keen insight into the realities of the situation. He had regarded the 'Punjab wrongs' as a memorial of national humiliation. The Hunter Report published on 28 May, 1920 was condemned by Gandhi as 'an attempt to condone official lawlessness' and he was shocked by its tendency to give 'page after page of thinly disguised official whitewash.'[36] He declared that 'a scandal of this magnitude cannot be tolerated by the nation, if it is to preserve its self-respect and become a free partner in the Empire.'[37] At a meeting in Bombay on 26 June he demanded the impeachment of Sir Michael O'Dwyer, the chief culprit of Punjab atrocities.[38] The remedy, Gandhi thought, was *Satyagraha*. According to Judith Brown, Gandhi linked the Punjab issue and Khilafat as "twin humiliating signs" which made it necessary to resort to Non-cooperation.[39] Gandhi was clear in his mind about the programme he was to launch on these issues.

From May 1920 onwards the Khilafat Movement entered a new phase of mass politics wherein religious appeal of the Ulama and vernacular journalists reached Muslims all over the country. The 'Punjab wrongs' provided the 'missing ingredient' which Gandhi brought forward and joined with Khilafat raising both the issues in this way to the All India dimensions. Gandhi's task now was to swing the Congress in favour of Non-cooperation and get over the resistance some of his distinguished colleagues had shown earlier in this regard.

The special Congress session took place at Calcutta on 4 September with Lala Lajpat Rai as its President. The subject committee took up the Non-cooperation resolution and it was passed there by a narrow margin of 144 to 132 votes. The next day the Non-cooperation resolution was moved by Gandhi before the delegates who gave Gandhi's programme a clear support of 1855 to 873 votes.[40] The Nagpur session of the Congress in December 1920 confirmed the Calcutta resolution of Non-cooperation. The agitation concentrated on the following items of the programme:

1. boycott of the law-courts by the lawyers;
2. boycott of schools and colleges owned, aided or recognised by the Government and establishment of national educational institutions as an alternative channel of education;
3. boycott of elections to the assembly and the provincial councils;
4. surrender of honours, titles, honorary posts and boycott of official functions;
5. boycott of British goods and encouragement of Swadeshi, especially *khaddar* or homespun, home cloth;
6. prohibition on drinking liquor.

The Non-cooperation programme electrified the whole country. It aroused strong sentiments among the people on a wide scale for the liberation of the country. Never before had any movement launched against the ruling authority stirred such anti-Imperial feelings in the country as the Non-cooperation movement. We need not dilate upon its mass character and the large scale participation of people in it. The Jamait ul-Ulama called upon the Muslims by the force of a *fatwa* to boycott elections, Government schools, colleges and law courts and also renounce titles and ranks. Jawaharlal Nehru captured the spirit of the time in the following words :

> Many of us who worked for the Congress programme lived in a kind of intoxication during the year 1921. We are full of excitement and optimism and a buoyant enthusiasm. We sensed the happiness of a person crusading for a cause. . . . Above all we had a sense of freedom and a pride in that freedom. The old feeling of oppression and frustration was completely gone.[41]

All through Azad remained closely associated with the Khilafat agitation and deeply involved in the programmes launched for giving it a momentum. During the war years, he had shown strong pro-Turkish leanings. When Gandhi took up the Khilafat cause, he found in Azad a staunch supporter who forcefully argued in favour of the observance of *hartal* on 9 March 1920. While some prominent Muslim leaders like Ajmal Khan, Abdul Bari and Hasrat Mohani had expressed reservations about Non-cooperation, Azad had no hesitation of doubts. The plight of Turkey had infuriated him, and he was determined to fight for the restoration of the Khilafat. He considered himself a citizen of historical Islamic brotherhood which was known as the Turkish Caliphate. When the British and Khalifa collided, Azad declared his loyalty to the Turkish sovereign. Often in his speeches he referred to the Covenant Prophet Mohammad had brought about between the inhabitants of Medina and the Jews. That Covenant had been negotiated by the parties after the entrance of Mohammad into Madina (627 A.D.). The object of the agreement was to forge a workable alliance for the common defence of the adherents of the Prophet and the Jews against the hostile Quresh who had persecuted the Prophet in Mecca and forced him to emigrate to Medina. By citing the relevant portions from the Quran and Hadith he enjoined upon the Muslims to join the Hindus against the British and forge what the Covenant had declared "*Ummat-i-Wahidaa*".[42]

Azad set at rest doubts entertained by some of his Muslim colleagues about the propriety of joining the Non-cooperation movement. By his scholarly interpretation of the Quran, he emphasised that the Quran permitted the Muslims joining the Hindus against the British on moral grounds. He enjoyed the full confidence of Gandhi and both supported each other on Non-cooperation. At the All India Khilafat Conference held in Calcutta in September, 1920, Azad justified Non-cooperation by the Islamic edict of *Tark-e-mavalat*. He emphasised the role the Ulama and Sufis ought to play in urging people to support Non-cooperation. Along with Muhammad Ali and Maulana Abdul Majid Badauni, Azad addressed a meeting in Amritsar on 24 October 1920 and exhorted people not to co-operate with the Government that disregarded their religious sentiments. Gandhi inaugurated the Madrassa Islamia in Nakhuda Jama Mosque at Calcutta where Azad had made arrangements for the study of Arabic as a part of Non-cooperation programme. Gandhi inaugurated the Madrassa and gave his blessings to this important venture.[43] On 13 December 1920 Azad delivered a highly inspiring speech on how students fired by a spirit of patriotism should join this institution.[44] Azad appointed Husain Ahmad Madni of Deoband (1879-1957), a zealous worker of the Khilafat, as its manager.

Azad was particularly active in organising the student population for Non-cooperation. His erudition and eloquence acted as magic on them. The Congress and the Central Khilafat Committee adopted a common programme of rectifying the Khilafat wrongs and establishing *Swaraj*. The Khilafat Conference held at Karachi on July 8-10, 1921 endorsed the *fatwa* urging people not to serve the British army.[45] The 7th Resolution of the conference read as follows :

> In the present circumstances the Holy *Shariat* forbids every Muslim to serve or enlist himself in the British army or to raise remits for it; it is incumbent on all Muslims in general and all ulama in particular to carry this religious commandment to every Muslim soldier in the British Indian army.

Other important resolutions passed were (i) determination to secure complete fulfilment of the Khilafat demands; (ii) rejection of any limitation on Turkish sovereignty; and (iii) refusal to accept non-Muslim control over *Jazirat ul-Arb*. The Khilafat Conference also declared the beginning of civil disobedience to attain complete independence.

In order to check the growing influence of Khilafat leaders, in mid-September, 1921, the Government arrested Muhammad Ali, Shaukat Ali, Dr. Kitchlew, Shri Shankarachary, Hussain Ahmad Madni, Nihar Ahmad and Pir Ghulam Mujjaddid. After Shaukat Ali's arrest, Azad took over as Secretary of the Central Khilafat Committee on 22 September, 1921. He had now to look after the organisation of Khilafat

Committee on 22 September, 1921. The major responsibility for propagating the Khilafat and Non-cooperation ideas fell on him. Because of his vast knowledge of Islamic history and culture he was to serve as guide on many sensitive issues which needed clarification. For intensifying the Non-cooperation campaign he began to tour the country to hold meetings and give lectures. He went to Delhi, Calcutta, Bombay, Karachi, Agra and other places to spread the agitation against the Government.

Azad marked the assumption of his office as Secretary of Central Khilafat Committee by publishing an article in his new Urdu weekly 'Paigham' which he launched in collaboration with Abdur Razzaq Malihabadi on 23 September, 1921 from Calcutta.[46] In the first issue he summarised the accomplishments of the Central Khilafat Committee – how it had adopted the Non-cooperation movement programme, mobilized public opinion by organising meetings in various parts of the country, and raised a fund for furthering the Khilafat cause. The paper propagated the view that the Muslims could no longer remain the subjects of a Government that suppressed religious freedom. It further urged that the real aim of the Khilafat movement was freedom of India for which the Muslims must fight. To achieve this object the paper exhorted the Muslims to order their life according to the *Sharia*, pray daily for God's mercy, promote communal harmony and remain in the vanguard of Non-cooperation.

Azad attacked the Government for arresting the Khilafat leaders. He said that every Muslim in India was committing the same crime for which the leaders had been arrested, and added that he and others who were outside would most willingly and joyfully go to jail for the same crime, the crime of defying the Government and fighting for the liberation of the country from the fetters of foreign rule. He declared that in Islam there was no choice, either the Muslim must remain free or die.[47]

Reiterating that the arrest of national leaders was unjustified and there was a strong resentment in the country, Azad called upon the people to follow the example set by the leaders :

> We have no sorrow for their arrest, but we should be jealous of their honour and should be more ready than before for the duty which was theirs as well as ours. In 1915 I was interned for nine months. After their internment I said at that time with sorrow that in this path they had stolen a march over me. Today instead of sorrowing, we should congratulate them and shall again say that they

have outstepped us all.[48]

Azad's speeches and articles during the campaign gave us an idea of the principles which he cherished on the Khilafat and Non-cooperation.

In the Presidential address delivered to the U.P. Khilafat Conference held at Agra on 25 August, 1921, Azad forcefully maintained that the Khilafat issue did not concern only a particular community or class but the whole country, and on it really depended the future of India.[49] He stated that the Quran makes a distinction between Muslims and Non-Muslims and directs that the non-Muslim nations that attack the Muslims are not to be befriended whereas those that are friendly to them should be invited to work for a common cause. Azad said in his picturesque diction that it was possible to be friendly, "with a snake or a scorpion but not with the British, it was possible to give milk to a snake on one's palm, it was out of the question ever to compromise with the British." What the country needed, above all, he emphasised, was Faith, Action and Sacrifice.

In another speech which was delivered at the Khilafat Conference in Agra on 26 October,1921, Azad condemned the Government action of arresting the Khilafat leaders. He termed this action as downright madness. He reiterated the position he had taken earlier on 28 February 1920 at the Calcutta Khilafat Conference that it was completely irreligious for the Muslim soldiery to serve in the British army and called upon it to resign from British service. Azad argued that it was the army that had enslaved the country and therefore it was necessary for the Muslim soldiers to quit the British service in order to liquidate the empire. While delivering his Presidential speech at Lahore on 21 November, 1921 at the Jamiat ul-ulama-e-Hind he appealed to the soldiers again to resign from service.[52] He also lamented that he had not been arrested by the Government.

It is clear from his speeches that Azad was fiercely attacking the Government for its misdeeds.[53] He was justifying the co-operation of Hindus and Muslims on the basis of his lucid interpretation of the Quran and he was organising the agitation against the British Government which had given an affront to their religion. Azad was speaking less like a pan-Islamist now and more like an Indian passionately devoted to the liberation of his country from foreign rule. His powerful eloquence had a profound impact on the audience. His choice of words was most effective. His speeches were scholarly in content, vigorous in diction, picturesque in form and rich in historical references evoking memories of the past that would inspire his audience.

In the speeches he delivered before the Jamiat-ul-Ulama-e-Hind at Lahore on 18 November, 1921, Azad had exhibited his erudition by surveying Islamic history and showing how great religious thinkers and leaders in the past had suffered privations, tortures and even executions in the cause of Truth.[54] He proclaimed that he saw no reason why the Ulama, the repository of true faith, should not emulate their example by fighting against oppression perpetrated by the British. Despite Azad's highly inflammatory speeches and his feverish anti-British activity the Government did not arrest him. He felt extremely unhappy about his not being arrested when many of his friends and colleagues were already in jail. But he did not have to wait indefinitely. When the Government decided to act, Azad had some premonition about it. On 8 December, 1921 he wrote down a message which was found laying in his papers after his arrest. The message read as follows :

> God knows best how painful it had become for me to stay out of jail. Those who go to jail first do not know the torments of the ones left behind. Muhammad Ali, Shaukat Ali, Lala Lajpat Rai and Pandit Motilal Nehru have completed their journey while I am still waiting for my destination. That destination is now in sight and my heart is full of joy . . . [55]

Azad was arrested on 10 December 1921 at 4.30 P.M. He was dictating a letter to his friend, Fazluddin Ahmad at that time. Azad was arrested without a warrant the same day as C.R. Das and they met in jail. The speeches delivered by Azad in Mirzapur Park at Calcutta on 1 and 15 July 1921 were used as a basis for his arrest.[56] He was produced before the Presidency Magistrate, M.D. Swinner. He was sentenced to a year's rigorous imprisonment on 9 February 1922 under section 124-A of the Indian Penal Code. On hearing the sentence, Azad smiled and said : "It is much less than what I had expected." Azad's wife sent a telegram to Gandhi complaining that the punishment awarded to her husband was mild.[57]

Azad presented a statement in the court which is one of the best ever made by a political prisoner in this country or elsewhere. Gandhi liked it immensely. In his journal *Young India* dated 23 February 1922 he hailed the statement as an "oration deserving penal servitude for life."[58] Azad gave his statement in chaste Urdu some portions of which

Mahadev Desai and Durlab Singh translated into English.

Azad made it clear at the outset that he expected no justice from the law court before which he had appeared because the law courts under the British regime were based on a system in which no magistrate could give justice to the accused person. He condemned the present system of Government as pernicious because it used the courts as weapons of vengeance and injustice. Azad went on to narrate how in history some of the greatest men like Jesus, Socrates and Galileo inspired by high ideas had suffered at the hands of courts. He spoke of the convict's dock as a "wonderful place" where the most righteous as well as the most criminal men are made to stand."[59] He then thanked the Almighty for the honour done to him by his arrest and trial in the court of law which he left 'could be an object of envy for emperors.'[60]

Admitting that he was fighting the British Government in the name of liberty and justice and that he was determined to provoke disaffection among people, Azad said :

> I am the first Muslim in India who invited this nation for the first time in 1912 to commit this crime and within three years succeeded in bringing about a revolution in their slavish mentality. Hence, if the government regards me a criminal and consequently desires to award punishment I earnestly acknowledge that it would not be an unexpected thing and that I will have absolutely no grudge against that.[61]

Azad pointed out that the real reason for his arrest was that the Government wanted to arrest him before the arrival of the Prince of Wales in Calcutta on 24 December so that there would be no *hartal* which they thought he would succeed in organising. The Government was convinced that Azad would threaten the peace of the town. Under the Criminal Law Amendment Act, 1908, the Government declared all the national organisations of volunteers unlawful. Azad maintained that he expected the Government either to withdraw the order banning meetings or to arrest him.

He attacked the Government fiercely for depriving the Indians of their fundamental rights of liberty.[62] To Azad the promise of liberty to be granted through 'graduated stages' by the Government was nothing but delaying tactics which added insult to injury. Such a procedure was like an owner of a property 'receiving it by bits and a creditor his dues by instalments'.[63] Analysing some of the liberal and egalitarian principles of Islam, Azad pointed out that Islam "constitutes a perfect system of freedom and democracy" where cardinal principle is that the "highest right is not might but right itself."[64] Personal monarchy and bureaucratic autocracy, Azad averred, were an anathema to Islam. Azad argued that as a Muslim it was his moral duty to stand up for truth and speak it fearlessly. He said :

> To expect from a Mussalman he should not pronounce what is right is to ask him to retire from Islamic life. If you have no right to demand from a person to give up his religion, then certainly you cannot require a Mussalman that he should not call tyranny a tyranny, because both the things are synonymous . . . .
> This is that vital organ of Islamic life, which if cut off, terminates the very existence of its best characteristics . . . . In the Quran – the Holy Book of Islam, the Mussalmans have been told that they are witnesses of truth in God's universe. In the capacity of a nation this is their national character.[65]

Azad saw no justification whatsoever for the perpetuation of British rule in India which was based on the exploitation of the people of India. Like Edmund Burke he believed that liberty is a natural and God-given gift of man and that no country, however benevolent, has any right to subjugate others because 'slavery is slavery and is opposed to the will and canons of God.' He maintained that it was his moral duty to fight for the liberty of his country from foreign rule. Azad reported how the Prophet extracted a promise of righteousness from any person by binding him to obey the Quranic command, "I will always proclaim the truth in whatever condition and wherever I may happen to be."[66]

Azad declared that to Mussalmans whose religious duties make it imperative on them to accept death rather than hesitate from proclaiming the truth, a case registered under section 124-A, the maximum punishment for which is seven years, can never be a frightful thing.[67] He cited some examples from Islamic history to show how humble men of lowly order dared to speak the truth against the mighty but surprisingly such cases did not incur the displeasure of the authorities in the past.[68] On the other hand, the Kings often appreciated the dissenting voices and rectified the wrongs. Azad pointed out that the Islamic Governments did not, as a rule, invoke ignoble laws like Section 124-A to crush the liberties of the people.

The struggle against a foreign power, Azad maintained, had to be waged, according to Islam either by the use of sword of Non-violence. He urged that in the present case the struggle had to be carried on in a true spirit of Non-violence. Admitting that he bore no grudge for having been involved by the Government in a case for punishment, Azad declared that "a true Muslim has either to immolate himself or to live as a free man; no third course is open to him in Islam."[69]

Azad made it clear that there was no question of his showing any loyalty to a Government that was tyrannical. He declared :

> During the last two years not a single day has passed when I had not proclaimed the tyranny of the Government with regard to the 'the Khilafat' and 'the Punjab affairs.' I admit having always said that for a Government which is bent on exterminating the Khilafat and is neither prepared to compensate nor is ashamed of the tyrannies of the Punjab there can be no loyalty in the heart of any Indian.[70]

Azad spelled out some of the basic principles which had governed his life, the principles which he would never sacrifice :

> Continuously in the last twelve years I have been training my community and my country to demand their rights and their liberty. I was only eighteen years old when I first started speaking and writing on this theme. I have consecrated my whole being to it and sacrificed the best of my life, meaning the whole of my youth, to my infatuation for this ideal. For four years I have suffered internment but even during my internment I never desisted from pursuing my work and inviting people to follow this national goal. This is the mission of my life, and if I live at all I elect to live only for this single purpose even as the Quran says : "My prayers and my observances and my life and death are all for my Lord, the Lord and the Universe."[71]

Azad wanted to be punished for another reason. In his statement he told the authorities that it was under his Presidentship of the Central Khilafat Conference on 28-29 February 1920 that a resolution was passed wherein it was declared irreligious for any faithful Muslim to serve in the British army. This resolution, he asserted, was thrice adopted under his Presidentship. He added, "So I am the proper person to deserve punishment in connection with this crime because I have done nothing except infringement of section 124-A many times by delivering speeches which contain all the things for which I have not been charged."[72]

Clarifying his position on the means to be adopted for the national struggle against the British. Azad said that in this 'war of liberty and justice' he would adopt the path of Non-violence and Non-cooperation. He made it clear that unlike Gandhi he believed in the use of armed force for liberty and justice because "violence is fully in harmony with the natural laws of God in these circumstances under which Islam permits the use of such violence." But so far India was concerned he thought that, "India can only triumph through a non-violent agitation and India's triumph will be memorable example of the victory of moral force."[73]

Azad maintained that what the authorities regarded as 'sedition' was in reality patriotism in his eyes. He argued :

> I am charged with 'sedition' but let me understand the meaning of 'sedition'. Is 'sedition' that struggle for freedom which has not as yet been successful ? If this is so, I confess frankly, but at the same time let me remind you that this very thing is called patriotism when it is successful. The armed leaders of Ireland were regarded rebels until yesterday but what title would the Great Britain suggest for Dr. Valera and Griffith today?[74]

Azad did not lament over the prospects of being sentenced to imprisonment. On the other hand, he regarded it necessary for the attainment of freedom of the country as would be evident from the following:

> I had said in these very speeches the seed of liberty can never yield fruit unless fertilised by the water of oppression. The Government has begun fertilisation. I had also said, "Don't be sad over the arrest of Khilafat volunteers. If you really want justice and freedom, get ready for going to the jails."[75]

The concluding part of Azad's statement, like Gandhi's statement in his trial on 18 March 1922, addressed to the magistrate reflects his passion for liberty and dignity of character :

> Mr. magistrate, I will not take any more time of the court now. It is an interesting and instructive chapter of history which both of us are engaged in preparing. The dock has fallen to our lot and to yours the magisterial chair. I admit that the chair is as much necessary for this work as this dock. Let us come and finish our role in this memorable drama. The historian is eagerly awaiting it and the future is looking towards us. Allow us to occupy this dock repeatedly and continuously and you may also go on writing the judgement again and again. For some time this work will continue till the gates of another court of law are flung open. Time will act as its judge and pass the judgement. And that verdict will be final in all respects.[76]

In his lengthy statement before the court Azad strengthened his argument by historical citations. Moreover, through his own interpretations of the Quran he justified his struggle against the alien rule. It was, he maintained, his mission to fight for the liberation of his country. His statement lacked Gandhi's brevity and Shaukat Ali's flamboyance and rhetoric. It did not possess Abdul Bari's fiery sallies. But it was remarkable for its erudition, gravity of tone, candour and clarity of thought. Translations are inadequate and never reach the force of the original, particularly in the case of Azad who was a master of chaste, elegant and powerful Urdu prose. *Qual-e-Faisal* which contained his original Urdu statement delivered before the court is written in a style whose rich eloquence will be more difficult to render in any translation.

Azad was placed in the European ward of Alipur Central jail, Calcutta. His other companions were C.R. Das, Subhas Chandra Bose and Birendra Nath Sasmal. During his prison days Malihabadi compiled a portion of his autobiography, known as *Azad ki Kahani khud Azad ki Zabani*. During the period of his imprisonment the political scene was changing fast. A serious riot took place in the village of Chauri Chaura in U.P., on 4 February, 1922. About 200 demonstrators led by Non-cooperation volunteers attacked a small force of twenty-two policemen. The police opened fire but was overpowered and the agitators set the police station ablaze, burning the entire police force alive excepting two who managed to escape the flames only to be beaten to death. This violence shocked Gandhi and he suspended the Non-cooperation movement. The Government had been thinking of taking stern action against Gandhi and sentenced him to imprisonment for six years in March, 1922.

What is clear beyond doubt is that throughout the Khilafat agitation and Non-cooperation movement, Azad gave Gandhi unstinted support and Gandhi too backed him. They were working together on the same wavelength in their anti-Imperial struggle. In fact Azad acted as the *ideologue* of Khilafat agitation. He gave legitimacy to the movement by justifying it through citations from the Quran. His views on the Khilafat question were embodied in a long treatise entitled *Masala-e-Khilafat wa jazirat-u-Arab* which was published in 1920. Azad's thesis was that it would be irreligious to support the British when Turkey was being humiliated and the Khilafat abolished. He put forward the thesis that Islam and Indian nationalism are not incompatible.

Azad's remarkable contribution was to bring the Hindus in support of this view and Muslims together on the same platform and he frequently quoted from the Quran. He emphasised that Islam did not produce a cleavage between the Hindus and Muslims, but, on the contrary, provided a strong base for their unity. When he brought Muslims into Indian politics he built the entire edifice of his ideas on religious grounds.

The abolition of the Khilafat disheartened Muslim leadership in India, but that was not the case with Azad who took a pragmatic view of the whole matter. He explained his viewpoint in his articles, 'The Khilafat Problem and the Turkish Republic' published in *Zamindar* in 1924. He stated that the Turkish Government by abolishing the Khilafat of the Ottoman dynasty had rectified a wrong which lay in an artificial division between spiritual and temporal powers. He thought that in reality the Khilafat had ceased to exist since 1922. The object now should be to organise Muslims in India on the foundation of Islamic ethics. Azad's exposition of the Khilafat in this light has been regarded as a piece of 'cool-headed casuistry.'[77]

The Ulama demanded that Indian Muslims be governed according to the principles of Quran. In Bihar Azad and Azad Sobhani, a lecturer and journalist, conceived the idea of setting up religious courts in the districts which were to administer the *Sharia*.[78] Finally the idea was to set up such courts in other provinces which would then elect an *amir-e-hind*.[79] But due to the opposition of Abul Bari and the Ali brothers the idea was dropped.

In October 1923 the Grand National Assembly declared Turkey as a Republic and Mustafa Kemal Pasha abolished the Khilafat on 1 March 1924. The symbol of Khilafat that had united the Hindus and

Muslims had now ceased to exist and mistrust and tensions between the two communities started growing fast. The Moplah riots occurred in Malabar in 1921. The years 1922-24 were marked by a series of communal riots which sullied the Hindu-Muslim relations. The *shuddhi*, *sangathan*, *tablig*, and *tanzim* movements launched with the object of converting people from one community to another greatly added to religious strife and tension in the country.

At the Gaya session in December, 1922, the Congress was split into two groups, 'no-changers' who were loyal to Gandhi's programme of Non-cooperation and 'pro-changers' who were known as Swarajists. The Swarajists led by Motilal Nehru, C.R. Das and Ajmal Khan favoured entry into the legislative council by participating in the coming elections in order to wreck them from within. Malaviya also supported Das. Most of the Muslim leaders stood by Gandhi's programme.

When Azad came out of jail on 1 January 1923 he was distressed to find the whole atmosphere in the country vitiated by the virus of communalism.[80] He felt that for meeting the challenge of communalism it was necessary to renew the spirit of Hindu-Muslim unity. Gandhi was in jail. Azad was upset to find a split within the Congress due to sharp differences between the 'no-changers' and 'pro-changers'. The first step to tackle the Hindu-Muslim riots and the Congress split was to call a special Congress Session at Delhi in September 1923.[81] Azad was elected as its President, and he was the youngest person elected to hold this high office. He was about thirty-five. M. A. Ansari acted as the Secretary. The Congress was facing a crisis like the one after the Surat Congress split of 1907, when the 'Moderates' and 'Extremists' had fought each other.

Azad delivered an eloquent Presidential address running into about forty-three pages.[82] At the outset he offered congratulations to Turkey on her victory and to Mustaffa Kemal Pasha for infusing a new spirit among his countrymen. He mentioned with special emphasis that for the sake of the freedom of Turkey thousands of Indians had gone to jail and suffered privations by resigning their jobs. Pointing out that the Non-cooperation movement had made Indians hold their head high and straighten their backs. Azad extolled the virtues of Non-violence as a technique for liberating Indians from British rule.[83] He repudiated the notion that Non-cooperation had failed. He elaborated on the benefits that India had derived from it.[84] According to Azad, Non-violence had inspired the Indians with lofty ideals and cultivated among them a spirit of solidarity, sacrifice and patriotism. Azad suggested some concrete steps for political education of the masses by setting up reading rooms, night schools and other institutions for adult education. He believed in the force of mobilizing public opinion by a wide circulation of newspapers.[85]

Azad emphasised in his speech that Non-cooperation movement was founded on the principles of truth and non-violence, the ideals which both Tolstoy and Gandhi had propagated on moral grounds to fight the wrongs which men were forced to suffer.[86] He assured his countrymen that there was no cause for dismay and urged them to stand united and continue their fight for the righteous cause of freedom. He regretted that Gandhi, the great leader of the Indian people, was in jail. He pointed out that Gandhi was venerated by the Turks and Arabs who had enshrined their faith in him and wished him a splendid victory in his fight for truth and justice. Azad expressed his anguish over communal riots and forcefully attacked the elements that were busy in injecting communal poison into the minds of the common people. This was one of the most eloquent and famous statements made by him and couched as it is in poetic imagery, it continues to ring in our ears even today :

> If an angel were to descend from the high heavens and proclaim from the heights of the Qutub Minar to abandon the mission of Hindu-Muslim unity and within twenty-four hours *Swaraj* will be yours, I will refuse the proferred *Swaraj* and not yield on my stand. The delay of *Swaraj* will affect Indians but the end of our unity will be the loss of the entire human race.[87]

Azad repudiated the idea of Hindu *sangathan* or Muslim *sangathan* (organisation). Only one type of *sangathan*, he declared, was needed, and that was the Indian National Congress.[88] He warned the British not to obstruct their march to freedom. If they continue to do so, the Indians, he warned, would be compelled to overthrow the obstacles placed in their way.

Azad saw the Congress caught up in a dilemma. At the Gaya Congress in September 1922, Das's resolution which had recommended the principle of Council entry was defeated by the combined strength of the followers of Gandhi and Khilafat leaders who wanted the Non-cooperation movement to continue. Das resigned on 1 January 1923, and along with Motilal Nehru founded the Swaraj party.

With his sedate realism, Azad wanted to bridge the gulf between the two rival groups. He was convinced that this conflict would weaken the Congress and help the ruling power. He refused to identify himself with either camp. About the differences in the Congress, Azad said :

> I fail tc understand why strict adherence to the creed of Non-cooperation should not accommodate several schools of thought. It is a case of difference in opinion regarding one of the items in the programme where too, it is not really a difference in principles but in details of their application, not in the goals but the means to be adopted for them. If there is a difference of opinion in the matter, the same significance cannot be attached to it as to a difference in principle.[89]

By his sobering influence, always a strong feature of Azad's personality, he tried to reconcile the 'no-changers' and 'pro-changers', the Gandhites and the Swarajists. He pointed out that both the groups instead of being antagonistic to each other should carry out their plans. There could be no conflict between them so long as both were solidly united in their common goal of freedom of India. As a result of Azad's plea, the Congress gave permission to the Swarajists, the 'pro-changers' to fight the Council elections and readmitted the followers of Das, Motilal and Vithalbhai Patel to the Congress fold. Gandhi's 'no-changers' followers included C. Rajagopalachari, Rajendra Prasad, Vallabhbhai Patel and M.A. Ansari.

Azad saved the Congress from a split. He reconciled both the groups to a compromise formula and made each group follow the programme it had wanted so. The Congress obtained large majorities in almost all the legislators. It secured forty-five seats in the Legislative Assembly and for the next few years the party functioned as a nationalist opposition at the Centre. Thus the fight for *Swaraj* was carried on both within and outside the Council. Azad's success in saving the Congress from split shows his sound political instinct and shrewdness of judgement. Gandhi was released on 5 February 1924 following an attack of appendicitis. He asked his followers the 'pro-changers' to take up constructive work in towns and villages. He also supported the Swarajists' Council entry. Thus he endorsed Azad's line.

The communal riots in 1924 reached their climax in Kohat (North Western Frontier) on 9 and 10 September, 1924. Gandhi was shaken by the communal outrages and to do penance for the sins of his country including his own, he undertook a twenty-one day fast. A Unity Conference was held on 26 September, 1924 at Delhi under the Presidentship of Motilal Nehru. It was attended by 300 delegates representing different parties. Azad took an active part in this conference and it was largely due to his initiative that the following resolution was passed:

> This Conference declares that it is not only wrong against law but also against religion for anyone to take the law into his own hands, either for the purpose of retaliation or punishment, and therefore, declares that all points in dispute shall be decided by reference either to private arbitration or where that is impossible, by reference to a court of law.[90]

At this Conference Azad clarified that cow slaughter was not an integral part of Islam. The Conference condemned the desecration of places of worship and the use of force for conversion.

The All-Parties Conference met at Bombay on 21 November, 1924 at the suggestion of Muhammad Ali, the Congress President, who wanted a united scheme to resolve the Hindu-Muslim rift. Nothing, however, came of this meeting. Another meeting of the All-Parties Conference took place on 23 January, 1925 at Delhi to bring about unity among the parties and to draw up a scheme for the representation of communities in the legislatures.

Politically the period from 1923 to 1927 was at a low ebb. The communal riots flared up and the worst of them took place in Calcutta for about six weeks in April and May, 1926. C.R. Das's death in 1925 was a terrible loss to the country. Azad had great admiration for Das and regarded him a statesman *par excellence*.[91] He thought that Das's Bengal Pact which had won the enthusiastic support of the Muslim intelligentsia was a *tour de force*. Das had firmly believed that so long as Muslims are not strongly represented in public life and services, there could be no possibility of Hindu-Muslim understanding. Azad published articles in *al-Hilal* and *Zamindar* on Das's contribution to Indian Nationalism. According to Azad, Das was not an idealist but a man of action who never mistook a shadow for the substance. Azad emphasised Das's liberality towards Muslims in Bengal as he offered to reserve eighty per cent of the new appointments in Calcutta Corporation.[92] He strongly felt that Das's passing away at a time when Hindu-Muslim antagonism was vitiating the climate of the country was a great blow to the cause of secularism. With Das's demise and Gandhi's withdrawal from active politics in 1926 the forces of unity and secularism were weakened.

The Muslim League under the Chairmanship of Abdur Rahim, a former judge of Madras High Court, in its session on 30 December, 1925, blamed the Hindus for communal disharmony in the country. On the other hand, the All India Hindu Mahasabha under the Presidentship of Lajpat Rai at its session of 11 April, 1925 opposed any scheme of communal representation and called for Hindu *sangathan*. Swami Shraddhanand's murder by a Muslim fanatic further accentuated the religious tension. It is a sad commentary on the development of the period that only eight years earlier Swami Shraddhanand had preached the gospel Hindu-Muslim unity from the pulpit of the Jama Masjid of Delhi.

The violent communal riots which occurred between 1923-27 vitiated the political atmosphere in the country. There were eleven communal riots in 1923, eighteen in 1924, sixteen in 1925, thirty-five in 1926 and thirty-one up to November in 1927. In 1926, the first year of Lord Irwin's term as Viceroy, forty riots took place. After the Kohat riot in 1924 Gandhi undertook a 21-day fast.

A unity conference representing various political parties was held under the chairmanship of Muhammad Ali on 26 September, 1924 to devise ways for combating the rising tide of communalism. The resolutions passed at the conference provided for the freedom of conscience and religion, condemnation of acts like desecration of places of worship and the prosecution of those who used compulsion in the matter of conversion.[93] The conference passed a resolution which stated that "all the points in dispute shall be decided by reference either to private arbitration or where that is impossible by reference to a court of law".[94] Azad declared at this conference that cow slaughter even for purpose of sacrifice was not an integral part of Islam and that the Muslims were reducing the habit of beef eating for promoting communal harmony.[95] The meetings of an All-Parties Conference were held on 21 November, 1924 and 23 January, 1925 to settle among the political parties the question of their representation in the legislature but no agreement was arrived at. As a third party it was natural for the British to exploit the Hindu-Muslim antagonism and use it to their advantage. The Non-cooperation movement had ended, the Swarajists had entered the Council, and the Congress too had followed suit in 1926. Its representation had been somewhat reduced in number but it was still the largest single group in the Council. The experience of the Congress leaders in the Council was one of bitter disappointment because they found that the British refused to oblige the Indians by promoting in any way the cause of 'self-government' or 'responsible Government for India.'

To quell the growing Hindu-Muslim communal tension in the country, Motilal Nehru and Abul Kalam Azad issued a manifesto in the form of a circular letter about the formation of the Indian National Union on 31 July. 1926 which was supported by influential leaders like Dr. Tej Bahadur Sapru, Hakim Ajmal Khan, Mrs. Sarojini Naidu, M.A. Ansari, Dr. Syed Mahmud, Lala Duni Chand and Choudhry Khaliquzzaman.[96] The manifesto aimed at organising those sections of enlightened Indians who agreed that communalism was a negation of nationalism and that continued national conflicts would lead 'to our utter political economic and social ruin.'[97]

Azad's object was to isolate and weaken the mischievous elements in our society which were poisoning the minds of Hindus and Muslims by spreading hatred among them through nefarious propaganda against each other.[98] The membership of the proposed Indian National Union would be open to those individuals who did not belong to any communal organisation. The Union was to be truly national and was also intended to be a non-political platform. It was also supposed to be giving training to village panchayats to settle disputes arising among different sections or individuals belonging to the village community.

A preliminary meeting to finalize the objects of Indian National Union took place on 10th December, 1926 in Delhi. The draft rules and regulations of the Union were defined as follows : (1) to promote and foster the growth of a united Indian Nation and to remove all causes of inter-communal discord and separatist tendencies; and (2) to launch a vigorous propaganda in order to foster the spirit of true nationalism and genuine patriotism among the people of India and to create an atmosphere in the country that would 'facilitate a settlement of all communal issues in a noble spirit of compromise and goodwill.[99] The office of the Union was to remain in Delhi with Lala Shankar Lal as its Secretary. Membership of the Union was to be open to anyone not under the age of 18 years and the annual subscription was one rupee. A pledge for enrolment of membership was to be signed by an individual whose guiding principle was to foster communal amity.

The inauguration of the Indian National Union was viewed with mixed feelings.[100] In Congress circles the proposal was commended but the Hindu newspapers in Punjab distrusted the Union and condemned it as another sinister move to sacrifice Hindu interests to appease rabid Muslim communalists.[101]

The appointment of the Simon Commission in 1927 to examine the constitutional question of India induced the Indian leaders to formulate a scheme of Indian constitution acceptable to all the parties. Lord Birkenhead, Secretary of State for India, asked the Swarajists to produce a Constitution 'which carries behind it a fair measure of general agreement among the great people of India'. From 1927 onwards it was the constitutional question which dominated Indian politics and various attempts were made by Indian political parties to resolve it.

The communal problem had become a bugbear for Indian leadership and seemed to defy any solution during the 1920s and 1930s. The Nehru Report (1928), Jinnah's Fourteen Points (March 1929), and the All-Parties Conference (December 1929), the Simon Commission proposals (May 1930) and the three Round Table Conferences (November 1930 to January 1932) could not settle the communal problem which in Gandhi's words became a 'problem of problems'.[102] The basic question was of Muslim representation as a minority community in the new constitutional arrangements that were to be made at the provincial and central level.

Historians have generally attributed the partition of India to the failure of Congress-League interim Government experiment and the recrudescence of communal riots in 1946 or to the Pakistan Resolution of 1940 which made a demand for a separate Muslim homeland. The failure to form the Congress-League Coalition ministry in U.P., in 1937 is also regarded as a real divide between the Congress and the League which paved the way for the creation of Pakistan. But the crucial period of the late twenties and early thirties when the seeds of partition were actually sowed is usually ignored. It is in this period when the real parting of ways between the Congress and the Muslim League took place.

We need not involve ourselves in a discussion of the various proposals made for resolving the constitutional problem but in order to understand how Hindu-Muslim rift widened in Indian politics, it would be helpful to focus on the Nehru Report because it was on this document of historical importance that all discussions for settling the constitutional question ultimately hinged. The Nehru Report was published on 15 August, 1928. The Report accepted two of the Delhi proposals (1927) about the formation of North-West Frontier province and Sind and rejected separate electorate and the principle of weightage. It recommended the unitary form of Government at the Centre. The Nehru Report took the view that adult franchise would solve the problem of Muslim representation in India because it was based on the assumption that if cultural autonomy and religious liberty were guaranteed, the communal problem would be solved.[103]

The Nehru Report debarred Muslims from reservation of seats in provinces where they constituted a majority. The Report worked on the principle that 'a minority must remain a minority, whether any seats were reserved or not.' Jawaharlal Nehru assured Dr. Syed Mahmud in his letter of 30 June, 1928 that a detailed examination of the Muslim population in Bengal and Punjab shows that the Muslims were 'certain of electoral majority at least equivalent to their number.'[104] According to R. Coupland, the constitution as recommended by the Nehru Report was 'dominated by the tradition of unitary government exhibited by British rule.'[105]

On the whole the Muslims of Bengal and Punjab welcomed the Report but Shaukat Ali, Hasrat Mohani and Muhammad Ali vehemently opposed it on the ground that the Muslims were denied the federal form of government and one-third representation in the Legislature. The Agha Khan and Mohammad Shafi rejected the Report saying that separate electorates were the only way to safeguard the interests of the Muslims.

In his letter of 26 April, 1929 Shaukat Ali complained to Syed Mahmud about the 'rift which the cursed Nehru Report has created amongst us Muslims' and the 'infidelity of the Hindus who have betrayed the Muslim interests.'[106] The nationalist Muslims like Azad, Ansari, Syed Mahmud and Saifuddin Kitchlew supported the Report.[107]

At the All-Parties Conference in Calcutta in the last week of December, 1928 Jinnah described the Nehru Report as 'neither helpful nor fruitful in any way.' He suggested three amendments — (1) In the Central Legislature Muslims should be given one-third of the seats; (2) The Residuary powers should vest in the provinces and not in the Centre; and (3) The Muslims in Punjab and Bengal be represented on the basis of population for ten years if adult franchise was not introduced, subject to subsequent revision of this principle.

At the Conference Jinnah declared that Hindu-Muslim settlement was essential to the political progress of the country. He said: 'I am not speaking as a Musulman but as an Indian. And it is my desire to see that we get seven crores of Mussalmans to march along with us in the struggle for freedom.'[108] The Hindu Mahasabha leaders and the Sikh representatives from Punjab rejected Jinnah's amendments. After this, Jinnah is reported to have wept and said to a friend, Jamshed, 'This is parting of the ways.'[109] This was Jinnah's formal farewell to Indian nationalism. The *entente cordiale* that had existed between the Congress and the League came to an end. The Ali brothers left the Congress and joined the reactionary wing of the League which was led by the Agha Khan and Muhammad Shafi. Jinnah submitted Fourteen Points to the First Round Table Conference which were supported by the Jamiat ul-Ulama-e-Hind.

The result of the failure of Indian leadership to submit an agreed constitutional plan was the Ramsay MacDonald's Award on 16 August, 1932 which retained separate electorates and the provision of a Muslim majority in Punjab and Bengal. The Hindu Mahasabha rejected it; the Muslims thought it a 'distinct advance' but the Congress adopted a neutral attitude toward it, neither accepting nor rejecting it.

It is evident from the above account that a great opportunity was lost by Indian leadership to settle the Hindu-Muslim problem through constitutional means. Absorbed in constructive work activities, Gandhi was looking to the Almighty for the light, hoping that He would show him the right path. He declared 'I dare not touch the problem of Hindu-Muslim unity. It has passed out of human hands and has been transferred to God's hands.'[110] Jawaharlal Nehru, a radical youth committed to socialism believed that the communal problem was essentially an economic issue and his father too adopted a similar attitude.

The Muslim leaders as representatives of their community wanted some concrete steps for the protection of their minority rights. They were dissatisfied with the Nehru Report. They wondered why the Delhi proposals of 20 March, 1927 which had been formulated among others by Jinnah, Muhammad Shafi and the Raja of Mahmudabad and accepted later by the Congress Working Committee in May, 1927 were being discarded. Motilal would not budge an inch from his position and regarded Jinnah as a big obstacle in the solution of the problem.

In retrospect, it seems that due to the intransigence of Hindu Mahasabha and the Sikh groups from Punjab the Congress refused to meet the Muslim demands. Jawaharlal Nehru admitted later that there were political reactionaries in the Congress who were 'communalists under national cloak.'[111] Men of such a mould would not concede Muslim demands. The Congress leaders like Gandhi, Motilal and Jawaharlal Nehru believed that concessions to Muslims would not solve the communal problem. It was not the satisfaction of minority demands that was important in their calculation but the fight for India's independence which would bring in the masses to unite for a common goal. It seems that whenever the Congress was confronted with the monstrosity of communalism the only way it saw for meeting the challenge was to launch a Civil Disobedience movement. The complex issues at this point of time might have been resolved through parleys round the table but alas! that was not be! And the communal issue was allowed to smoulder so that later it needed only a spark to ignite it into a conflagration.

Because of the sectarian attitude of the Muslim League on the Minority problem, the nationalist Muslims broke away from it and founded on 27 July, 1929 the All India Nationalist Muslim Party with Azad as its convener. Other prominent members of the group were M.A. Ansari, Abdul Ghaffar Khan, Dr. Syed Mahmud, Dr. Saifuddin Kitchlew, the Raja of Mahmudabad, T.A.K. Sherwani and Choudhary Khaliquzzaman. The aims of the party were:

1. To promote among the Muslims of India the spirit of nationalism and to develop a mentality above communalism and to inspire into them confidence in Indian national ideals.
2. To induce the Muslims to take their proper share in national struggle; and
3. To create such relations between majority and minority communities as would lead the former to consider the right of minorities in a spirit of broad-minded patriotism and the latter in that of true nationalism.[112]

Azad and Ansari published a manifesto on behalf of the Nationalist Party explaining its main objectives. In April 1931 at a conference of Muslim Congress members in Lucknow a resolution was adopted calling for adult franchise, abolition of separate electorates and guarantees for the protection of national languages and religious minorities. The other important recommendation was the reservation of seats; minorities which constituted less than 30 per cent of a province's population should have the right to additional seats. These efforts to come to an agreement with the League on the minority question failed once again. The Nationalist Muslims Party did not have an independent identity and was guided by the Congress ideology and programme.

The Congress had declared complete independence as its goal at the Madras Congress of 1927. Gandhi launched two Civil Disobedience movements at short intervals (1930-31 and 1932). The British Government announced the consideration of constitutional problems which needed to be resolved before preparing India for self-government. Much debate went on among the official and non-official circles regarding the form of government suitable for India. The British declared that it was the communal problem that really thwarted the question of India's political advancement. In fact the British made full capital out of it because of the differences on this issue among the political parties. On the communal question a deadlock seemed to have been created. The Simon Commission Report was published on 23-24 June, 1930. It omitted any mention of Dominion Status as the goal of India.However,it did suggest among other things maximum devolution of responsibility to provincial ministries and a strong government at the centre but it maintained that the Governor-General's executive would not be responsible to the Assembly.

Lord Irwin, the Viceroy, announced on 31 October, 1929 that the natural issue of Indian constitutional progress was the attainment of Dominion Status. The Congress challenged the statement and asked for clarification whether a Dominion Status was to be granted immediately. The Congress session at Lahore in December, 1929 declared independence of the country as its goal and authorized the All India Congress Committee to start Civil Disobedience movement whenever it thought it necessary. The Congress insisted on the government to accept the Nehru Report. Gandhi was convinced that the Government was indulging in delaying tactics to hoodwink the Indian people. He launched the Civil Disobedience campaign on 12 March, 1930 with a view to paralysing the Government by mass performance of specific illegal acts like violating the Salt Tax, boycott of English goods, etc. Gandhi was arrested and taken to Yeravda jail in May 1930.

It is not necessary for our purpose to analyse the Civil Disobedience movement, its nature or impact. Suffice it to say, over 60,000 persons courted arrest in the first six months. The movement damaged the British economic interests, reducing the Indian imports from England considerably, especially textiles and yarn where the reduction was nearly to the extent of 31 to 45 per cent. Azad was also arrested on 21 August, 1930. In the Civil Disobedience, the Jamiat ul-Ulama-e-Hind, Ahrar party of Punjab, the nationalist Muslim groups and Khudai Khidmatgar organisation of North-West Frontier province cooperated with the Congress. The Civil Disobedience was a popular movement and its base was strong in Bihar, Orissa, U.P., Bengal and Bombay. It acquired rural adherents, and the women participation in it was quite striking.

On Gandhi's arrest, Irwin announced the Round Table Conference. Being under arrest Gandhi could not attend this conference which took place in London on 12 November, 1930. It could not resolve the communal problem. Gandhi was let out on 26 January, 1931. The Gandhi-Irwin Pact was signed on 5 March, 1931 under which the British Government agreed to release the prisoners, and the Congress to suspend the Civil Disobedience. Azad was released on 11 May, 1932. Gandhi attended the second Round Table Conference on 7 September, 1931. He insisted on the premise that the Round Table Conference should draw up a scheme for a responsible government at the Centre as in the provinces with immediate effect. He tabled the Congress scheme which was a reproduction of the Nehru Report. He admitted his utter failure to bring about any agreed settlement acceptable to the parties concerned.

The British Prime Minister Ramsay MacDonald announced the Communal Award which introduced separate electorates for the depressed and backward classes and allowed reservation of seats for Muslims in every province. Gandhi undertook a fast unto death on 20 September, 1932 in Yeravda jail against the Award. Ultimately an agreement was reached by what is known as the Poona Pact which reserved certain seats for the depressed classes.

Within three weeks of Gandhi's return in January, 1932 he was again back in prison. During his absence from India, the Government clamped a number of severe and drastic Ordinances and made a number of arrests including those of Jawaharlal Nehru, Sardar Patel, Abdul Ghaffar Khan, Syed Mähmud and others. The Civil Disobedience was resumed on 1 January, 1932. The Viceroy had refused to grant an interview to Gandhi for negotiations. According to official statistics 14,800 arrests were made in January and 17,800 in February. Gandhi was released on 8 March, 1933 and at his recommendation Mr. M.S. Aney, the Acting President of the Congress, suspended the Civil Disobedience movement.

Azad was upset over the Communal Award. He was deeply concerned about the minority problem and he took the initiative of bringing about an agreement among the communities on the communal question and he was supported in it by Madan Mohan Malaviya, Syed Mahmud and Shaukat Ali. Gandhi was in jail at that time. These leaders tried to persuade the Muslim League to arrive at a settlement on the basis of the acceptance of the Thirteen Points (out of Jinnah's Fourteen) and Muhammad Ali's formula. But this effort proved fruitless. Due to Malaviya's initiative the Unity Conference held at Allahabad on 3 November, 1932 did not oppose the concessions made to the Muslims by the Communal Award. It also accepted the separation of Sind with certain conditions. But at the All-Parties Muslim Conference in Allahabad on 11 December, 1932, prominent Muslim leaders from Punjab rejected the Award. The British Government too accepted the Muslim representation in the federal chambers and the separation of Sind.[113]

The British used Jinnah's Fourteen Points to inflame the existing religious differences. The three Round Table Conferences provided the material for the Joint Committee of both Houses of Parliament whose proposal formed the basis of the Government of India Act 1935. India was to become a federal State, though what is known as the federal part of the Act never came into operation. The Act of 1935 established effective responsible government in the provinces giving it control over a large number of subjects. Of course communal representation and safeguarding of interests of the minority communities were ensured. A White Paper was published on the recommendation of Simon Commission but there was no mention of Dominion status. Both the Congress and the League strongly criticized the Act. Nevertheless, the Act brought peace to the country for the present and the political parties decided to work it out by contesting the elections which they found round the corner.

After the Khilafat movement Azad was actively engaged in promoting the cause of Hindu-Muslim unity. He supported the Nehru Report but thought that it could be accepted only with certain modifications. He was instrumental in the establishment of Indian National Union and was the moving spirit behind the formation of All India Nationalist Muslim Party. He participated in the meetings of Unity Conferences to bridge the differences between Hindus and Muslims and negotiated with the League leaders for the settlement of communal issues. He was now a confirmed nationalist whose watchwords were freedom, national unity and cultural harmony.

In his *Autobiography*, Jawaharlal Nehru has discussed the role of nationalist Muslims in Indian politics. He wrote : "The collapse and elimination of Nationalist Muslims as a group – as individuals they are, of course, important leaders of the Congress – forms a pitiful story."[114]

Nehru thought that the nationalist Muslims had practically lost their political hold on the masses by 1934. He added : "They (the Nationalist Muslims) were all upper middle class folk, and there were no dynamic personalities amongst them – they lost touch with the masses - - - Indeed they never went to the masses."[115]

This harsh judgement of Nehru on the nationalist Muslims is unfair. The Ali brothers during the Khilafat movement had swayed the masses. Azad's eloquence on Turkey and her misfortunes during the war had moved his audience almost to tears. Hakim Ajmal Khan, a poet of distinction and philanthropist, was highly respected among people, and Ansari, a surgeon by profession, became a front-rank leader. Abdul Ghaffar Khan had a large following in the North-West Frontier province.

The Muslim communal leaders gained popular support by rousing fears in the minds of their co-religionists about their future being threatened by the Hindu-majority rule. The Congress, on the other hand, failed to offer any alternative course to allay these fears. The nationalist Muslims were supposed to act as a pressure group on the Congress but they failed in this role because they were not listened to by Congress leadership. When Ansari expressed his misgivings about the Civil Disobedience movement in February 1931 he was snubbed by Gandhi and he had to resign as President of the Delhi Provincial Congress Committee. Later the Congress policy of approaching Jinnah directly over their heads weakened their influence. Motilal boasted that Ansari dared not defy him on his Report.

Sadly enough, even the loyalty of nationalist Muslims in the Congress began to be questioned and their community did not hesitate to vilify them. Perhaps men of such idealism and strong convictions as nationalist Muslims who suffered much at the hands of their own community and became suspect in the eyes of others could never be found. They sacrificed so much and gained so little, but they never swerved from the path they had chosen. The history of nationalist Muslims which is yet to be written is the history of great suffering in a noble cause neglected by historians.

Azad too was reviled and castigated by his co-religionists and his *bona fides* began to be questioned in the Congress. To understand the character and force of India's struggle for freedom it is necessary to realize the predicament of nationalist Muslims like Azad who were remarkable men but who were prevented from playing an effective role of which they were really capable by the wrong turn events took in the late twenties and early thirties.

*References*


1. *IWF*, p. 5.
2. Sumit Sarkar : *The Swadeshi Movement in Bengal (1903-1908)*, pp. 217-243 & 367.
3. *IWF*, p. 6.
4. *Ibid.*
5. Rajat Ray, 'Revolutionaries, Pan-Islamists, and Bolsheviks : Maulana Abul Kalam Azad and the Political Underworld of Calcutta 1905-1925' in Mushirul Hasan ed., *Communal and Pan-Islamic Trends in Colonial India*, pp.103-05.
6. *Foreign and Pol., Frontier B-Confidential, A Proceeding; 1914*, pp. 241-430; Proceeding, 271.
7. *Ibid.*, See *Home Pol.*, A, June, 1919, 517-527.
8. *Ibid.* Letter to Col. C. Wilson from Sir Charles Cleveland, No. 3923, XI, 7 Dec., 1916; Appendix to the Silk letter Conspiracy, See *Foreign and Pol. Dept. Frontier B.A. Proceeding, 1914*, pp. 241-430.
9. *Home Pol.*, June, 1919, A, 517-525. See also *Home Pol.*, May, 1916, A. 455-456.
10. *Home Pol.*, 1919 A. 517-525.
11. James Campbell Ker, *Political Trouble in India*, 1907-17, p. 314.
12. *Home Pol.*, June, 1919, A, 517-525.
13. For the impact of these movements, see VN Datta, *Jallianwala Bagh*, particularly the last chapter.
14. Jawaharlal Nehru, *An Autobiography*, p. 44.
15. Douglas's treatment of Azad's role in Freedom struggle is superficial; see Douglas, *op. cit.*, pp. 172-78 and 234-38. Editors' conclusions too offer a cursory survey of his political activity in thirteen pages, 293-305. This survey is based on information drawn from a few pages of Nicholas Mansergh's *Transfer of Power* volumes.
16. Judith M. Brown, *Gandhi's Rise to Power*, pp. 190-230. See also V.N. Datta and S.C. Mittal, *Sources of National Movement*, pp. XIX-III.
17. R.A., Gordon, 'Non-Cooperation and Council Entry', in *Locality, Province and Nation, Essays on Indian Politics, 1870 to 1940*, p. 13.
18. Minault *op. cit.*, p. 87.
19. Judith Brown, *op. cit.*, pp. 205-06.
20. *Ibid.*, *op. cit.*, 207; Minault, *op. cit.*, 93.
21. *Ibid.*, p. 207. See Francis Robinson, *op. cit.*, p. 307 and Minault, *op. cit.*, p. 93.
22. Minault, *op. cit.*, p. 94; This account of Azad's speech is based on Minault, *op. cit.*, See pp. 93-95; See Francis Robinson, *op. cit.*, p. 307.
23. *Zikr*, pp. 24-25, Minault, *The Khilafat Movement*, p. 101, *Paigham*, 25 November, 1921.
24. Mushirul Haq, *Muslim Politics in India* p.94, see *Makatib-e-Azad*, (ed. Abu Salman Shahjahanpuri), p. 103.
25. *Ibid.*, p. 98.

26. Maulana Sayyid Ahmad Akbarbadi, *Maulana Abul Kalam Ki Sirat aur Ilmi Karnamey*, p. 61.
27. Malik Ram, *Kuch Abul Kalam Azad Kay Barey Main*, p. 168.
28. Minault, *op. cit.*, pp. 95-96.
29. Judith Brown, *op. cit.*, pp. 207-09.
30. *IWF*, pp. 8-10. See Francis Robinson, *op. cit.*, p. 308.
31. Judith Brown, *op. cit.*, *Ibid.*, Francies Robinson, *op. cit.*, p. 308.
32. Judith Brown, *op. cit.*, p. 218; Francis Robinson, *op. cit.*, p. 311.
33. Francis Robinson, *Separation among Indian Muslims*, p. 327.
34. *Ibid.*
35. Mushirul Haq, *Muslim Politics in Modern India*, p. 124.
36. Judith Brown, *op. cit.*, p. 244.
37. *Ibid.*
38. *Ibid.*
39. *Ibid.*
40. *Ibid.*
41. Jawaharlal Nehru, *An Autobiography*, p. 69.
42. Abul Kalam Azad, 'Khutabat-e-Sadarat, Majlis-e-Khilafat', Agra, 25 Aug., 1921 in Azad, *Khutbat-e-Azad*, p. 51. For the Covenant see Sir William Muir, *The Life of Muhammed*, p. 184.
43. *Zikr*, p. 45; Minault, op. cit., p. 119.
44. Azad, *Khutbat-e-Azad*, pp. 37-39. See Abu Salman Shahjahanpuri, *Makatib-e-Azad*, p. 115.
45. Francis Robinson, *op. cit.*, p. 330, Minault, *op. cit.*, pp. 169-72.
46. *Paigham*, 23 Sept., 1921.
47. *Ibid.*
48. *Ibid.*, 22 Sept. 1921; 14 Oct., 21 Oct., 1921. See Minaulet, *op. cit.*, p. 125.
49. *Khutbat-e-Azad*, pp. 40-68.
50. *Ibid.*, pp. 59-62.
51. *Ibid.*, p. 72
52. *Ibid.*, pp. 139-157.
53. This account is based on analysis of his speeches and articles on the Khilafat, published in *Paigham* and *Khutbat-e-Azad.*
54. Abul Kalam Azad, *Khutbat-e-Azad*, pp. 83-156.
55. A.G. Noorani, *Indian Political Trials*, p. 41. See *Qaul-e-Faisal*, p. 7.
56. *Ibid.*, p. 160.
57. *Ibid.*, p. 161.
58. Mahadev Desai, *Maulana Abul Kalam Azad*, p. 44.
59. A.G. Noorani, *op. cit.*, p. 164.
60. *Ibid.*
61. *Ibid.*, p. 165.
62. *Ibid.*, pp. 167-68.
63. *Ibid.*, p. 168.
64. *Ibid.*, p. 169.
65. *Ibid.*, p. 170.
66. *Ibid.*, p. 171.
67. *Ibid.*
68. *Ibid.*

69. *Ibid.*, p. 173.
70. *Ibid.*, p. 174.
71. *Ibid.*, p. 175.
72. *Ibid.*, p. 177.
73. *Ibid.*, p. 178.
74. *Ibid.*
75. *Ibid.*
76. *Ibid.*
77. Minault, *The Khilafat Movement*, pp. 204-05.
78. Francis Robinson, *op. cit.*, p. 327.
79. *Ibid.*, pp. 153-54.
80. Azad mistakenly states that he was released in May 1923. See *TQ*, Vol. I, p. 24.
81. In *Khutbat-e-Azad*, the date of this session is wrongly given as 15 December; see p. 157.
82. *Ibid.*, pp. 157-210.
83. *Ibid.*, pp. 180-81.
84. *Ibid.*, pp. 191-93.
85. *Ibid.*, pp. 202-03.
86. *Ibid.*, pp. 181-82.
87. *Ibid.*, p. 205.
88. *Ibid.*, pp. 207-08.
89. *Ibid.*, pp. 196-97.
90. Mahadev Desai, *op. cit.*, p. 62.
91. *IWF*, pp. 24-25.
92. *Ibid.*, p. 25.
93. R. Subramania Iyer, *The Role of Maulana Azad in Indian Politics*, p. 37.
94. *Ibid.*
95. *Ibid.*
96. *The Indian Quarterly Register*, 1926, pp. 90-94.
97. *Ibid.*
98. *Ibid.*
99. *Ibid.*, p. 94.
100. *Ibid.*
101. *Ibid.*
102. Mushirul Hasan (ed.) *Muslims and the Congress*, p. 266.
103. *The All Parties Conference, 1928, Report of the Committee appointed by the Conference to determine the Principles for the Constitution, for India* 1928, p. 43.
104. V.N. Datta and B. Cleghorn, *A Nationalist Muslim and Indian Politics*, p. 89. The portions relating to communal problem and the statistical position in Bengal and Punjab were compiled by Jawaharlal for the Nehru Report. See David Page, *Prelude to Partition*, p. 172.
105. R. Coupland, *The Constitutional Problem in India*, p. 94.
106. V.N. Datta and B. Cleghorn, *op. cit.*, p. 92.
107. *The Indian Quarterly Register*, Jan-June 1929, Vol. I, No. 1-2.
108. David Page, *op. cit.*, p. 191.
109. Aziz Beg, *Jinnah and His Times*, p. 370.
110. *Collected Works of Mahatma Gandhi*, Vol. 32, p. 511.

111. Jawaharlal Nehru, *An Autobiography*, p. 136.
112. *The Indian Quarterly Register, 1929*, Vol. II, p. 350.
113. Moin Shakir, 'The Muslims and the Freedom Struggle in India, 1919-1935', p. 333. In B.B. Pande (ed.) *A Centenary History of the Indian National Congress*, (1919-1935), Vol. II.
114. Jawaharlal Nehru, *An Autobiography*, p. 139.
115. *Ibid.*

# 5

# AS CONGRESS CHIEF

After M.A. Ansari's death in 1936 the Congress depended mainly on Azad for guidance on the problems concerning Muslims. In fact from now onwards he emerges as a front-rank political leader. He was elected a member of the Congress Working Committee on 16 April 1936 under the Presidentship of Jawaharlal Nehru and, became with Vallabhbhai Patel and Rajendra Prasad a member of the parliamentary Sub-Committee which came to be known as 'High Command'. As a member of this Committee it became his responsibility to supervise the working of the legislatures and ministries in the provinces. The Muslim majority provinces, Bengal, Punjab and North-West Frontier were put under his charge. Later U.P. was also placed under his supervision.

The Congress contested the elections in February 1937 to combat the 1935 Act, which resulted in a striking Congress success securing an overall majority in five provinces and emerging as the single strongest party in two others. Over 54 per cent of the electorate went to the polls and out of the total of 1581 seats in the Provincial assemblies, the Congress won as many as 711. The Congress won 26 out of 58 Muslim seats contested against the total of 485 reserved separate seats. The Non-Congress Muslims won 424 seats. The Muslim League contested a little less than half the seats reserved for Muslims in separate constituencies and won about sixty per cent of them. The Congress was able to form ministries in seven provinces: U.P., Bihar, Bombay, Central Provinces, Madras and North-West Frontier. Assam had a Congress ministry in September, 1938, after the first cabinet was thrown out and Sind formed a cabinet supported by the Congress Party. The League was extremely weak in Muslim majority provinces and was routed in Punjab. It failed to form ministries even in Sind, and North-West Frontier Province. However, it showed better results in U.P., and Bengal. It won 108 out of 482 total Muslim seats but was nowhere able to form a ministry.

Azad was by nature a man of moderate disposition. In his political thinking he had been close to C.R. Das and Moti Lal Nehru. He firmly believed in settling political issues through negotiations. He had succeeded in resolving differences between the 'No-Changers' and 'Pro-Changers' in 1923-24. On the Nehru Report, too, he had tried to bring together the contending parties. As a politician his mind was always active in devising alternatives for resolving political issues. On the formation of provincial ministries after the election in 1937, he was keen on the Congress and the League sharing power in the experiment of self-government. In his view this opportunity for working together might prove helpful in resolving the communal question. Even if we do not take Humayun Kabir's account in *India Wins Freedom* seriously, it is clear that in the negotiations for Congress-League Coalition Ministry in U.P., Azad played a leading role.[1]

The issue of the Congress-League coalition ministry in U.P. has provoked much controversy among historians. For a proper understanding of the entire sequence of developments in this regard, we must place the issue in a historical perspective. Unfortunately, there has been a general tendency amongst us to insert our present day prejudices in the assessment of this crucial issue which was not properly handled by our leaders and for this the country had to pay a heavy price. It must be recognised at this point that the Muslim League of 1935-36 was different in its approach to national issues from what it became later in 1938-39. Jinnah's own stand underwent a great change in the late thirties from his earlier thinking on the question of political rights of the minorities.

Increasingly dissatisfied with what he considered the smugness and obtuseness of Indian politics, Jinnah went to London in 1930 and practised there at the Privy Council. He was later persuaded to return to India by Liaquat Ali Khan to organise the Muslim League. A former Prime Minister of India gave an explanation of Jinnah's return to India to this writer an allusion to which will be in order here. He said that when a prominent Congress leader told Nehru that Jinnah was practising law at the Privy Council, he is reported to have said, 'good riddance'. This comment was carried to Jinnah who felt enraged so much at this 'impudence' that he returned to India to settle his accounts with Nehru.[2] Whatever be the reasons for Jinnah's return, he started taking active part in Indian politics and began to organise the Muslim League.

As a leader of the Independent party, Jinnah congratulated the 'Hindu-Brethren' for protecting the rights of depressed classes on 1 February, 1935. He complimented Gandhi for serving the cause of the minorities by his 'fast unto death' which compelled the Government to come to a settlement known as the "Poona Pact.' Jinnah's speeches before the elections reflect his abiding faith in Gladstonian liberalism, and his political idiom was not religious but secular and constitutional. At this stage of his political career, he thought in terms of the political rights of minorities. The *Mullas* and *Moulvis* nowhere existed in his political vocabulary. In the election manifesto of the League prepared under his direction the emphasis was on the cultivation of 'Victorian Liberalism' among people which means the preservation of their democratic rights of equality and justice. Jinnah fought the elections on the basis of co-operation with the Congress. He said, "There is really no substantial difference between the League and the Congress and we shall always be glad to co-operate with the Congress in their constructive programme."[3]

If we compare the 1937 electoral manifestoes of the Congress and the League we do not find in them any substantial differences on social and economic matters such as industrial development, uplift of the rural population, relief from rural indebtedness and civil liberty.[4] The Congress manifesto was drafted by Jawaharlal Nehru. In the League manifesto special emphasis was laid on fighting the reactionary forces (meaning the National Agricultural Party), upholding the ideals of 'Victorian Liberalism', nationalising the Indian army and reducing the cost of administration.[5]

The League manifesto stressed the need for co-operation with the Congress in self-rule. The only difference lay in its insistence on separate electorates and the protection and promotion of Urdu.[6] The League's demand for safeguarding the minority rights cannot be regarded as communalism. In fact there was nothing in the League's programme to obstruct a political "entente' between the Congress and the League.

Nehru's letter to Dr. Rajendra Prasad dated 21 July, 1937 is very significant on the Congress-League relations.[7] Nehru makes it clear that there was no conflict between the Congress and the League during the elections and the desire was to avoid it.[8] According to him the tussle was wholly with the Government Party meaning (the National Agricultural Party) and there was hardly any problem in practice 'in promoting good relations with the League.' Nehru wrote that he even 'supported the League candidate if he was not reactionary.'[9]

Hailing the Lucknow Pact of 1916 as a unique demonstration of the purpose, earnestness and co-operation between the two great sections of the people of India, the League manifesto emphasised that from that time onward the Muslims had stood shoulder to shoulder with the Hindus in the task of the attainment of self-government.[10] The manifesto further stated that the Muslims did not lag behind in patriotic co-operation with the Hindus and hoped that they 'can rely on the majority with a complete sense of confidence.'[11] It is in this background of cordiality of relationship between the two political parties before the 1937 elections testified by both Jinnah and Nehru that Azad's efforts for a negotiated settlement on the ministry formation in U.P., have to be seen.

It is now acknowledged that for the Congress-League coalition in Bombay Jinnah approached K.M. Munshi who later became a Minister in the cabinet but his offer was turned down by the 'High Command.'[12] Even after a fierce controversy with Nehru on this issue, Jinnah approached B.G. Kher, the Premier in Bombay for Congress-League coalition. As Jinnah's lieutenant, Khaliquzzaman, a prominent Muslim league leader of U.P., who, as a staunch Congressman earlier was closely associated with Nehru, could not have come up without Jinnah's approval with an offer to negotiate with the Congress on the formation of a coalition ministry. Jinnah himself was in favour of a coalition ministry in Bombay. As a member of the Congress Parliamentary Board, Azad met Khaliquzzaman on 5 July, 1937 and initiated the talks for the Congress-League ministry in U.P.[13] Thereafter he held several meetings with Khaliquzzaman on this issue.

According to Khaliquzzaman the Muslim League Parliamentary Board had authorized him to continue talks with the Congress provided (1) The Muslim League Legislature party did not join the Congress in wrecking the Constitution; (2) the Congress and the League were to agree upon a programme in accordance with the programme of the League; and (3) the Communal Award and separate electorate in the local self-governing bodies were to continue till an all-India settlement of the communal problem was arrived at.[14] To say therefore that Khaliquzzaman negotiated behind Jinnah's back or that Jinnah would have wriggled out because he was not consulted is contrary to facts. Jinnah of 1937 cannot be regarded as a diehard communalist. We know that he had accepted the principle of an all-India federation at the Round Table Conference in 1930. During the interim period before the 1935 Act, Congress and Muslim League had combined against the Government. In 1937 the Muslim League was a small organisation run with inadequate resources both in terms of men and material. After the elections it was natural for the League to think of sharing power with the Congress in U.P., when both the parties had fought the elections on a common platform with more or less identical programmes on major social and economic issues.

After the elections the Congress emerged as the strongest party to form an independent ministry in U.P. But out of the 64 Provincial Assembly seats reserved for Muslims chosen by separate electorate, 26 were won by Muslim League, 28 by independent Muslims, 9 by the National Agricultural Party and only 1 by the Congress.[15] Hafiz Muhammad Ibrahim defected from the League to join the Congress later.

Khaliquzzaman, leader of the Muslim League Party in U.P., was negotiating on the coalition-ministry formation with Azad in July, 1937. What Sri Prakasa, a detached observer of contemporary events who became later the Governor of Bombay wrote shows that Azad was deeply committed to the formation of coalition Ministry in U.P.[16] On Pant's query how many ministerial seats the League would want, Khaliquzzaman replied '2' out of 6, 3 out of 8.' The conditions stipulated by the Congress for the League joining the Ministry came as a rude shock to Khaliquzzaman. According to these conditions the Muslim League group in U.P. Provincial Legislature would cease to function as a separate group and become a part of the Congress party and Muslim League and the Muslim League Parliamentary Board would also be dissolved.[17] In fact what the Congress wanted was the merging of the League with the Congress. When Azad proposed these conditions to Khaliquzzaman he said, "You want me to sign the death warrant of the Muslim League."[18] These were impossible demands which no political party worth the name could accept unless it had decided to liquidate itself. These conditions were a clear threat to the League that they must abandon their separate political identity before they could think of sharing power with the Congress.

Khaliquzzaman made an alternative proposal which looks more reasonable: (1) on communal matters the League should have complete freedom of action; and (2) in the Ministry there should be two members of the League, himself and Nawab Ismail Khan.[19] The Congress rejected this proposal and the U.P. Congress Ministry was formed with two Muslims, one, the only Congress Muslim elected and the other who had deserted the League to become a Minister.

Heavens would not have fallen if two ministerial seats had been offered to the League. Politics is the art of the possible. Thus a good opportunity of active co-operation between the Congress and League was lost for which the country was to pay a big price later. If the coalition ministries supported by the League could work satisfactorily in Bengal and later the Unionist Ministry in Punjab with the Congress alliance, why could it not do so in U.P. It is possible that the irritating problems like the future of Urdu, *Vande Matram*, music before mosques, the unfurling of national flag and Gandhi's Basic Education could have been resolved by a mutual spirit of give-and-take. Recalling how the Congress rule had harassed the Muslims, Jinnah told Lord Mountbatten in early 1947, 'Well, look, what they did to us in 1938-39 they oppressed us,.[20] A successful working of the Congress-League coalition would have prevented the possibility of the Pakistan resolution of 1940. The newly published material of Iqbal-Jinnah correspondence in Pakistan shows that the poet-philosopher was urging Jinnah in May 1937 to fight for the establishment of an autonomous Muslim state in north-western India but Jinnah was rather cool to this proposal.[21] The Aligarh professors prepared a comprehensive thesis on the two nation-theory and submitted it to Jinnah. This they did to strengthen his hands for building up a separate state of Muslim majority areas but Jinnah was not inclined to encourage it.

Jinnah had left the Congress during the Non-cooperation on the Mahatma's mixing religion with politics. The rejection of the U.P. coalition proposals by the Congress was a bitter pill for him to swallow and at the Lucknow Muslim League conference which took place in the middle of October, 1937, after the talks on the coalition issues had failed, he chose what Gandhi then called 'a war path.' In Jinnah's politics the conference, in fact, marks the beginning of a new militant phase based on strong mistrust of the aims and objectives of the Congress Party. Leaders like Sir Sikandar Hayat Khan of Punjab, Sir Fazl-ul-Haq of Bengal and Sir M. Saddullah of Assam gave Jinnah fullest support by advising the members of their respective parties to join the League. The U.P. Muslim leadership including Shaukat Ali, Khaliquz-zaman and Liaqat Ali using Aligarh Muslim intellectuals as their base infused an entirely new spirit in the League.[22] A few months after the Lucknow conference, 40 League branches were set up in U.P., and the League membership rose to 100,000. Jinnah came to be a symbol of Muslim destiny and began to be greeted in the country as a spokesman of the urges and aspirations of the Muslims. There was a swift and striking increase in his popularity. He said, 'Muslims can expect neither justice nor fair play under Congress government.' In the light of the Muslim League's growing popularity S. Gopal's view that "no weighty consequences followed the failure of U.P. talks" is not justified.[23] In a recent study it has been shown that the talks for Congress-Muslim League coalition in U.P. failed due to the stringent conditions imposed by the Congress and that the failure of these talks strengthened the arguments in favour of a separate Muslim State.[24]

A perusal of the conditions laid down by the Congress for the coalition ministry would show that the Congress was not at all serious about any compromise with the League. Swayed by its euphoria over its election success, it refused to compromise with the League and showed lack of political realism. In the words of the Raja of Mahmudabad, the Congress wanted the League 'to commit suicide at the steps of Anand Bhawan.' The real decision on the coalition ministry rested with members of the Congress Parliamentary Sub-Committee like Vallabhbhai Patel, Rajendra Prasad and the leader of U.P. Legislative Party, Govind Ballabh Pant. Intellectually and temperamentally Jawaharlal Nehru loathed the idea of negotiating with any communal organisation particularly the League which he condemned as a reactionary organisation led by feudal landlords for their vested interests.

Nehru had been one of the chief organisers of his party's elections in U.P. Because of his high political stature in the country and his closeness to Gandhi, his word on political matters carried great weight. On the Congress-League coalition in U.P., his letter to Prasad shows clearly that he was firmly opposed to it from the beginning.[25] In this letter he was influenced by what Azad called 'theoretical considerations.' Nehru wrote that he did not like, to use his own expression, 'angling for ministries,.[26] He opposed the idea of giving two ministerial berths to the League. He added that he 'disliked the bargaining of seats.'[27] He asked : 'What about those who severed their connections with the League and joined us?' He anticipated 'risk of conflict' by 'this bargaining' in his own party. To give greater emphasis to the matter which strongly agitated his mind Nehru stated very emphatically that he was ' repelled by this talk on opportunistic basis.' In reality Nehru favoured the entry into the cabinet of his friend Rafi Ahmed Kidwai and Hafiz Ibrahim who had defected from the League. Nehru frankly admits that the conditions imposed on the League for merging itself with the Congress were stringent, the underlying idea being to prevent the League from accepting these terms.[28]

Nehru wanted nothing short of winding up of the League. Khaliquzzaman was willing to negotiate further but the Congress withdrew its offer. Khaliquzzaman wanted to call another meeting of the Muslim League Legislature Party to consider the matter further. On the Congress-League coalition Nehru had consulted Dr. K.M. Ashraf, Acharya Kripalani, Narendra Deva, members of the Congress Socialist Party and Purshottamdas Tandon, a staunch Hindu revivalist who too refused co-operation with the League. Khaliquzzaman calls this group a motley crowd of the Leftists and a Hindu reactionary, and thinks that Nehru was influenced on the coalition issue by their views. M.C. Chagla holds Nehru responsible for not allowing the coalition in U.P.[29]

Thus Azad's efforts for a Congress-League coalition did not succeed.[30] His wise counsel was disregarded though he had Gandhi's support on this issue.[31] Sri Prakasa in his letter to Khaliquzzaman says that Azad who was the 'zonal dictator' at the time could never overcome his regrets on the failure of the Congress-League coalition.[32] Khaliquzzaman further points out that Azad being influenced by Nehru took away the Jamiat ul-Ulama from the League on 17 May, 1937 which sealed the fate of further negotiations with the Congress for any political understanding.[33]

Before the 1937 elections the League had worked for safeguarding the minority interests of the Muslims but after the elections it began to think of a separate homeland. A man of moderate disposition, Khaliquzzaman had made earnest efforts to bring about a rapprochement between the Congress and the League. Khaliquzzaman said, "I ran from pillar to post, begging the Congress leadership to realize the dangers they were courting but this was taken as a weakness."[34] After the failure of these talks on the coalition, Jinnah was altogether a different man. Bellicose in his speeches, he refused to have anything to do with the Congress. Now Gandhi, Nehru, Subhas Bose and Prasad were desperately keen to open unity talks with Jinnah but he was not willing to listen to them. The great opportunity for collaboration of the two parties in the task of safeguarding the minority interests within the political framework of united India was lost. I am inclined to agree with the view that the Congress policy on the coalition issue was to put it in Hodson's words, a blunder of the first order.[35]

Lord Mountbatten, the Viceroy, while analysing the circumstances leading to the Partition also thought that the Congress attitude towards the U.P. coalition problem was most unreasonable. Recalling the events he said in an interview :

> Instead of having enough sense to have coalition government and

> bringing in the Muslim League (and even at the worst if they did not do that, they should have gone out of the way to give the Muslims the best possible treatment), they (the Congress) in fact did not allow them in anywhere and opposed them. They convinced the Muslim League that that was the kind of treatment they in fact would get if they did not try and stand out for independence.[36]

The year 1940 opened with Azad's election as President of Indian National Congress on 17 March and the Muslim League's Pakistan Resolution of 23 March for a separate homeland. Earlier Azad had presided over the Congress session at Delhi in September, 1923. When Subhas Chandra Bose was contesting the Presidential election against Pattabhi Sitaramayya, Gandhi proposed Azad's name. Azad had agreed first but later withdrew on 21 January, 1939 leaving Bose and Pattabhi Sitaramayya to contest. As was his wont, Azad avoided embroiling himself in any such controversy. But now when critical decisions were to be taken there were sound reasons for Azad being called upon to take up Presidentship of the Congress. He was known for his quiet temper, sobriety of judgement and physiographic tact to grasp the essentials of political problems. He was elected President of the Congress at Ramgarh (in Chotta Nagpur area in Bihar) by 1864 votes against M.N. Roy who polled only 183.

Azad remained at the helm of the Congress for about six years at a critical juncture in the country's history when momentous political decisions were taken. He took up his new responsibility with great elan. He reconstituted the Congress Working Committee and brought back Nehru who had been excluded in Prasad's committee. He also included C. Rajagopalachari, Dr. Syed Mahmud and Asaf Ali as members. He delivered an eloquent and forceful Presidential address at Ramgarh on 19 March which dealt with vital national and international issues. His treatment of various issues he touched upon in this address was marked by passionate energy as well as logical clarity and precision.[37] He delivered his speech in chaste Urdu and it was translated into English by Nehru. Azad greatly liked Nehru's translation of his speech which showed how Nehru had captured the true spirit of the original and rendered it into English with felicity and accuracy of phrasing. Azad thought that the English translation was a real improvement on his original text which he attributed to Nehru's first rate intellect' and 'exceptional talents.'[38]

In his address Azad focused mainly on India's immediate political problems in the context of the prevailing international crisis. He strongly attacked the rise of fascism in Europe but showed no mercy for British imperialism either since it continued to deny the right of self-determination to the subject people. He declared that India's fight was not directed against the British people but British imperialism which even at that critical moment withheld from the people their fundamental rights.

Azad protested that without consulting the Congress Britain had the impudence to push the country into war.[40] He made it clear that British rule was not to be tolerated any longer. He said :

> So far as the question of war is concerned our position is quite clear. We see the face of British imperialism as clearly now as we did in the last war. Our case is crystal clear. We do not wish to see British Imperialism triumphant and stronger and thus lengthen the period of our own subjection to it. We absolutely refuse to do so.[41]

About the future of India Azad made it clear that his country was no longer willing to be duped by any British assurances of 'safeguards' or 'promises of concessions' after the termination of the war. Azad dispelled the impression from the minds of his countrymen that the 'third power' – meaning Britain, was going to quit India. The need of the hour, he felt, was to see the goal clearly and to unite the people to fight the battle for India's freedom.[42]

Azad also covered the communal problem at great length. He admitted its stark reality but said that it had been created by the British for serving their sinister designs. He firmly believed in the unity of Hindu-Muslim composite culture. According to Azad, Hindus and Muslims professed different religious faiths but as a nation they were one, an integral part of the common heritage for which any nation could be legitimately proud. He pointed out that there was no contradiction in being a good Indian and a devout Muslim, in owning the common heritage of Islam and India. He said emphatically that the inexorable logic of history had fused the Hindus and Muslims into a nation and no power on earth could sunder that indissoluble bond. On the Hindu-Muslim question, he declared :

> Full eleven centuries have passed by since then. Islam has now as great a claim on the soil of India as Hinduism. If Hinduism has been the religion of the people here for several thousands of years,

> Islam also has been their religion for a thousand years. Just as a Hindu can say with pride that he is an Indian and a Hindu, so also we can say with equal pride that we are Indians and follow Islam.[43]

Azad then assured the Muslims that their fears of being swamped by the Hindus were groundless because the strength of any community did not depend on the sheer brutality of its numbers but on its own internal resources to stand for its rightful place in national life.[44]

Discussing how the Muslim interests would be protected, Azad explained two basic principles which, he maintained, had guided the Congress policy throughout its history.

1. Whatever Constitution is adopted for India, there must be the fullest guarantees in it for the rights and interests of minorities.
2. The minorities should judge for themselves what safeguards are necessary for the protection of their rights and interests. The majority should not decide this. Therefore the decision in this respect must depend upon the consent of the minorities and not on a majority vote.

Azad firmly believed that the rights of minorities could be protected in a Federation which he explained as follows :

> The recognized minorities have a right, if they so please, to choose their representatives by their votes. Their representatives will not have to rely upon the votes of any other community except their own. So far as the question of the rights and interests of the minorities is concerned, the decision will not depend upon the majority of votes in the Constituent Assembly. It will be subject to the consent of the minority. If unanimity is not achieved on any question, then an impartial tribunal, to which the minority have also consented, will decide the matter. This last proviso merely in the nature of a provision for a possible contingency is most unlikely to be required. If a more practical proposal is made, there can be no objection to that.[45]

Azad reminded the British Government that with the formation of the ministries in 1937 the Congress had stretched forth its hand of cooperation to the Government but they were forced to withdraw it after the unilateral declaration of war. The question facing the Indian people, Azad asked, was 'where do we go from here?' Azad thought that not much had been lost yet and the situation could be salvaged provided the Government understood the political climate in the country.[46] Placing his faith in the leadership of Gandhi, Azad hoped that the deadlock between the Congress and the Government could still be resolved.

On Hindu-Muslim unity and composite culture of which he was a symbol, Azad delivered some strikingly lyrical passages remarkable for their intellectual range, convictions and sensitivity. Azad said :

> I would remind my co-religionists that I stand to-day exactly where I stood in 1912 when I addressed them on this question (Hindu-Muslim unity). I have given thought to the innumerable things which have helped since then. My eyes and my mind did not fail to watch them and to think about them. I was in their midst and I examined every circumstance with care. I cannot belie my experience, I repeat today what I had said throughout the entire period that the ninety-nine millions of Indian Muslims have no right course of action except the one to which I invited them in 1912.[47]

On the theme of 'composite culture' there appears in his diction a kind of bold and noble purity as he invoked the idea of human brotherhood forged between the two great streams of Indian civilizations, that is, Hinduism and Islam.[48] The following passage shows his pride as an heir to India's rich cultural heritage.

> I am a Muslim and proud of the fact. Islam's splendid traditions of thirteen hundred years are my inheritance. I am unwilling to lose even the smallest part of this inheritance. In addition, I am proud of being an Indian. I am part of the indivisible unity that is Indian nationality .... I am indispensable in this noble edifice. Without me this splendid structure of India is incomplete. I am an essential element which has gone to build India. I can never surrender this claim.[49]

Azad admired the virtues of 'composite culture' but he condemned strongly the Hindu and Muslim tendency to revive exclusively their own narrow past to the neglect of rich heritage of common culture which they have jointly evolved through the centuries. He warned :

> If the Hindus think of reviving their thousand years old way of life, then they must be living under an illusion. Similarly if the.Muslims believe in adopting their hundred years old beliefs which they had brought from Persia and Middle East then they are mistaken. The earlier the Hindus and Muslims discard these notions the better. Such mode of thinking is unnatural.[50]

Azad believed that 'revivalism' of the true spirit of religion may be justified but any idea of reproducing the old social and cultural pattern of life was fraught with dangerous consequences for the progress of any society.[51]

Azad emphasised that for the freedom of their country, unity and discipline, the leadership of Mahatma Gandhi was absolutely necessary.[52] The Presidential address delivered by Azad was distinguished by its firm grasp of contemporary national and international issues which reflected his strong denunciation of fascism and British imperialism, his deep concern for Hindu-Muslim unity, his firm faith in Gandhi's leadership and his still lurking hope of resolving the Indian political question with the British through negotiations and goodwill on both sides.

To check the rising tide of communalism the Congress launched a Muslim mass contact programme. The idea of this campaign was initiated by Nehru to which the Congress lent its approval in October, 1937. In this campaign the Congress was supported by the Ahrars, Khudai Khidmatgars and the socialists. Dr. K.M. Ashraf was put in charge of the Muslim mass contact campaign. In a recent study it has been shown that the campaign had success initially in some parts of U.P., Bihar, Bengal and Punjab.[53] Largely urban-based it failed to generate Muslim confidence in the Congress in rural areas. From the beginning Gandhi had strong reservations about it.

Azad too worked for the Muslim mass contact programme and enlisted for it the support of Jamiatul-Ulama-e Hind. It was the alliance of the right wing in the Congress with the Hindu Mahasabha which wrecked the campaign.[54] With the termination of the tenure of Nehru's Presidentship of the Congress, all zeal for it was gone. Dr. Ashraf complained that he was sitting idle in his office doing nothing.[55] The upshot was that this campaign, though inspired by good intentions, proved ill-conceived, and unproductive and further aggravated the already deteriorating relations between the Congress and the League.

When the Congress was in office, the Muslim League launched a virulent tirade against it by condemning it as a purely HIndu organisation and oppressing the Muslims by its anti-Muslim programme and policies. The League approached the Government for the appointment of a Royal Commission to inquire into the alleged atrocities on the Muslims. The League published the Pirpur Report at the end of 1938 which highlighted the oppression inflicted on the Muslims during Congress rule. As a member of the Congress Parliamentary Board, Azad knew the working of the ministries and he found that the League's allegations of the Congress discriminating attitude towards Muslims were absolutely baseless. Azad condemned the Pirpur Report which he thought had made all sorts of false allegations.

A crisis developed in the Congress on the question of the election of the Congress President in November 1938. Gandhi was keen on Azad's election to the Presidency as he thought that in the prevailing atmosphere of communal tension this might help in curbing the growth of communalism.[56] Meanwhile, Subhas Chandra Bose declared his candidature for the second term of Presidency. The right-wing leadership in the Congress headed by Gandhi opposed this move because they disapproved of Bose's militant policy on national issues. Azad had agreed first to contest the election but later withdrew his candidature on 20 January 1939. In the elections a lot of acrimony was generated but we need not go into details on this issue. Bose was re-elected at Tripura on 29 January 1939 defeating Pattabhi Sitaramayya. On 22 February twelve members of the Congress Working Committee including Azad resigned requesting the President to select a homogeneous executive. Due to his illness Bose could not preside over the Congress session. Azad conducted the meeting.

Bose's Presidential Address was read out. Bose wanted an ultimatum on national demands for independence to be submitted to the Government and a time-limit prescribed for the Government's reply failing which the Congress would be forced to resort to Civil Disobedience.[57] This did not attract the right-wing of the Congress which was more concerned with organisational matters rather than with launching a mass movement at this juncture. Govind Ballabh Pant moved a resolution which was passed by a majority declaring their faith in Gandhi's leadership and requesting the Congress President to nominate the Working Committee in accordance with Gandhi's wishes. Despite Bose's negotiations with Gandhi no settlement between the contending parties could be possible. Bose resigned on 29 April 1939.

Azad supported the right-wing leadership in its fight with Bose. He did not think that it was the proper time for an open confrontation with the British. In his letter to Nehru dated 17 April 1939 Azad wrote :

> I consider the affair of Subhas Babu to be neither a struggle between the right and left, nor the question of a composite and homogeneous working committee. It is only a matter of Subhas and some of his supporters. It matters little in what form tangle comes to an end, we have to consider these questions independently and specifically, in order to reach a solution.[58]

When the question came up for taking disciplinary action against Bose for his defiance against the Congress, Azad favoured taking a lenient view of the matter. With Bose's resignation, Rajendra Prasad was elected as President, with a new Congress Working Committee which included Azad as a member.

On the outbreak of War, the Viceroy Lord Linlithgow declared on 3 September 1939 that 'War has broken out between His Majesty and Germany and that a state of war emergency has existed.'[59] In this way India went into the war as a belligerent country against Germany. This unilateral declaration of war without consulting the Congress and the League was strongly resented by the political parties in India. The Congress voiced a strong protest against it. By its resolution of 14 September, 1939 the Congress Working Committee insisted that the issue of war and peace must be decided by the Indian people and no outside authority could impose any decision on them nor could the Indian people permit their resources to be exploited for imperialist ends. The Congress emphasised that if Britain was fighting for democracy, it must give the right of self-determination to the people of India. It firmly believed that no genuine support for defence would be possible without the establishment of self-government in India. The Congress asked the British Government to specify precisely its war aims in regard to 'democracy and imperialism and the new order that is envisaged.' The Committee posed the question : 'Do they (the British Government) include the elimination of imperialism and the treatment of India as a free nation whose policy will be guided in accordance with the wishes of her people'?[60]

In his statement of 17 October, the Viceroy declared Dominion Status, as enunciated by Lord Irwin in 1929, to be the goal of British policy in India, but the immediate step for associating Indian opinion with the prosecution of war seemed to be 'the establishment of a consultative group representative of all major political parties in British India and of the Indian princes over which the Governer-General would preside.'[61]

The Congress Working Committee, at a meeting held at Wardha on 22 October 1939, regarded the Viceroy's statement as 'in every way unfortunate' and called upon the Congress ministries to tender their resignation. The Government thought the Congress ministries had resigned on the pretext of India's participation in the War. By November 1939 all the ministries resigned. Jinnah declared 23 December 1939 as a 'Day of Deliverance and Thanksgiving' and a mark of relief that the Hindu Raj as established by the Congress regime had at last come to an end. The resignation of the Congress ministries in 1939 was a hasty and ill-conceived act which was likely to damage the Congress and the country. It was a blunder of great magnitude. There was still a possibility of further negotiations with the Government. This decision of the Congress left an open field for the League to strengthen itself and capture power in Bengal, Punjab, Sind and North-West Frontier Province which it could not have dreamed of earlier.

The war took a serious turn for the Allied powers during April 1940 - December, 1942. Holland, Belgium and France had collapsed by mid-April 1940. France sought armistice and the British were forced to evacuate Dunkirk. The Allied powers were engaged in a desperate fight for their survival. The U.S. declared war against the Aris powers towards the end of 1941.

The first problem that confronted the Congress under Azad's Presidency was to define its attitude towards the European War which provoked much controversy in the Congress and brought it almost on the verge of a split. Gandhi's attitude of non-participation of India in the war was firm. A pacifist by conviction, he was not prepared to involve India into war. Non-violence was an article of faith with him. He would not entertain using armed force even for defending the freedom of his country against a threat of aggression. He made it plain that his non-participation in war was not based on political expediency but strictly on moral grounds. He would not lend support to British efforts in war even though such a positive response should draw his country closer to freedom. Such bargaining counters were alien to his temperament. But other Congress leaders did not share Gandhi's views on non-violence and India's non-participation in the war.

At Ramgarh session of the Congress, the issue of Civil Disobedience was evaded but faith in Gandhi's leadership was strongly affirmed. At the Wardha Congress Session, 17-20 June, 1940, things took a different turn altogether. There was no meeting ground between Gandhi and other members of the Congress Working Committee on India's participation in the war. The Congress Working Committee resolved that it could not make non-violence a matter of policy in meeting external aggression.[62] It stated further that "Gandhiji should be free to pursue his great ideal in his own way and therefore absolve him from responsibility for the programme and activity which the Congress has to pursue under the conditions at present prevailing in India and the world in regard to external aggression and internal disorder."[63]

The question of the Congress attitude on war came up again at the Congress Working Committee meeting in Delhi, 3 July - 7 July 1940. The Committee decided to support effective organisation of the defence of the country provided the British made an immediate un-euivocal declaration of the full independence of India. To support the British war efforts the Congress demanded the setting up of a provisional national government which "commands the confidence of all the elected elements in the Central legislature and secure the closest co-operation of the responsible governments in the Provinces."[64] The underlying idea was that India would take up armed defence if her national demands were conceded. It was a bargaining counter.[65] In sum, it meant the Congress assurance to the British : 'we will support you in the war if our demands are met.' This resolution was drafted by C. Rajagopalachari and supported by Azad and Patel. Gandhi said that Patel was 'Rajaji's greatest prize' who lent his support to the Delhi resolution.[66] Abdul Ghaffar Khan resigned in protest against the resolution. The All India Congress Committee meeting held at Poona on 27 and 28 July, 1940 confirmed the Delhi resolution by 95 votes to 47, the opinion in the Congress Working Committee being divided. At the meeting Azad said "The Indian National Congress is a political organisation pledged to win the political independence of the country. It is not an institution for organising world peace."

Soon after the Poona Congress, Azad received a letter from all but four members of the Congress Working Committee saying that they doubted whether they should continue as members of the Congress Working Committee because of their disagreement with the Congress on India's participation in the war.[67] They would continue to be members so long as the differences had no immediate effect on the Congress policy but in case the British government accepted the terms of Delhi-Poona offer of Congress participation in war efforts, they would have no alternative but to resign.[68] Nehru, C. Rajagopalachari, Dr. Syed Mahmud and Asaf Ali did not sign this letter. This letter written by the majority of the members of the Congress Working Committee knocked out the basis for Delhi-Poona offer of the Congress to the Government.

Azad felt deeply hurt at this letter from his colleagues who, he thought, could have talked over the matter with him or called another meeting of the Working Committee for it.[69] Almost a similar situation had confronted Subhas Chandra Bose. The letter from his colleagues threatened Azad's position as President and warned him not to negotiate with the Government for India's participation in the war. It asserted a firm confidence in Gandhi's leadership. What was Azad to do in such a situation? He was not Subhas who would revolt, quit the Congress and organise another party. He had not a large following. He knew that even Nehru who shared his views and who enjoyed great popularity among the masses would not go that far. Azad preferred to lie low. He would not tackle a problem that was too much for him. He did not show the strength to take up cudgles with the Congress leadership. He had no option left but to yield.

Not by any means on idealist, Azad's approach to politics was pragmatic. For the solution of any problem, he would ask himself, 'What is the principle involved and what are the chances of its success?' When Nehru expressed his reservations about launching Satyagraha on the ground that this would be contrary to the *shan* (dignity) of India to take undue advantage when Britain was involved in war, Azad wrote a strong letter on 25 May, 1940.

> I do not know what is the *shan* of India? What is the considered decision? I want to know. We can't grope in the dark like blind men. We should adopt a way with open eyes even if it embarrasses England. ... You interpret the Ramgarh decision against the honour and dignity of India. I do not understand how this confused and illogical conception could find a way to your mind.[70]

Azad believed in non-violence only as a matter of policy, not as an article of faith. He justified even the use of armed force for the cause of liberty. In his attitude towards the present war, Azad's sympathies lay entirely with the Allies who were fighting Nazism. At this critical juncture he disfavoured any Civil Disobedience movement. He was conscious of the growth of the strength of Muslim League which was demanding a separate homeland. As one who had an acute historical sense reinforced by his knowledge of Bismarckian diplomacy and the study of the Balkans, he thought that negotiations with the British when they were involved in a desperate situation for their survival might prove advantageous to India politically and also curb the ascendancy of communal politics. Like Rajagopalachari he regarded the Congress mainly as a political organisation meant to fight for the liberation of his country and achieve self-rule. Therefore at this critical stage when circumstances seemed favourable to India, he thought that parleys and negotiations might help in resolving the Indian political problem. The immediate need was to demand, as the Congress did, a provisional national government enjoying the confidence of the people.

On July 9, 1940 Jinnah reacted strongly against the Delhi Congress Resolution of 7 July, 1940 which had demanded the setting up of a national government. He condemned this Congress move as a sinister design to establish Hindu Raj. Azad sent his clarification in a telegram to Jinnah :

> I have read your statement of July 9. The Delhi Resolution of the Congress means by national government a composite cabinet not limited to any single party. But is it the position of the League that they cannot agree to any provisional arrangement not based on two nations scheme? If so, please clarify by wire.

In his reply, Jinnah rebuked Azad :

> I have received your telegram. I cannot reciprocate confidence. I refuse to discuss with you by correspondence or otherwise as you have completely forfeited the confidence of Muslim India. Cannot you realize you are made a Muslim show-boy Congress President to give it colour that it is national and deceive foreign countries. You represent neither Muslims nor Hindus. The Congress is a Hindu body. If you have self-respect resign at once. You have done your worst against the League so far. I know you have hopelessly failed. Give it up.[71]

On the Delhi-Poona offer Azad and his supporters could not have their way and were forced to retreat. As a pragmatist, he realized that non-violence could not be a policy against external aggression and it would not become a cardinal principle in deciding about political action in a world governed by human wilfulness. Rajagopalachari had told Gandhi that he was 'obsessed with non-violence,' and that 'his vision had got blurred.' Gandhi was determined to disallow the Congress from participating in the war and this view was to influence the entire Congress policy during the war. He may have thought that the allied powers were going to lose the war. So when Lord Linlithgow invited Azad as Congress President to discuss with him the ''August Offer,' he declined the invitation on 10 August even without consulting his colleagues. He knew that the Congress had denied him the authority to negotiate with the Government. Was it for nothing that Jinnah had called him the 'show-boy' (Congress President)?

Encouraged by the conciliatory attitude of the Congress which was reflected in the Delhi-Poona offer and by his anxiety to enlist India's support for war, Linlithgow made the August 8 offer inviting the Congress to join the new Advisory Defence Council and the Governor-General's Council, but as regards self-government, there was to be no constitutional advance until after the war. R.J. Moore has shown in his studies that this proposal was drawn up by Winston Churchill, the Prime Minister. The proposal recommended an extended executive council in which the Congress representatives would be included. The Muslim League received a pledge that the British "would not transfer power to any system of government where authority is directly denied by large and powerful elements in India's national life." By this declaration the Muslims had something like 'the veto on constitutional advance that the 1935 Act had given to the provinces.' Sikandar Hayat Khan, the Punjab Premier, thought that this declaration had 'removed the spectre of Hindu Raj,.[72] The 'August Offer' said nothing about national government but a firm 'no' to the Congress demand for independence, and gave a mere promise for constitution-making after the war. As noted earlier, Linlithgow wanted Azad to meet him for discussions on the 'August Offer' before 21st August, but he declined the invitation.

Gandhi regarded Azad's refusal to meet the Viceroy as 'God inspired.'[73] He feared that there might be a settlement between the Congress and the Government. At the Wardha Congress on 18 August, the 'August Offer' was rejected and regarded as 'opposed to the best interests of the country.' In Congress circles there was a talk about suspending the Working Committee and electing Rajendra Prasad as Congress President.[74] Obviously, this was a reaction against Azad's views on non-violence. In mid-September, 1940 the AIIC met at Bombay and affirmed its full confidence in Gandhi's leadership. The Congress resolved on 15 September, 1940 that it firmly "believed in the policy of non-violence not only in the struggle for *Swaraj* but also insofar as this may be possible of application in a free India." By this resolution the Congress was thrown back on Gandhi's pacifism and non-cooperation. The Muslim League neither accepted nor rejected the 'August Offer', but the League's cooperation in the conduct of the war was still made 'conditional on the Viceroy's acceptance of the 'fifty-fifty principle.'[75]

Gandhi launched a limited Satyagraha movement on 18 September, 1940. The immediate issue on which the movement was started was to protect 'civil liberty', i.e., the right of the freedom of speech. In practice it meant the right to propagate that India does not believe in the war waged by the Allied powers and dissuading people from assisting war efforts. Azad was arrested on 31 December, 1940 and sentenced to imprisonment for two years. By May, 1941 about 14,000 Congressmen had been put in prison. The Viceroy had expanded in July 1941 his Council to fifteen, of which eleven were Indians. Due to the advancing tide of the Japanese conquest in the East and the pressure of the Indian members of the Viceroy's Executive Council on the Government to adopt conciliatory attitude towards the Congress, all the Satyagrahis were released. Azad came out of the gaol somewhat frustrated. He felt as though nothing had been gained in the cause of India's freedom since the beginning of the war.[76]

The Congress Working Committee met at Bardoli in the Surat district of Gujarat on 23 to 30 December, 1941 and at Wardha on 13 and 14 January, 1942. The Japanese were advancing on India and the danger of their penetration in the country was real. The issue of non-violence and non-participation of India in the war came up again at Bardoli. Gandhi was again inflexible in his commitment to non-violence. The impression created by the Bardoli resolution was that the Delhi-Poona offer was being revived again by the Congress.[77] The Bardoli Congress resolved that the 'Bombay Resolution of 16 September, 1940 still holds to-day.' Gandhi realized that the Bombay Resolution was contrary to his views on non-violence and he resigned from the leadership of the Congress. He wrote to Azad that he found :

> great error in the interpretation of Bombay Resolution. I had interpreted it to mean that the Congress was to refuse participation in

> the present or all war on the ground principally of non-violence. The discovery of this error makes it impossible for me to lead the Congress. The resolution contemplated material association with British in the war effort as a price for guaranteed independence of India. If such was my view and I believed in the use of non-violence for gaining independence I would consider myself guilty of unpatriotic conduct. It is my certain belief that only non-violence can save India and the world from self-extinction.[78]

So Gandhi resigned from the Congress leadership and decided to continue Civil Disobedience for 'free speech against all war with such Congressmen and others whom I select.'[79] Abdul Ghaffar Khan also resigned from the Congress Working Committee. Explaining the differences between Gandhi and the Congress Working Committee, Azad said that Gandhi would not like to obtain India's freedom by participation in the war. He declared: "But I am prepared to accept the independence of my country at any moment. The only thing is that it should be real independence.'[80]

The winter of 1941-42 brought the war close to the Indian borders due to the Japanese advance. This impending danger of invasion combined with Roosevelt's and Chiang Kai Shek's efforts made the British Government take another initiative to resolve the Indian problem. Churchill was in the United States and Attlee was in charge of the Cabinet. Sir Stafford Cripps whose diplomatic success with the Russians had enhanced his reputation and who was Lord Privy Seal and leader of the House of Lords, came to India to negotiate with the Indian leaders a settlement of the political question.

Azad was a hard negotiator. As Congress President he held consultations with Sir Stafford.[81] He carried the impression from his talks that the Indian question could be resolved. He was prepared to accept certain limitations on the normal powers of the Defence Minister but he was firm on the question of national government which he thought should function as a cabinet with the Viceroy as a constitutional head. It seemed to him that Cripps was making a positive response to the Congress proposals but this hope proved an illusion.

The Congress rejected the Cripps proposals because they provided nothing tangible and immediate and left things to the future. The Congress insisted that the new Government must immediately have full powers of the Dominion status and strongly urged for giving more powers to the executive council and reducing the role of the Secretary of State. The Congress also objected to the provincial option and the inclusion of the princes instead of the people of the states in the constitution-making body. The actual breakdown of the Cripps proposal which is evident from Azad-Cripps correspondence, was not on the formula about defence responsibilities but on the Congress demand that the national government must be a cabinet government with full powers and not merely a continuation of the Viceroy's Council.

The Cripps proposals were meant to act as a sop to the Indian aspirations and at the same time to mollify public opinion in USA and England. The recently published Amery diaries show that Churchill and Leopold Amery, Secretary of State for India were pulling strings from behind. Moore also has shown how Linlithgow prompted Cripps to withdraw the offer.[82] At one time Churchill called for the resignation of Cripps 'from the war council with impunity.' But the Cripps proposals conceded Pakistan in principle in recommending that once the constitution was drawn up any province might opt out from the Indian Union and become a separate dominion. Such a political concession to the League, Azad could not accept. Percival Spear thought that the rejection of the Cripps offer was a prelude to Pakistan.[83] The implication is that the Congress should have shared power with the League which might have settled the communal problem and paved the way to self-rule after the war. To Azad the question of national government with certain limitations in view of Britain's precarious military position was of paramount importance. That is why he rejected the Cripps proposals. These proposals might have led to the balkanization of India which the Congress could not have accepted. The failure of the Cripps proposals was a prelude to Quit India movement. According the Moore, once again Churchill barred the road to India's freedom.[84]

Increasingly dissatisfied with the British attitude, the Congress demanded their withdrawal on pain of a new Civil Disobedience movement. The All India Congress Committee passed the Quit India Resolution on 8 August 1942 and only 13 votes were cast against it. Azad and Nehru had serious reservations about launching a Civil Disobedience movement. They wished to cooperate in the war provided they had real responsibility. However, Gandhi held different views and in early July told Azad that they could not work together.[85] In fact Gandhi demanded Azad's resignation but Patel intervened and averted the crisis.[86] Nehru moved the Quit India Resolution and Azad also fell in line with him. Gandhi declared at the meeting: 'There is no question of one more chance. This is an open rebellion.' Nehru had coined the phrase 'open rebellion.' The closing words of Gandhi's speech were 'Do or die.'

Justice Wickenden's report published recently shows that Gandhi started the movement due to the failure of Individual Satyagraha, and Cripps Mission, the growing Muslim demand for Pakiṣtan, the presence of American troops in India and the Japanese victories.[87] He chose the time which he thought appropriate for forcing Britain to concede freedom to India. But the overwhelming consideration, as noted earlier, which weighed with him was to save India from the ravages of war and keeping her out of it. He knew that the country was not non-violent and anticipated violence as a consequence of his movement.

In his press interview to the Congress workers Azad said in Delhi on 17 July, 1942 : "Gandhiji has been made to promise that the new movement will not be stopped merely for the reason that violence might be displayed. However, Congressmen should never resort to or encourage violence."[88]

The Government took stern action by arresting the members of the Congress Working Committee including Azad, Nehru, Patel, Asaf Ali, Syed Mahmud and Narendra Deva and on 9 August they were dispatched to Ahmednagar fort.

It is not our purpose here to discuss the character of Quit India movement at length. Suffice it to say that violent disturbances flared up in rural areas of U.P., and Bihar where railway stations were burnt, communications disrupted and policemen killed. It was the left-wing element in the Congress that stimulated a violent form of revolutionary activity. In his letter to the Prime Minister Churchill, Linlithgow, the Viceroy, wrote on 31st August 1942, "I am engaged here in meeting by far the most serious rebellion since that of 1857, the gravity and extent of which we have so far concealed from the world for reasons of military security." Churchill even told the King in desperation that he would give up India after the war though he changed his mind on the termination of the war when he was out of power.

The Quit India movement was ruthlessly suppressed with 1000 lives lost and 60,000. people arrested. From a larger angle the movement had profound results as it sowed the seeds of the ultimate British withdrawal from India. The prestige of British rule received a rude jolt by the hard blow given by this movement. But some ironies which attended this movement cannot escape our notice. Gandhi's non-violence turned into violence and with the Congress leaders in jail, the Muslim

League got a golden opportunity to seize power. By 1945 the League enjoyed the status of being the party controlling governments in Sind, North-West Frontier Province, Bengal and even in the Hindu majority province of Assam. When the Congress leaders were released, they saw in the League their potential rival.

Azad was arrested on 9 August, 1942 in the early morning at Bhulabhai Desai's residence where he usually stayed. He was taken to Ahmadnagar Fort where he remained till April 1945. Thereafter he was removed to Bankura in Bengal and released on 15 June, 1945. During this period of his prison life, his wife died at Calcutta. When she was seriously ill the Government of India was inclined to release him but he declined. In his prison life he wrote a bunch of letters published later as *Ghuber-e-Khatir*, considered by literary critics to be a masterpiece of Urdu prose.

Azad's health lay shattered in prison. He had lost forty pounds in weight. After his release he contemplated relaxing and recuperating but that hope remained unfulfilled. As Congress President hectic political activity was to consume his entire time. He went to his home town Calcutta from Bankura. He knew that his wife Zulekha was no more there to receive him. On reaching Calcutta he went first to his wife's grave where he said the *fateha*.

The political deadlock had lasted through the war. At the end of the war Lord Wavell, the Viceroy, made a new offer to Indian political parties. Wavell called a meeting of Indian leaders at Simla on 25 June, 1945 to resolve the Indian problem. His first object was the formation of a new Executive Council as contemplated in the Cripps proposals. The question was how the Executive Council was to be composed.

Jinnah wanted all five Muslim members in the Council of fourteen to be members of the Muslim League. In other words, every Muslim on the Executive Council had to be from the Muslim League.[89] Jinnah declared that the Muslim League alone represented the Muslims and no other party had the right to nominate a Muslim on the Council. Neither the Viceroy nor the Congress accepted this view.

Azad repudiated Jinnah's contention of nominating all the Muslims on the Council.[90] He emphasised that to yield to Jinnah's demand would mean reducing the Congress to a communal organisation, a position which he was not prepared to accept.[91] He said that the issue was political but was being given a religious turn to mislead the people. Challenging the League's contention that Muslim League was the sole representative of the Muslims, Azad said that in the Muslim majority province of Punjab the Unionist Ministry was in power; in North-West Frontier it was the Congress that ruled and in Sind Congress support had brought a Non-League ministry into the saddle.[92]

When pressed by correspondents to confirm whether he had agreed to the inclusion of Non-Congress Muslims in the Council, Azad said that for resolving the deadlock he suggested that should the League agree to the inclusion of able Muslim nationalists who belonged neither to the League nor the Congress, he would not insist on the inclusion of Congress Muslim nationalists in the Council.[93] He added that if the League had approved his proposal he would have persuaded his colleagues to accept it. Azad went so far as to suggest that the League should accept the right of the Congress to choose whomsoever it wanted but in practice the Congress would not do so. This proposal shows that Azad was willing to stay out of power. Whether or not the Congress would accept such a proposal was another matter. He blamed Wavell for not dealing firmly with the League.[94] He would have liked Wavell to proceed in the matter and constitute the Executive Council with or without the League. Azad said, "Those who are prepared to go forward should be allowed to go and those who wish to be kept out should be left out."

Wavell being a soldier was comparatively straightforward and well-intentioned in his attempts to solve the problem. He put the cards on the table but lacked what Attlee called suppleness in dealing with political problems.[95] Wavell and Azad got on well with each other. Attlee thought Wavell a 'curious silent bird.'[96] Azad too was reserved by nature. Wavell found Azad, 'honest, moderate and a gentleman but not a strong character.'[97] He wrote to King George VI on 8 July 1946 that Azad was a gentleman who stood for good sense and moderation 'as far as he was able, in spite of poor health and a naturally weak character.'[98] Azad was also struck by Wavell's sincerity of purpose and frankness. Wavell records that in his presence at Simla, Azad stretched forth his hand to shake it with Jinnah but he refused.[99]

Jinnah's view was that if other political parties start claiming to represent Muslims, this would seriously hit his position as the sole spokesman of Muslims and thereby weaken his authority to establish his claim for a separate homeland. The Simla conference failed not on the basis of conflicting political objectives but on account of the communal question, which created division among different Indian groups. Jinnah was willing to tolerate the continuation of British rule rather than have a Congress monopoly of power. He scuttled the Simla Conference by his intransigence.

Before we discuss the last-ditch efforts made by Azad to retain the unity of country and avoid the creation of Pakistan, it is necessary to focus on the political changes contemplated by the British government to resolve the Indian question. To any student of transfer of power to India it should be clear beyond doubt, a fact which nevertheless is usually ignored – that from 1942 to 1947 Cripps meets us almost at every critical turn whenever any constitutional issue arises about India. He drafted almost every statement, suggested alterations and held frequent consultations with Indian political leaders. Cripps viewed the Congress President, Azad as 'the foundation and basis of India's future destiny.'[100]

With the advent of the Labour Party in power in England the Indian national leaders in the Congress party became optimistic about India's future and thought that the Labour Government would fulfil their commitment to the cause of India's self-rule. Azad regarded the Labour Party in power as 'an event of historic importance and a prelude to a constitutional settlement.'[101] In the words of the Secretary of State, Lord Pethick-Lawrence, the Cabinet Mission was 'dispatched to India with the object of taking immediate and positive steps to provide full self-government for India." The Mission was to hold discussions with the elected representatives of British India and the Indian states in order to arrive at an agreement about the forming of a constitution, setting up of a constitution-making machinery and an interim government having the support of the main Indian parties. The Cabinet Mission arrived in India on 23 March 1946 with a three-man team, the Secretary of State for India, Lord Pethick-Lawrence, Sir Stafford Cripps, now President of the Board of Trade and A.V. Alexander, the First Lord of the Admiralty. The mission announced their plan on 6 March 1946.

Azad took special interest in the Cabinet Mission proposals and thought them reasonable enough for resolving the Indian problem. The democratic process had been set in motion and elections were held for the provincial assemblies in 1945. The Congress won over 91.3 per cent of the general votes and the League nearly 75 per cent of the Muslim vote, thereby securing all the Muslim seats.[102] The Congress emerged victorious in all the non-Muslim majority provinces, Assam, U.P., Bombay, Madras, Orissa, the Central Provinces and Bihar and also in the Muslim majority province of North West Frontier. The Muslim League formed Governments in Bengal and Sind but was frustrated in Punjab. Thus the League governed only in two provinces and its strategy lay in toppling the coalition government of Punjab. The election results showed that the League had gained a spectacular success. While in 1937 the League had won only 4.4 per cent of the Muslim votes, in 1946, it captured about 75 per cent. On the basis of these election results Jinnah could declare with confidence that only the League represented the Muslims and no one else had the right to speak on their behalf.

The Cabinet Mission proposals provided a compromise between 'Jinnah's sovereign Pakistan and Congress's strong and organic Centre.' The Cabinet Mission scheme was a modification of the Cripps proposals. It envisaged a federal union controlling defence, foreign affairs and communications. The states were to be included in the federal union after negotiations. The powers of the federal union were reduced and the individual provinces had the liberty to form a subordinate union of their own. Each of these was to decide for itself the powers it would exercise outside the range of federal subjects. On the basis of this arrangement a Constituent Assembly would be convened to complete the constitution-making process. The Cabinet Mission Plan opened an avenue for reconciling united India with Muslim autonomy, though the powers of the federal government were reduced and the provinces were at liberty to form subordinate groups of their own.

The Muslim League accepted the Cabinet Mission plan on 6 June, 1946 in the belief that the formation of Pakistan was inherent in the grouping of the Muslim areas in Sections B and C.[103] The Congress accepted the plan with reservations and queries on 24 May, 1946 and 25 June, 1946. The Congress was entirely opposed to any executive or legislative machinery for groups of provinces – the three tier system which the Cabinet Mission regarded as an essential feature of the plan.[104] Azad made it clear to Wavell that North West Frontier, Assam and the Sikhs in Punjab were entirely opposed to the compulsory grouping of provinces. Clarifying the position to Azad, Wavell wrote that 'grouping was not compulsory in the statement of 16 May, 1946 but the decision for it has been left to the elected representatives of the groups sitting together in sections.[105] To Jinnah prior formation of the Muslim groups was fundamental so that once the groups were formed he could negotiate with the Congress groups, but to the Congress prior acceptance of an all-India Union was fundamental.[106] To the Cabinet Mission the grouping of provinces was the crux of the problem which could be modified only by an inter-party arrangement. The chief concern of the Congress was to gain power at the Centre. The League's fear was that in an all-India federation the four Muslim majority provinces would be outweighed by the seven Hindu majority provinces.

The Congress was opposed to the grouping of provinces and this issue soon came out in the open. Gandhi mistrusted Azad because he had been carrying on negotiations with the Cabinet Mission without the knowledge of his colleagues. Azad was replaced by Nehru as President of the Congress. In his speech to the All India Congress Committee on 7 July, 1946, Nehru said : 'We are not bound by a single thing except that we have decided to go into the Constituent Assembly.'[107] At a press conference on 10 July, Nehru elaborated upon his A.I.C.C. speech :

> We have agreed to go into the Constituent Assembly and we have agreed to nothing else . . . what we do there, we are entirely and absolutely free to determine . . . . The big probability is that from any approach to the question, there will be no grouping. Speaking in betting language, there was 4 to 1 chance of the North-West Frontier Province deciding against grouping. The group B collapses. It is highly likely that Assam will decide against grouping with Bengal, although I would not like to say what the initial decision may be, since it is evenly balanced. But there is going to be finally no grouping there, because Assam will not tolerate it under any circumstances.[108]

Nehru added later that the Congress would enter the Constituent Assembly 'completely unfettered by agreements and free to meet all situations as they arise.'

After Nehru's statement Jinnah protested against complete repudiation of the basic terms on which the long-term scheme rested. The Cabinet Mission tried to clarify that the parties could not go outside its terms in the Constituent Assembly. Jinnah condemned the 'pettifogging and haggling attitude of the Congress.' He issued a strong statement, "I find we have exhausted all reason. It is no use looking to any other sources for help or assurance. There is no other tribunal to which we can go. The only tribunal is the Muslims. This day we bid goodbye to Constituent Assembly and Constitutional methods."[109] Jinnah went further and said, 'Today we have forged a pistol and are in a position to use it.'

The Congress was invited by Wavell to enter into the Interim

Government on 10 August, 1946. Jinnah protested against the formation of the Interim government. He declared 16 August as a Direct Action Day. Within three days of its declaration, 20,000 people were killed and seriously injured in Calcutta.[110] Communal riots flared up in different parts of the country. The brutal killings brought the country almost on the verge of a civil war. The Muslim League had called in the *mullahs* and *pirs* who held meetings in and around the mosques and aroused the dormant passions of the Muslims against the Congress provoking them into violence.[111]

Nehru's emotional outburst on the grouping question did incalculable harm to the possibility of cooperative working of the Cabinet Mission plan. It was taken by Jinnah as a declaration to wipe out their identity as a separate independent unit in the All-India Federation. Michael Brecher, Nehru's biographer, regards Nehru's statement as the 'most fiery and provocative statement in his forty years of public life.'[112] Mosley wrote that Nehru's remarks were a direct act of sabotage.[113] Azad's reactions to Cabinet Mission plan were completely opposed to Nehru's. Azad thought that Nehru's provocative speech turned the tables by giving Jinnah the handle to withdraw his commitment to the Cabinet Mission Plan. S. Gopal, however, rejects Azad's contention as stated in *India Wins Freedom*.[114]

Another opportunity for settling the constitutional crisis was lost in this way by the Congress through its tactless handling. It could be argued that if the Cabinet Mission plan had not been repudiated, there would have been no Direct Action, no Calcutta killings and no cutting of the country into two. The Congress tried to salvage the situation by issuing certain clarification on the Cabinet proposals but it was too late. It must be said in favour of Azad that all through he was working behind the scenes to make the Cabinet Mission proposals acceptable as is evident from the *Transfer of Power* volumes.

Like most of his Congress colleagues, Azad was firmly opposed to the partition of the country which he thought would create problem instead of solving them. He realized that the Cabinet Mission plan was the best option available. On the basis of this understanding he lent it full support as would be evident from his correspondence with Wavell included in the *Transfer of Power* volumes. Azad made it clear to Wavell that the Congress would not accept parity with the League in the formation of government as this would lead to perpetual conflicts.[115] He wanted an immediate declaration from the Government about complete independence with the Viceroy remaining only as its constitutional head.[116]

Azad thought that the Cabinet Mission Plan despite some limitations was a sound formula to work on for preventing partition. Even after Nehru's provocative statement on the Constituent Assembly Azad continued his efforts to save the Cabinet Mission proposals although they had already been rejected by the League. He held the view that the decentralisation of power in a federal government with autonomous units which the Cabinet Mission proposals offered was the only feasible alternative to Pakistan. Azad also admitted the right of a province to step out under certain conditions.[117] The League joined the Interim Government in October 1946. Azad was convinced that once the League had come in the cabinet the question of its withdrawal from it would not arise. He knew Jinnah's tactics.

Azad felt so desperately involved in the idea of preserving the unity of India that he carried on negotiations with the Cabinet Mission even without the knowledge of Gandhi and Congress Working Committee which shocked Gandhi so much when he came to know about it that he could not sleep for a whole night.[118] According to Sudhir Ghosh, such dealings on the part of the Congress President meant to Gandhi a 'moral death to the Congress.' Azad had assured the Cabinet Mission that he could get the Congress Working Committee agree to a single Federation which would be broken down into parts legislating separately for optional subjects.[119] He suggested discussions between the Congress and League representatives on the basis that "the Congress started from the position he had described and that the Muslim League started from the position that they wanted two legislatures on the second tier." Azad made this move on his own and did not want anything to be said about it to Gandhi. When Gandhi asked Azad whether he had been writing to the Cabinet Mission on his own, Azad denied it. Ghosh notes that the copy of Azad's letter to the Mission was lying at that time just at a little remove on Gandhi's desk. F.F. Turnbull's Minutes dated 13 February, 1947 show Azad's sustained endeavour to see the Cabinet Mission proposal through. Turnbull wrote, "Azad is more than anyone else the person who sought to get the Cabinet Mission proposals accepted and he tends to outrun what his colleagues on the Working Committee are prepared to accept."[120]

A man of moderate disposition, Azad was not influential enough to change the attitude of his colleagues towards the Cabinet Mission Plan. Wavell had hinted at it in his letter to King George VI. Azad had ceased to be the Congress President. He told Lord Mountbatten that if he had not relinquished his office as President of the Congress, he might have saved the country from partition.[121] He suggested to Mountbatten to take up the Cabinet Mission proposals and work for their acceptance by the parties concerned and in case of dispute on their interpretation he should use his personal influence to bring about an agreement between the contending parties.[122] Azad's advice to Congress leadership was disregarded and his hopes for the preservation of the unity of India were shattered. The Mountbatten Plan of Partition was accepted by the Congress Working Committee on 2 June, 1947. The atmosphere in the Committee was tense. Abdul Ghaffar Khan voted against the Partition Plan and said : "We have been destroyed (*Hum to tabha ho gaye*). You are throwing us to the wolves." Azad whispered to him with bitter irony, 'You should now join the League.'[123] For the rest sitting in a corner he uttered not a word and was puffing away at his endless cigarettes.

It is not our purpose here to undertake an analysis of the circumstances leading to Partition but it would not be out of place to draw attention to some vital factors that strengthened the process of partition. Jinnah claimed to have forged a pistol and declared his intention to use it while the Congress adhered to its policy of non-violence without taking effective steps to counter the virulently communal propaganda launched by the League. The Congress's vacillation on critical issues offered a sad contrast to Jinnah's consummate policy of blackmail and bellicosity. Jinnah ruthlessly used the two nation theory as a psychological weapon for gaining power. Thus Congress leadership was caught up in 1947 in a flurry of events beyond their control and had to accept partition since it could offer no alternative proposal acceptable to all concerned.

To some leaders in the Congress only *Ram-Rahim* approach could resolve the communal problem which was threatening to split the country; to others it was an economic issue requiring long-term action. To Azad who seemed to have a clearer understanding of communal politics, the immediate requirement was sharing power with the minorities and safeguarding their interests. The basic questions were : "How do you treat the minorities? What status do you give them in Free India?" It was this crucial issue that provided the League the real ammunition for its politics. Azad believed that political problems are not resolved by Utopianism or pious resolutions. The leadership must be in touch with the ground realities and be prepared to work out compromises which would promote the well-being of the society as a whole. In his political approach Azad knew what objectives could be achieved in the given circumstances and how far miscalculations and mistakes caused by hurry or stress of conflicts could be harmful. For him politics was not to be adjusted to human reasoning alone but to human nature in its totality. That is why he showed extraordinary sagacity in understanding contemporary politics. At many critical points his standpoint turned out to be right and it was vindicated by subsequent developments.

### *References*

1. Choudhry Khaliquzzaman, *Pathway to Pakistan*, pp. 160-03; *IWF*, pp. 170-02. H.W. Hodson, *The Great Divide*, pp. 66-67; and Jawaharlal to Rajendra Prasad, RPP; file No. 1/37,. Letter No. 42.
2. V.N. Datta, *Madan Lal Dhingra and National Movement*, Appendix III, p. 94.
3. R.S. Symonds, *The Making of Pakistan*, p. 53.
4. For the Congress election manifesto see, S. Gopal (ed.), *Selected Works of Jawaharlal Nehru*, Vol. VII. pp. 459-67. See also AICC File No. 41/1936 629-64 and for the League manifesto, see Sharif Ali Mujahid, *Quid-I-Azam Studies in Interpretation*, Appendix, pp. 482-89.
5. Sharif Ali Mujahid, *op. cit*., p. 486.
6. *Ibid*. See H.V. Hodson, *op. cit*., p. 60.
7. Nehru to Prasad, 21 July, 1937, *RPP, File No. 1/37*, Letter No. 42.
8. *Ibid*.
9. *Ibid*.
10. Sharif Ali Mujahid, *op. cit*., p. 483.
11. *Ibid*.
12. Rajmohan Gandhi, *India Wins Errors*, pp. 21-33.
13. Choudhry Khaliquzzaman, *op. cit*., pp. 160-63.
14. *Ibid*.
15. R. Coupland, *The Constitutional Problem of India*, Part II, p. 111.
16. Choudhry Khaliquzzaman, *op. cit*., pp. 187-88.
17. *Ibid*.
18. *Ibid*.
19. *Ibid*., pp. 162-63.
20. Larry Collins and Dominque Lapiere, *Mountbatten and the Partition of India*, p. 43.
21. C.M. Naim, ed. *Iqbal, Jinnah and Pakistan*, pp. 88-89.
22. Choudhry Khaliquzzaman, *op. cit*., pp. 170-74.
23. S. Gopal, *Jawaharlal Nehru*, Vol. I, p. 20.
24. Bimal Prasad, 'Congress versus the Muslim League, 1935-37' in Richard Sisson and Stanley Wolpert (ed.), *Congress and Indian Nationalism*, pp. 320 & 326.
25. Nehru to Prasad, RPP, *op. cit*.
26. *Ibid*.

27. *Ibid.*
28. *Ibid.*
29. M.C. Chagla, *Roses in December, Autobiography*, pp. 81-82.
30. Rajmohan Gandhi, *Indian Wins Errors*, p. 23.
31. *Ibid.*
32. Khaliquzzaman, *op. cit.*, pp. 187-88.
33. *Ibid.*
34. *Ibid.*, p. 167.
35. H.V. Hodson, *op. cit.*, p. 67.
36. Larry Collins and Dominique Lapiere, Interviews; *Mountbatten and the Partition of India*, p. 22.
37. *Khutbat-e-Azad, op. cit.*, pp. 269-322.
38. Azad to Nehru, 27 March, 1940. *A Bunch of Old Letters*, Letter No. 300, pp. 424-25.
39. *Khutbat-e-Azad, op. cit.*, pp. 272-73.
40. *Ibid.*, pp. 274-75.
41. *Ibid.*
42. *Ibid.*, p. 295.
43. *Ibid.*, p. 298.
44. *Ibid.*, p. 292.
45. *Ibid.*, p. 288.
46. *Ibid.*, p. 289.
47. *Ibid.*, pp. 283-84.
48. *Ibid.*, pp. 285, 296.
49. *Ibid.*, p. 299.
50. *Ibid.*, p. 299.
51. *Ibid.*
52. *Ibid.*, pp. 284, 300.
53. Mushirul Hasan, 'The Muslim Mass Contact Campaign : Analysis of a Strategy of Political Mobilization' in Richard Sasson and Stanley Wolpert (eds.), *Congress and Indian Nationalism*, p. 214; see for details, pp. 198-222.
54. *Ibid.*
55. Bimal Prasad, 'Congress versus the Muslim League, 1935-37' in Richard Sasson and Stanley Wolpert, *op. cit.*, pp. 314-35.
56. Pattabhi Sitaramayya, *History of the Indian National Congress*, Vol. II, p. 105.
57. For the decision on Bose's conflict see Atul Chandra Pradhan, 'Socialist Stirrings within the Congress' in B.N. Pande, *A Centenary History of the Indian National Congress*, pp. 256-60.
58. Jawaharlal Nehru, *A Bunch of Old Letters*, pp. 381-82.
59. R. Coupland, *The Constitutional Problem in India*, Part II, p. 211.
60. *Ibid.*
61. *Ibid.*
62. Pattabhi Sitaramayya, *History of the Indian National Congress*, Vol. II, pp. 192-93.
63. *Ibid.*
64. R. Coupland, *The Constitutional Problem in India*, Part II, p. 240. See for discussion Bhupen Qanungo, 'Preparations for Civil Disobedience Jan.-Sept., 1940 in B.N. Pande, *A Centenary History of the Indian National Congress*, p.

353.

65. *The Amrita Bazar Patrika*, 28 July, 1940.
66. Pattabhi Sitaramayya, *op. cit.*, p. 201.
67. Bhupen Qanungo, *op. cit.*, p. 358.
68. *Ibid.*, p. 361.
69. *Ibid.*, see *IWF*, pp. 35-36.
70. Jawaharlal Nehru, *A Bunch of Old Letters*, p. 433. See Sulaiman Shahjahanpuri, *Maktubat-e-Azad*, p. 19.
71. Pattabhi Sitaramayya, *op. cit.*, p. 202. Even Khaliquzzaman, Jinnah's favourite regards this telegram as impolite. see Choudhry Khaliquzzaman, *op. cit.*, p. 250.
72. R.J. Moore, *Escape from Empire, The Attlee Government and the Indian Problem*, p. 58.
73. *IWF*, p. 42; see Bhupen Qanungo, *op. cit.*, p. 363.
74. B. Pattabhi Sitarammayya, *op. cit.*, p. 210.
75. R. Coupland, *op. cit.*, p. 246.
76. *IWF*, p. 45.
77. Bhupen Qanungo, 'The Individual Civil Disobedience,' *op. cit.*, p. 440.
78. Gandhi to Azad, 30.12.1941, *RPP* 2-A/41.
79. *Ibid.*
80. *The Hindu*, 16 January, 1942.
81. The account of the Cripps proposals is based on *IWF*, pp. 54-75, 267-78, R. Coupland, *op. cit.*, pp. 263-86, and R.J. Moore, *Escape from Empire*, pp. 69-75.
82. R.J. Moore, *op. cit.*, p. 72.
83. Percival Spear, *Oxford History of India*, Vol. III, p. 828.
84. R.J. Moore, *op. cit.*, p. 104.
85. *IWF*, p. 90.
86. *Ibid.*
87. Justice Wickenden's Report, *Historic Judgement on Quit India*, ed., P.N. Chopra, p. 255.
88. *Ibid.*, p. 71.
89. Ayesha Jalal, *The Sole Spokesman*, pp. 16-17, R.J. Moore, *op. cit.*, pp. 16-17, 34-35, *IWF*, pp. 119-38.
90. *The Hindustan Times*, 18 July, 1945.
91. *Ibid.*
92. *Ibid.*, 18 July, 1945.
93. *Ibid.*
94. *Ibid.*, 21 July and 31 July, 1945.
95. R.J. Moore, *op. cit.*, p. 149.
96. *Ibid.*, p. 149.
97. Penderel Moon (ed.), *Wavell, The Viceroy's Journal*, p. 315.
98. *Ibid.*, p.495
99. *Ibid.*, p. 257.
100. R.J. Moore, *op. cit.*, p. 75.
101. *Ibid.*, p. 60.
102. Ayesha Jalal, *op. cit.*, p. 101.
103. H.V. Hodson, *op. cit.*, p. 153.
104. Azad to Wavell, 14 June, 1946 *TP*, Vol. VII, p. 169.

105. Wavell to Azad, 15 June, 1946, *TP*, pp. 171-72.
106. H.V. Hodson, *op. cit.*, p. 145.
107. R.J. Moore, *op. cit.*, p. 157; *IWF*, pp. 181-82.
108. *Ibid.*, p. 158.
109. See Ayesha Jalal's analysis of Jinnah's reaction to Nehru's statement, *op. cit.*, pp. 209-13.
110. H.V. Hodson, *op. cit.*, p. 166, Ayesha Jalal, *op. cit.*, pp. 215-16.
111. Ayesha Jalal, *op. cit.*, p. 217.
112. Michael Brecher, *Jawaharlal Nehru*, p. 316.
113. Leonard Mosley, *Last Days of the British raj*, p. 28.
114. Sarvepalli Gopal, *Jawaharlal Nehru*, Vol. I., pp. 227-229.
115. Azad to Wavell, 14 June, 1946, *TP*, Vol. VII, pp. 171-72.
116. *Ibid.*, 25 May, 1946; *TP*, Vol. VII, pp. 163-64, p. 169.
117. H.V. Hodson, *op. cit.*, p. 108.
118. Sudhir Ghosh, *Gandhi's Emissary*, pp. 105-110.
119. Alexander's Diary in *TP*, VII, pp. 145, 149 & 150.
120. Minute by F.F. Turnbull, *TP*, IX, 13 Feb., 1947, p. 676.
121. Mountbatten's note on 27 March, 1947, *TP*, Vol. X; pp. 33-34.
122. Azad to Mountbatten *TP*, Vol. X, No. 142.
123. Abdul Ghaffar Khan, *Thrown to the Wolves*, p. 97.

# 6

# RELIGIOUS IDEAS

To understand Azad's religious ideas it is necessary to trace their genesis and see how he came to adopt them. His commitment to Islam remained firm throughout his life. In fact, Islam became the motive force of his entire existence. He battled with himself to lead the life of a devout Muslim but he fell short of the high standard of conduct laid by the injunctions of Islam, and made a bold confession of his human frailties in his early youth. In reading Azad we enter into the world of Islam just as we enter into the world of Hinduism when we read Vivekananda.

We have seen how as a child Azad was initiated into the study of Quran by his father. At Nadwat ul-Ulama in Lucknow during 1905-06 under the guidance of Maulana Hamid-ud-Din, a great authority of Quran, Azad further developed and enriched his understanding of Islam. Except for a short period when the turned a heretic he remained a firm votary of Islam up to the end of his life. Mahammad Abdah and Rashid Rida hnd moulded his religious thinking. His short composition *Sarmad* (1910) was a concentrated expression of a bold spirit confessing its profound love for Islam and its readiness to die for it. In *Al-Hilal* he preached eloquently the message of Islam and in *Al-Balagh* he entered into spiritual communion with Quran and the Prophet. In these journals he preoccupied himself with the interpretation of *Surat al-Fatiha* and emphasized that Quran was God's book. He said that 'This is the only book that matters' and even went so far as to say that 'This (The Quran) is my book.'

The *Tazkira* that he wrote in his confinement at Ranchi is a portrait-gallery of the profoundly religious men who embodied in themselves the true virtues of Islam for whose preservation they did not hesitate even to lay down their lives. The Quran and the life of the Prophet deeply absorbed him. He always responded to the teachings of the Prophet with devotional fervour and even felt inspired to write his biography. There was nothing to distract him from his devotion to Islam, neither the standards of society nor the temptation of worldly success. When he was editing *Al-Hilal* and *Al-Balagh* he assimilated all that was pertinent and spiritually meaningful in Islam and its history and was now capable of producing his celebrated work *Tarjuman al-Quran* which was a natural fulfilment of his honest efforts to understand the spirit of Islam. In his introduction to the *Tarjuman*, he wrote :

> The zest of search for truth never forsook me. There is hardly a single conviction in me which has not had to bear the test of denial. I have gulped in poison mixed with every drought applied to my lips and also administered to myself Elixer coming forth from every quarter. Whenever I felt thirsty, my parched lips did not resemble the lips of others who were equally thirsty and when I quenched my thirst, it was not from the same fountain as others did. Whatever I could gather in this lengthy period of my life in my search of the Quranic truth I have tried to understand to the best of my ability, and have spread over the pages of this volume.[1]

Azad made an announcement in 1915 about his forthcoming publication of the Urdu translation of Quran which he called *Tarjuman* along with a commentary which he called *Tafsir al-Bayan*. He did not realize that his reading public would have to wait for about fifteen years to see his *Tarjuman* in print.[2] In the issue of *Al-Balagh* dated 1 November, 1915, he mentioned that *Tafsir al-Bayan* was under preparation. He wrote in *Al-Balagh* on 26 November, 1915 that the *Tarjuman* would be printed in lithograph and priced at Rs.6/- but in its issue of 12 January, 1916 he regretted that it would take a little more time to publish these works.

Azad's original idea was to produce three volumes on Quran, first an explanatory translation of the Quran called *Tarjuman al-Quran*, secondly the *Tafsir al-Bayan* providing an interpretation of the significant parts of the Quran in the text and thirdly, the *Muqaddama-i-Tafsir* to serve as prolegomena, to the two volumes embodying the fundamental teachings of Quran.[3] Thus Azad had a big project in hand to handle but like his other literary works this work too remained unpublished.

Azad tells us in his Introduction to the *Tarjuman* that during his confinement in Ranchi and his imprisonment during the non-cooperation movement the police ransacked his residence at Calcutta and seized these manuscripts which despite his best efforts he could not recover. Thrice he encountered this bitter experience of losing his manuscripts of *Tarjuman* and *Tafsir* at the hands of the Government. The loss of these manuscripts on which he had toiled so hard did not however dampen his spirits. He remembered how Thomas Carlyle's manuscript of the French Revolution had been consigned to fire due to the negligence of his friend John Stuart Mill.[4] But Carlyle took it as a big challenge and produced his *magnum opus de novo*. Azad too decided to start his work afresh but his hectic political life left him hardly any time for undertaking any serious literary work. The conflicting loyalties between his scholarly pursuits and political commitments subjected him to acute mental tension which is evident from the following passage in his Introduction to *Tarjuman* :

> The uproar of political activity and the calmness of literary life could not proceed together. Conciliation between fire and flake of cotton is never possible. I wished to bring the two together : on the one hand, I went on piling up the efforts of my thought and on the other involved myself in inviting the scorching lightning to touch them. I know the result. I have therefore no right to complain.[5]

Azad picked up the thread for starting his work on *Tarjuman* and completed it on 30 July, 1930 in Meerut gaol.[6] In this work he completed his translation of *Surat al-Fatiha*, the first chapter of the Quran to which he gave prime importance. The second volume of *Tarjuman* including the translation and commentary and covering Surahs 7-23 was published in 1936. Instead of translation and notes it included commentary and discussion at the end of each Surah. Both these volumes take us to chapter 23 of the Quran and cover a little more than half the book. These volumes were revised in Ahmednagar fort and republished in 1945. The third volume of *Tarjuman* never appeared.

From Azad's correspondence with Ghulam Rasul Mihr it is evident that Azad was engaged in writing the third volume of *Tarjuman*.[7] Ajmal Khan, Azad's Secretary, in reply to queries about the third volume of *Tarjuman* confirmed that this work was under preparation.[8] The question arises why the third volume if prepared and announced in *al-Balagh* was not published. In fact, one might ask whether the volume even existed.

Azad was a painstaking scholar who always tried to maintain a high level of meticulous scholarship in his literary and religious productions. He sought perfection in his literary creations. After his release from gaol in 1945 he was so deeply involved in political activity that he found no time for his literary work for the next two years. Thereafter his official duties as Education Minister and Congress party work made heavy demands on his time. Douglas says categorically that Azad never wrote the third volume of *Tarjuman.*[9] It is believed in some circles that Azad's boxes were removed after his death to Calcutta and it is likely that the manuscript of the third volume may be gathering dust there.[10]

Perhaps it would not be out of place of mention a similar case which relates to Professor H. Butterfield, formerly Regius Professor of Modern History, University of Cambridge. His colleagues and friends anxiously looked forward to the publication of his biography of Charles James Fox on which Butterfield said that he had been engaged for over a decade. Butterfield died in 1977. G.R. Elton who later became the Regius Professor at Cambridge mentioned in the first Butterfield memorial lectures delivered at Dublin that despite his best efforts he could not find a single scrap of paper after his death relating to Butterfield's biography of Fox in his private collection. What Elton suggested was that only the idea of writing Fox's biography existed in Butterfield's mind. Perhaps, Azads' mind also worked the same way. Being a meticulous scholar, Azad found writing an arduous task which his political commitments made all the more difficult for him to pursue. Perhaps he also realized that he had nothing more to say than what he had already said in the two volumes which took him about thirty years (from 1915 to 1945) to complete.

Azad's *Tarjuman* is not only a translation of parts of Quran but also a commentary on it which offers a highly pertinent interpretation of its basic teachings. It serves as a treatise on some of the significant episodes in Islamic history. *Tazkira* was meant for the learned but *Tarjuman* Azad wrote for the general reader. Shah Waliullah had translated the Quran into Persian making it acceptable to the Ulama, but his sons Shah Rafiuddin (1749-1817) and Shah Abdul Qadir (1753-1827) translated it into Urdu. Sir Sayyid Ahmad Khan also wrote a commentary on the Quran in *Tafsir ul-Quran* which also remained incomplete. Azad repeatedly argues in *Tarjuman* that Quran's true message has been misrepresented by the medieval commentators who inserted in their interpretation the Greek, Roman, Iranian, Byzantine and Indian categories of thought and gave meanings to Quranic exegesis which were alien to the true spirit of Islam. Azad emphasizes that the commentators of Quran usually trained in a narrow theological discipline and stifled by antiquated erudition indulged in hair-splitting arguments on insignificant points, strained fallacious arguments by imposing personal option (*tafsir bil-rai*) and fabricated such an elaborate maze on scholastic syllogisms and terminology that the real meaning of Quran was lost.[11] By importing esoteric elements of reasoning and terms the commentators skirted the real issues and gave a wrong notion of Islam.

Ibn Taimiya had held similar views about the commentators who, he thought, were lacking in a broader perspective for understanding the real meaning of Islam. In this category of commentators who distorted the true message of Islam Azad included Fakhruddin al Razi (1149-1210), author of *Mafatih al-Ghaib*.[12] Azad believed that as Quranic teachings are based on nature (*fitrat*) so the application of man's inventiveness (*waziat*) would not be a proper way to understand the true meaning of Islam.[13] Azad thought that religious values remain eternal while scientific investigations could not be regarded as an adequate instrument to understand the spirit of religion. The right thing for understanding Islam was not to depend on the interpreters of Quran but to return to the original message of Islam as understood in complete simplicity by the Prophet and his Companions. In his attitude towards religion Azad was never satisfied with the traditional doctrines upheld by his family.[14] He regarded blind adherence to religious beliefs and practices and following them tenaciously (*taqlid*) a hindrance to his search for truth. According to Azad, Quran lays down that wisdom and insight, but not imitation of traditional beliefs lead to the cultivation of true religious faith.[15]

Our interest does not primarily lie in Azad's translation of Quran but in his interpretation of it. The first volume of *Tarjuman* deals entirely with the *Surat al-Fatiha* which he regards as the essence of Quran. The opening chapter consists of seven verses of Quran on which Azad elaborates. At the outset Azad stresses that the prayer 'Praise be to God' in *Surat al-Fatiha* is the most beautiful form of praise for God which expels fear of God from the mind of man and fosters love for beauty and goodness, the values which the ancient Greeks too, had cherished. Azad points out later that the Jews had invested God with the attributes of anger and vengeance which Islam completely rejects.[16] In the next three verses Azad presents Quran's image of God as *Rabb al Alamin* (Lord of the entire universe), *al-Rahman* (Lord of the Being), *al-Rahman al-Rahim* (The Benevolent, the Merciful) and *Malik Yaum al Ḍin* (Master on the Days of Recompense) which represent God's attributes as providence, mercy and justice, and all-pervading sustainer of life which he illustrates by subjecting the evolutionary scheme of life rationalistically.[17] He argues that the existence of a coherent world order with its regularities, balance and harmony provides a cogent proof of the controlling power of God. Such a secular conception of God stripped of narrow religious attributes knocks out the common anthromorphic view of God. In the sixth verse emphasis is laid on honesty and good conduct which help men to choose the straight path of truth. The last verse emphasizes that it is only by loving God that men find true direction. In his inimitable style Azad wrote :

> Look, so far as the question of God's worship and its image are concerned what can be said simpler than what has been set out in seven verses. Just only seven verses and each verse not containing more than four, five words, and each word is a gem set in a ring that captures the heart . . . nothing difficult, nothing mysterious, all simple and plain. Reality and truth are always expressed like that . . . what could be easier or simpler than that.[18]

What is the substance of Azad's interpretation of Quran? According to him the guiding principle of Quran is that *Din* is but a direct worship of God and righteous action.[19] The Quran visualises God as *Rabbal Alamin*, the master of the entire universe. *Din* is *Al-Islam*, submission to the will of God.[20] The Quranic conception of the divine as explained by Azad does not bear the slightest similarity to human qualities.[21] Thus devotion to one God and righteous action is the *summum bonum* of the teachings of the Quran. Faith in one God is fundamental to Islam from which there is to be no deviation.

An important feature of Azad's interpretation of Islam is that, *Din*, as he sees it, is the essence of all the religions of the world which brings mankind closer to God and unlocks the seals of the universe. He emphasizes that *Din* is not a monopoly of any particular country, nation, community or sect. There is no separate *Rabb* for Muslims, Christians and Jews but one *Rabb* for all and he who is devoted to him and performs good deeds is a true follower of *Din*. Righteous action, Azad explains, is *amar bil ma ruf wal nahy an al-munkar*, meaning 'enjoining the Good and forbidding the Evil.' Righteous action is also the guiding principle recommended for the salvation of man in Buddhist thought and the *Bhagavad-gita*. Azad argues that an individual born as a Muslim is not *ipso facto* superior to others. It is not birth but devotion to God and furtherance of good deeds that determine the virtues of an individual. From this premise it follows that a person born in a religious faith other than Islam, cannot be branded a *kafir* if he follows *Din* as expounded in the Quran.

According to Azad, people have adopted wrong notions about religion. Even after eliminating the artificial forms of religion like hereditary (imbibed from family conventions), geographical (determined by territorial considerations), customary (based on rituals) and census (column in a register), there is something precious left which, according to Azad, is *Al-Islam*, the essence of all religions to which mankind must submit for their moral and spiritual regeneration.

Azad emphasizes that Islam does not offer anything new to the world.[22] It confirms what has been already said in other religious faiths. The Quran says :

> This is no tale of fiction but a confirmation of previous scriptures and an explanation of all things and a guidance and mercy to those who believe.

Thus Quran does not repudiate what other religious faiths have professed and preached.[24] Islam does not deny the Prophets already sent for the salvation of man. When it comes to giving an account of the Prophets and their role Azad becomes particularly eloquent and he writes in a poetical style.[25] He cites the examples of Noah, Moses, Christ and Luke who delivered the message of God to mankind.[26] In the light of Quranic direction Azad affirms that to deny one prophet is to deny them all.[27] As all prophets preached the unity of God, so they are to be revered. In his letter to Ahmad Sabat, Azad wrote that it would be unjust to show any bias against a prophet as they are all messengers of God.[28] But Azad makes it clear that the prophets are to be regarded as human beings who have a distinct role to play for the benefit of mankind. Azad justifies prophethood as the word of God has to be revealed in a language human beings can understand and delivered in a manner that makes it available to men for active guidance in their social conduct.

In the light of Quranic notion of God and the Prophet, Azad states that there is no justification whatsoever for imposing one religion on another because the fundamentals of *Din* are one and the prophets have taught mankind the worship of the same God.[29] If follows from this view that each individual has a right to stick to his own religious faith.

There is no justification for people belonging to different religious faiths to revile or upbraid each other on grounds of professing different faiths. Azad pleads that people should return to the true spirit of their religious faith which is forgotten due to ignorance and blind adherence to obsolete customs practised in the name of religion.

If *Din* is one, the question arises why in that case religious faiths exist in the world. Why is there not a single religious faith embracing the entire world so that there are no religious strifes and conflicts which have riven the world? Azad feels that there are different faiths because people tend to deviate time and again from the true path of *Din* and they forget the significance of its essential spirit making it necessary to reformulate this true spirit in a new idiom for their guidance. Azad argues that differences do not lie in *Din* itself but in mode of worship, customs and religious practices which vary in accordance with the social and economic environments. It is changes taking place in the environment which account for the diversity in religious beliefs. The Quran makes a distinction between *Din* and *Shariat* which consists of the whole body of rules guiding the life of a Muslim in the fields of law, ethics and other areas of social life. Azad emphasizes that these differences in *Shariat* do not negate the oneness of all religious thought.

Azad offers a historical explanation for the existence of different religious faiths in the last portion of *Surat al-Fatiha*.[30] According to him the teachings of Quran are based on the progressive evolution of human society. It is through man's encounter with his environment that he began to pursue the path of truth. Explaining how different religious faiths originated in the world, Azad wrote in *Surat al-Fatiha* :

> In early times people led a simple and natural life entirely free from any antagonism and rivalry. They were bound by common ties of fraternity but with the growth of population and increasing demands conflicts arose which led to the creation of separate groups. Things reached such a pass that conflicts led to bitter hostilities among people and the physically stronger individuals subjected the weaker section of society to servitude and untold misery. In such circumstances, it was natural for Divine Light to manifest itself to mitigate the sorrows of man. Hence originated the chain of Prophets to disseminate God's message of love and piety among people.[31]

The Quran says that each country and nation has been blessed with the grace of a prophet for delivering God's message to mankind. But only a few prophets have been mentioned in the Quran. Azad points out that these few prophets are mentioned not as an exhaustive enumeration but as examples to characterize their role as God's messengers. They have been selected due to the geographical proximity to the areas where they delivered the message of God.[32]

Azad argues that as patterns and conditions of human society are not similar, there can be no uniformity in the mode of religious beliefs and customs of all people. Uniformity in religious habits of life, he adds, would not give people the opportunity to develop their natural faculties like tolerance and freedom of expression. Azad elaborates on differences in the modes of religious worship and customs of people and reverts to his favourite theme that the cementing force that binds men is *Din*-devotion to God and righteous action.[33] God is one but the paths people follow to reach Him are different. An Urdu poet expresses the same idea in the following verse :

*Shaik Kaaba ho key pohancha ham kanisht-e-dil say ho*
*Dard manzil aik thi tuk rah hi ka pher tha*

Tr. The Shaikh reached the state of bliss through Kaaba but we followed the dictates of our heart.
O Dard, (the poet's pen-name), the goal was one but the ways were different

A similar view is expressed in the Rigvedic hymn :

*Ekam sat Viprah Bahudha Vadanti*

Tr. God is one but wise men describe Him in various ways.

The Quran also emphasizes that all may worship the same Truth but they quarrel over the use of different terms, one calls it *Shahid* (honey), and the other calls it *asl* (honey) which are different words having the same meaning.

Like Ranke, Azad discerned God's vicissitudes in the world and we could give dozens of passages from his *Tarjuman* proclaiming that every deed in life is a witness of God or application of the law of divine purpose. Azad was fully acquainted with the debate going on in the West on religion versus science. He quoted the words of Sir Oliver Lodge with approval to the effect that the pre-determined natural laws inexorably operate in the universe.[34] But Azad also held the conviction that the mystery of the eternity of life lies beyond the reach of human intellect and cannot be grasped by rational philosophy.[35] In this connection Azad brings into the discussion two words, *Mutashabha* (by which human efforts fail to apprehend Reality) and *Mukhamat* (by which man is invested with extraordinary powers to grasp the Truth). While urging the cultivation of *Mukhamat*, Azad argues that the attributes of God are outside the reach of human mind and no purpose will be served by trying to comprehend Reality which lies beyond our range of thinking.[36] In other words, Azad believes that religious truths cannot be proved at the scientific level. Even leading scientists are puzzled over the mystery of the universe. But this does not mean that Azad bade goodby to rationality in the comprehension of Reality. In dealing with religious matters Azad thought it necessary to exercise *tadabbur*, i.e., to go deeply into the meaning of Quran.[37] Douglas states that Azad was influenced in his notion of God and Reality by the ideas of Wilhelm Schmidst's *The Origin and Growth of Religion* in twelve volumes.[38]

Azad introduces in *Tarjuman* the subject of divine guidance (*hidayat*) which man seeks for his salvation. The Quran has specified four sources which could help man to understand the nature of Reality. They are (1) Instinct (2) Perception (3) Reason and (4) Revelation. Azad has shown in his analysis that the first three of these sources have been used by man to enhance the material and moral quality of his life. Through their interaction, civilization advances. They interact with each other and serve as powerful weapons in the hands of man to advance in the scale of human civilization. Azad illustrates the working of each of these sources. He points out, for example, that if instinct tells us that the sun has the size of the golden dish then rationality must subject this notion to minute scrutiny in order to arrive at the truth. Revelation, Azad regards, as the highest form of guidance which intellect cannot grasp in its own terms. Azad believes that revelation flashes on the mind of a man like lightning to make him see the vision of Reality. This spiritual experience which illumines the mind and soul of man also fortifies his faith in the omnipotence, ominiscience and omnipresence of God.[39]

It seems that before taking up his *Tarjuman* Azad had done his own foundational reading of different religions in the world. That is why we find in the *Tarjuman* direct or indirect references to the Chinese, Zoroastrian, Judaic, Greek and Hindu concept of God.[40] He also traces the evolution of religious ideas from animism to monism.[41] Azad does not find any essential difference between the teachings of Islam and Christianity. Like Ram Mohun Roy he denies the divinity of Christ but accepts the Biblical version of his birth.[42] Azad warns that while interpreting religious literature it is necessary to see the real meaning behind the use of figurative and symbolical terms. For example, he says that in the Bible, the words 'turn thy cheek' or 'love thy enemy' should not be taken to mean that one must surrender abjectly to one's adversaries. Such Biblical expressions, Azad maintains, are used only to emphasize the virtues of compassion and piety in life.

In *Tarjuman* Azad showed great interest in Hindu philosophy and spoke of it with appreciation, something rare among the Ulama in his time. He discerned the good not only in Christianity but in Hinduism as well. He admired the Vedic hymns which described the phenomenon of nature but he did not think they would further the cause of religion as such. He was impressed by the philosophical speculations of the *Upanishads* which were concerned with the ultimate reality and sought to define the highest values of life. He wrote that in the *Upanishads* the Hindu mind "had reached such heights that we can scarcely find a parallel in the ideologies of the ancient people."[43] According to Azad, the doctrine of negation expounded in Hindu philosophy offered an advanced notion of transcedentalism without affirming any positive belief.

Jainism and Buddhism did not appeal much to Azad because of their ascetic character. The *Bhagavad-gita*, he regarded, as an echo of the *Upanishads*.[44] It puzzled him to see how the Hindu mind which created such profound philosophical systems for apprehending Reality also built pantheons that tempt men to observe the external forms of religion to the neglect of the inner depth of spiritual experience. According to Azad, there are no differences between the teachings of Jews and the Prophet Mohammad. The difference lies only in the outward nature of utterances on account of the difference in occasions when they were made. Both Islam and Judaism stood for purity of spirit, cultivation of virtue and exercise of compassion. On the necessity of retaliation, however, differences do exist.[45]

Azad raised the question of authenticity of *Hadith*, particularly of the juridical directives on political matters.[46] He realized that difficulties in establishing the veracity of *Hadith* were created by theologians who adopted a partisan attitude, sided with the ruling powers and tried to provide them legitimacy by means of twisted interpretations of *Hadith*. On the question of *Hidith* Azad followed Ibn Taimiya who judged the authenticity of *Hadith* by strictly subjecting them to scientific scrutiny.[47]

In *Tarjuman* Azad deals with a number of topics such as *Haji*, *Zakat*, *jaziya*, and the conflicts between the Jews and Muslims. He also offers comments on various religious faiths regarding the issues which form a part of his theme. While discussing the 'Art of War' Azad shows how at the battle of Badr in his encounter with Abu Safyan by sheer force of his inspiring leadership and disciplined followers the Prophet won victory with his feeble escort over the numerically superior yet undisciplined rivals.[48]

Azad's mind occasionally went beyond the principles of Islam and commented on the problems of general history. He discussed the theme of 'Chance in History' an issue which received particular attention from historians like J.R. Seeley, Regius Professor of History, Cambridge. Azad's thinking on historical issues is, however, not as impressive and authoritative as his explication of Islamic principles. Azad takes the position that if there had been no torrential rains on the 16 and 18 June, 1815, Napoleon would not have been defeated by Wellington and the Prussian General Bliicher.[49] This is an oversimplification of a complex problem. Churchill, an expert on military warfare, thought that Napoleon's defeat stemmed primarily from Wellington's strategic retreats and tactics which trapped Napoleon.[50] A deeper analysis by 'Elie Halevy, a distinguished French historian, explains that Napoleon lost the battle for two reasons: (1) he fought the battle in old style; and (2) his troops at Waterloo no longer possessed the old elan they had displayed at Austerlitz and Jena.'[51]

Azad also discussed the sanctity of treaties in international politics and showed how the British broke them one by one with the ruling Chieftains in India, Siraj ud-Daula, Mir Jafar, Mir Qasim, Chait Singh of Benaras, the Begums of Oudh, Hyder Ali, the Amirs of Sind and others.[52] By giving a detailed accounts based on literary and archaeological evidence, Azad showed that Dhul Qarnain was the title of Cyrus, the celebrated conqueror, King of Media and Persia. Azad accepted Xenophon's evidence without realizing that his *Cynopoedie* wrongly considered a historical source on the life of Cyrus was really a philosophical romance.[53]

What is our estimate of Azad's *Tarjuman*?[54] What stature does he attain on the strength of his interpretations of Quran? It is difficult to answer these questions. For one thing, Azad could complete just half of his work, and secondly, *Tarjuman* is basically a translation venture and not an independent interpretative work. It would, however, be unfair to regard *Tarjuman* as a mere exercise in translation. It is a combination of both translation and interpretation and as it proceeds, interpretation recedes into the background. The first volume of *Tarjuman*, *Surat al-Fatiha,* to which Azad gave prime importance as he regarded it as an essence of Quran itself is largely an interpretative work. The third and fourth volumes of *Tarjuman* are filled with large historical data connected with Islam, Judaism and Christianity. The question is whether we could form a sufficiently clear notion of Azad's point of view from a work which remained incomplete and is interpretative only in parts.

Azad treats Quran as a primary determinant of Islam to which all else is secondary. Sayyid Ahmad Khan had interpreted Quran in the light of reason to meet the exigencies of his times. Jalaluddin al-Afghani had attacked his interpretation as serving the interests of the British administration. S. Abid Husain has described Sayyid Ahmed Khan a 'romantic apologist' in his approach to the interpretation of Quran.[55] Sayyid Ahmad Khan's interpretation, it has to be admitted, was lacking in historical perspective and Sufi fervour.

In his interpretation of Quran, Azad was deeply influenced by Abduh and the *Al-Manar* School. Douglas says that the *Tarjuman* was like *Al-Manar* in many ways.[56] Sayyid Ahmad Akbarabadi, an authority on the study of Quran, also thought that Azad's work was cast in the mould of Rashid Rida.[57]

It would be clear from Azad's commentary of *Tarjuman* that he viewed Islam from the wider perspective of a great humanist. He brought to the interpretation of Quran a liberal approach which emphasised that Islam stands for *Wahdat-I-Adiyan* (Unity of Religion), the major theme of *Surat al-Fatiha.* His entire work is free from any trace of theological narrowness or dogma. He could never take the view that Truth could exclusively be found in Islam alone, nor that a Muslim by virtue of his birth would *ipso facto* be superior to others. Azad showed in his study that the Prophet had believed in a multi-religious state 'Ummat-Wahidaa', a federal religion in which tolerance and goodwill prevail.

To put Azad's view in the simplest terms would be to say to the world: "Look, Islam asks you to submit to God and do good deeds, but if you don't, then that is your look out. We have done our duty. For your action you shall be accountable to God. He will be your judge." Azad's favourite verse from Raumi given below is an epitome of the same idea.

*Tu Baraya vasl Kardan amdi*
*Na Baraya fasl kardan amdi*

Tr. you have come to unite people but not to divide them

In his assessment of Azad's interpretation of Islam, Professor Mohammad Habib says eloquently that "in spite of the fact that it is not complete, there is nothing like *Tarjuman* in the whole range of religious literature."[58] Habib adds that *Tarjuman* should be carried to every home. Sayyid Sulaiman Nadwi who held orthodox views on Islam wrote that in his interpretation Azad followed the path shown in Ibn Taimiya and Ibn Qayyam.[59] He considered Azad's translation of *Tarjuman* to be 'agreeable, effective and dignified.'

Azad's *Tarjuman* had its critics too. *Tarjuman* has been branded as a 'Congressi Tarfsir,' i.e., the Indian National Congress's interpretation of Quran.[60] Douglas writes that Azad's political association with Hindus 'may have encouraged him to emphasise unity of religion.'[61] But in his defence Azad would say that he only asked his co-religionists to return to the word of God as understood by the Prophet and his Companions. Douglas has also faulted Azad for making the belief in the Prophet non-essential.'[62] In other words, the criticism against *Tarjuman* is that it is a reformist's commentary, a tendentious work designed with eye on the present which suffers from the same *tafsir bil rai* (subjective element) that Azad had attacked in works of earlier theologians. According to this view, *Tarjuman* reflects the conflicts and tensions that assailed his mind because of the Hindu-Muslim rift in politics. This criticism leads further to the charge that Azad restricted himself to a certain kind of data which accorded with his pre-conceived notions and would be used to lend support to them.

In view of the above criticism Azad is branded a lost leader who took a wrong turning after his release in Ranchi in 1920. Azad's critics maintain that the real interpreter of Islam was the Editor of *Al-Hilal* and *Al-Balagh* but thereafter his vision got blurred because of his obsession with the Congress propaganda of Hindu-Muslim unity. That is why *Tarjuman* never became influential among the Muslims in pre-Independence India.

Some of the questions to which Muslims attach great importance like revelation, free will, faith and doubt and the exclusive role of Muslims as an independent community do not find adequate explanation in *Tarjuman*. One would have expected Azad to elaborate on the dissimilarities that exist between different religious faiths and how Islam could eliminate them. Azad is also assailed for not being the sole author of *Tarjuman* as he was assisted in this venture by a number of other scholars.[63] It is possible that some of Azad's associates helped him in the collection of data or gave him material on points he needed for his elaboration in his work. But there is no doubt that the entire work bears the stamp of his personality and he presents a distinct point of view within a framework which he had himself evolved after a deep study of religions of the world.

*Tarjuman* is the work of a supple mind backed by solid scholarship. It is enriched by aphorisms and brilliant illustratious taken from Islamic history. The entire work notable for its high seriousness is exquisitely sensitive and finely tempered. Azad made a definite contribution through this work which cannot be easily ignored by students of Islam and historians of the independence movement in India. It opened a 'moral and spiritual path' for many ardent Muslims who were humanistically inclined and carried a great deal of nationalistic fervour among them.[68] Azad's work makes a powerful impact on the mind of any non-Muslim who reads it and he begins to feel that if he were not subjected to the rigours of *Sharia*, he would be as convinced a Muslim as one who was born in this faith and brought up under its influence.

It is unfortunate that Azad could not complete his work. Possibly he thought that he had nothing more to say, possibly he thought that the Muslim community he was addressing would not listen to him as his influence among his community was diminishing after he became the Congress President in 1940. When he was free from political activities, his readings of books consumed so much of his time that he found little time for writing. A noted Indian scholar who was close to Azad and who does not wish to be quoted told this writer that Azad was compelled by financial difficulties to write his books and that he was a lazy person by nature who derived great pleasure from extensive reading. This is not an unusual attitude on the part of a scholar. Dr. Johnson had said that he wouldn't write unless he was paid for it. Whatever be the reason, Azad's *Tarjuman* remained incomplete like his life. *Tarjuman* is not profound or original but it is a scholarly work of great merit and remarkable for its high moral integrity and rectitude. He could not see the flaws in his own case, though in an adversary nothing could escape his discerning eye.

*References*

1. *TQ* (ET) Vol. I, p. XIIII, *TQ* (SA). Vol. I, p. 53.
2. *TQ* (SA), p. 18.
3. Syed Abdul Latif, 'An Unpublished Masterpiece' in Humayun Kabir ed., *Maulana, Abul Kalam Azad*, pp. 122-129. See *TQ* (SA), p. 26.
4. *TQ* (SA), p. 26.
5. *TQ* (SA), Vol. I, XXIV, XXIX, *TQ* (SE) Vol. I, p. XXIX.
6. *Ibid.*, (SA), p. 27.
7. Ghulam Rasul Mihr, *Naqsh-e-Azad*, pp. 29, 40, 42, 62, 78, 88, 133, 226; See also Abu Salman Shahjahanpuri, *Maktubat-e-Azad*, pp. 224, 246, 283 and 288.
8. Dr. Mohammad Abdur Rashid in *Ifadat-e-Azad* ed. Abu Salman Shahjahanpuri, p. 131.
9. Douglas, *Abul Kalam Azad*, p. 201.
10. *TQ* (ET), Vol. I, XVI.
11. *TQ* (SA), Vol. III, p. VII, Qazi Mohammad Abdul Ghaffar, *Aser-e-Abul Kalam*, p. 135, Mohd. Habib, *The Revolutionary Maulana*, *op.cit*, pp. 83 & 88.
12. Douglas, *op. cit.*, p. 168.
13. Mohd. Habia, *op. cit.*, p. 83.
14. *GK*, pp. 100-02.
15. *TQ* (SA), Vol. II, pp. 125-26.
16. *TQ* Vol. I, pp. 10-13.
17. *Ibid.*, p. 10.
18. *Ibid.*, pp. 8-9.
19. This study of Azad's interpretation is based on *TQ* (SA) and *TQ* (ET).
20. *TQ* (SA), Vol. I, pp. 190-317, 361 and 371.
21. *Ibid.*, pp. 71-72, 76 and 79.
22. *Ibid.*, p. 47.
23. *TQ* (SA), Vol. III, in *TQ* (ET).
24. *TQ* (SA), Vol. I, p. 155.
25. *Ibid.*, Vol. III, p. 698.
26. *Ibid.*, Voi. I, p. 40.
27. *Ibid.*, pp. 190-357, 364 & 408.
28. *Ifadat*, *op. cit.*, pp. 20-21.
29. *TQ* (SA), Vol. III, pp. 633-35 & 690.
30. *Ibid.*, Vol. I, p. 352.
31. *TQ* (SA) Vol. I, pp. 352-53, 360, Vol. IV, pp. 660-61.
32. *Ibid.*, pp. 356-57.
33. *Ibid.*, p., 374.
34. *Ibid.*, Vol. I, p. 467.
35. *Ibid.*, Vol. III, pp. 308-09; Vol, IV, pp. 932-47.
36. *Ibid.*

37. K.G. Saiyidain, *Maulana Azad's Contribution to Education*, the Maharaja Sayajirao Memorial Lectures, University of Baroda, p. 18.
38. Dougles, *op. cit.*, p. 202.
39. *TQ* (SA), p. 174.
40. *Ibid.*, pp. 285-314,
41. *Ibid.*, f. 285-300, See *TQ* (ET), p. 105.
42. *TQ* (ET), Vol, III, p. 404.
    *TQ* (SA), Vol. IV, p. 563.
43. *TQ* (SA), Vol. IV, pp. 109-10.
    *TQ* (ET), Vol. I, pp. 190-92.
44. *TQ* (ET), Vol. I, p. 114.
45. *TQ* (SA), Vol. I, pp. 109-10.
46. *al-Hilal*, pp. 13-20, May, 1914,*al-Balagh*, 24 December, 1915.
47. Gulam Rasul Mihr, 'Bai Hasiyet-e-Muhddith', in Abu Salman Shahjahanpuri, *Abul Kalam Azad*, pp. 108-20.
48. *TQ* (SA), Vol. III, p. 168.
49. *Ibid.*, pp. 168-69.
50. Winston S. Churchill, *A History of the English Speaking Peoples*, p. 322.
51. Elie Halevy, *A History of the English Peoples in the Nineteenth Century, England in 1815*, p. 91.
52. *TQ* (SA), pp. 221-22.
53. *Ibid.*, pp. Vol. IV, pp. 430-542.
54. This discussion is based on the *Tarjuman* in 4 volumes published by the Sahitya Akademi.
55. S. Abid Husain, 'Modern Trends in Islam' in *Islam*, p. 85.
56. Douglas, op. cit., pp. 216-18. See Manzur Ahmad, *Abul Kalam Azad, Fikr-o-Fun*, p. 428.
57. Syed Ahmad Akbarabadi, 'Azad' *Tarjuman al-Quran*' in *Ajkal*, August, 1958, p. 81.
58. Mohammad Habid, 'The Revolutionary Maulana' in Humayun Kabir, *op. cit.*, p. 93.
59. Quoted in the above.
60. Mufti Abul Ghaffar Khan, *op.cit.*, p. 167.
61. Douglas, *op. cit.*,,p. 210.
62. *Ibid.*, p. 211.
63. Jamel Khawaja, *Quest for Islam*, p. 57.

# 7

# A SCHOLAR EXTRAORDINARY

What is striking about Azad's scholarship is the disparity between the massive erudition he possessed and the absence of sustained monumental work. His output began slowly as editor for *Lisan al-Sidq* when he was about fifteen, grew in volume and quality when he became editor of *Al-Hilal* and *Al-Balagh* and declined after *Tazkira.* He picked up the thread of his writing in 1927 and published two volumes of *Tarjuman* in the thirties. And finally appeared *Ghuber-e-Khatir* and *Karwan-e-Kheyal* in forties. There were some shorter pieces, the addresses he delivered, his marginal notes on books and letters which have been compiled after his death.

Thus the output of his scholarly works is not impressive but it is the quality of his erudition and the motives that inspired him to creative activity which are worthy of great commendation. Naturally his feverish political work hampered his scholarly pursuits. The question is whether Azad continues to be read or has already become 'dated' as an author. What position does he hold in the world of literature? Who will today read *Al-Hilal* or *Al-Balagh* except those interested in understanding the history of Indian journalism or the spread of Muslim resurgence? *Tazkira* was meant for the specialists in theology, and the *Tarjuman* for the moral uplift of the average Muslim.

We have seen how in his early life Azad had elevated journalism to the level of a literary activity. *Tazkira*, a work of restless imagination, was a short discursive history of Muslim religious thought. *Azad Ki Kahani Khud Azad Ki Zabani* was compiled by Abdur Razzaq Malihabadi who was working with Azad as Assistant Editor of *Paigham* in 1921. Malihabadi had finalised this work by 1923. Then why should he have waited for thirty-six years to publish it ? Malihabadi published the work after Azad's death. *Kahani* is a diffuse, predestrian work, the best we can say about it being that it throws light on Azad's religious and intellectual development. Malihabadi says that Azad did not write this work. He only spoke at some lengtyh about his past and he recorded what Azad spoke. It is thus Malihabadi's reconstruction of Azad's life on the basis of what Azad seems to have spoken. This work does not show Azad's usual rigour of mind, his literary flair and refined wit. It would not be fair to view it as Azad's autobiography. None has seen its original manuscript. Not even Malihabadi's son, as pointed out earlier, has any knowledge of it. From what we know of Azad, it is difficult to believe that he would speak so much to anyone however close he might have been to him.

Azad's letters addressed to Nawab Sadar Yar Jung Bahadur Maulana Habibur Rehman Sherwani were composed by him during his prison life in Ahmednagar Fort, 1942-45 and came out later in the form of a book entitled *Ghubar-e-Khatir.*[1] The first edition of this book was published by Hali publishing House, Delhi in May 1946. *Ghubar-e-Khatir* is Azad's dispersed meditations on various themes of general interest without any special design or set purpose. When Azad wrote them he had no intention of publishing them, but after his release, his Secretary, Ajmal Khan persuaded him to do so. Malik Ram says that it was Montesquieu's *Persian Letters* published in 1721 that put the idea of writing these letters in Azad's mind .[2] The *Persian Letters* had been translated into many languages including Arabic. Azad may have read the book but this remains merely a hypothesis unsubstantiated by evidence.

It is doubtful whether Azad ever read Charles-Louis Montesquieu's *Persian Letters.*[3] There is little similarity in content and style between the *Persian Letters* and *Ghubar-e-Khatira. The Persian Letters* contain the correspondence of two Persian travellers in Europe with their wives in the *harem* and the eunuchs that guard them. This work is a forerunner of Montesquieu's political treatise, *Of the Spirit of Laws (1748).* It echoes the anti-establishment sentiments of the eighteenth century and criticises the traditional French institutions by viewing them with mock-innocent eyes. It conveys the atmosphere of the Regency of Philipe d'Orleans from 1715 to 1723 following the death of Louis XIV and attacks Hobbes's doctrine of the state. A combination of the erotic and exotic, and written in a rhapsodic style, these letters contain Montesquieu's reflections on a variety of themes such as sex, women, marriage, religion, government, justice, virtue, some features of French life, the Ottoman empire, etc. These letters ran into ten editions in the first year of its publication. Montesquieu sees by flashes and does not think connectedly. His avowed purpose was moral.

*Ghubar-e-Khatir* belongs to a different category; it is never episodic. Azad wrote these letters to please and satisfy himself in gaol life. His letters are free from politics and sex, and he does not come out of them as a debunker of established authority like Montesquieu. Unlike Montesquieu who wrote in a lighter vein and chose the simple phrase, Azad's letters exude a literary and scholarly flavour. But both offer their reflections on general themes of human interest which arouse our curiosity even today.

Douglas complains that Azad refused the advice of his fellow prisoners to complete his *Tarjuman*.[4] The implication in this statement is that Azad in his prison life had ample time to complete his *Tarjuman* but did not utilize his stay in the prison for this purpose so that the task so dear to his heart remained unfinished. But Douglas forgets the peculiar circumstances in which Azad was placed. For translating the *Quran*, Azad had to consult a large collection of specialised works which for him or anyone else it was impossible to obtain in gaol. The translation also involved a highly specialized kind of scholarship which could not be maintained in the absence of readily available theological works of high standard for citations and explanations. Prison life has certain inherent limitations for the pursuit of scholarly studies. Political prisoners during their confinement in jail have usually tended to write their autobiographies, confessions, testaments or reflections but seldom minute scholarly works. Thus prison was not a suitable place for Azad to undertake the *Tarjuman*. He could dabble only in a dilettantish fashion in curious and recondite matters which became a theme of *Ghubar-e-Khatir*.

Azad was too proud to request for any favour during his imprisonment, far less for books. The Inspector-General of Police, Bombay asked Azad whether he would like to procure books from his own library at home. Azad gave his consent first but withdrew it the next day.[5] Due to the non-availability of theological works needed for completing his *Tarjuman*, what was Azad to do? How was he to spend his time? He had no interest in taking physical exercise. Nor did he share his fellow-prisoner Nehru's passion for gardening, 'the purest of human pleasures.' He was used to living a sedentary life. Nehru was then engaged in writing his *Discovery of India*, Sardar Patel whiled away his time mostly with newspapers and chess.[6] Dr. Syed Mahmud could scarcely read due to his eye trouble. Asaf Ali composed Urdu poetry. The only thing Azad could seek refuge in was to find comfort in his past, reconstruct it in his mind and express it in a literary form. Cut off from the outside world, a man of profound scholarship and exquisite literary taste, the remembrance of things past provided an escape from his present dreariness of life and evoked nostalgic memories. These Azad poured out in the letters.

But to whom should he address his letters? Surely to someone worthy enough to understand his thought and idiom and share his confidence. Who could deserve this honour better than Nawab Sadar Yar Jung Bahadur Maulana Habibur Rehman Sherwani of Bhikampur (1867-1950).[7] Azad and Sherwani had known each other since 1905 when they had met in Lucknow through Shibli Numani when Sherwani was co-editor of *al-Nadwa*.[8]

Nawab Sadar Yar Jung Bahadur Habibur Rehman, an aristocrat with a large landed property, a scholar and a poet with 'Hasrat' as his pen name was the author of several literary works including his Urdu poetical works, *Karwan-e-Hasrat*, the Persian anthology of poems, *Bostan-e-Hasrat, Tàzkira-i-Babur, Makalat-e-Sherwani* and *Ulama-e-Sair*. A former Head of Religious Studies at Aligarh College, he was appointed later by the Nizam of Hyderabad as *Sadr-us-Sudur* (Head of the ecclesiastical department in Nizam's Government) and the first Vice-Chancellor of Osmania University, Hyderabad. The Nizam conferred on him the coveted title of 'Nawab Sadar Yar Jung Bahadur.' A trustee of Aligarh College, he was also associated with Nadwat ul-Ulama.

Douglas states that Nawab Sadar Yar Yung was a loyalist to the British Government but offers no evidence in support of this assertion.[9] The Nawab kept himself discretely aloof from politics and was a man of independent character. It was his passion for learning that brought him close to Azad. If the Nawab had been a loyalist the British Government would have conferred on him some title as a mark of their appreciation of his loyalty to them. They did no such thing. Azad too would have desisted from cultivating friendship with anyone hobnobbing with the British. It appears that Azad had no close association with Nawab Sadar Yar Jung Bahadur between 1920 and 1940. In his letter of 4 September, 1940 to the Nawab, Azad throws light on how the old association between the two was revived after a period of about two decades.[10]

Azad tells us how one day while he was looking for a book in his shelves, his eyes fell suddenly on the old files of *al-Nadwa* which kindled memories of his long-cherished association with Nawab Sadar Yar Jung. He wrote that on seeing the *al-Nadwa* volumes :

> At once I thought of meeting you in retreat from the tears and toil of the world to sit quietly and recapitulate our past not over the goblets of wine but cups of tea.[11]

Azad recalls also with warmth of feeling his previous meetings with him in 1909 or 1910 and 1920.[12]

The Sahitya Akademi edition of *Ghubar-e-Khatir* contains twenty-four letters including twenty which Azad wrote in prison, three after his release and one before his arrest. The prison letters were written between 10 August and 16 September, 1943. When his wife died on 9 April, 1943, letter-writing, as he says, no longer interested him.[13] He could force himself to write just three more after his wife's death.

Azad's mind soars on a variety of themes in *Ghubar-e-Khatir*. The subject matter is life itself in all its complexity which he views from different angles in these letters. They give faithful expression to his intense personality and convey his inward feelings and thoughts in varied moods. He describes vividly how he was arrested at Bhulabhai Desai's residence in the early hours of 9 August 1942 and taken to the Victoria Terminus from where he was bundled off along with his colleagues to Ahmednagar. The history of the Ahmednagar fort is also unfolded evoking the memory of the stirring events connected with its past.[14]

Here in Ahmednagar fort where the world is quiet, sitting alone with his white paper and black ink, Azad enjoys his white jasmine tea and starts talking to himself. Thoughts crowd round him, he lets his pen flow and pours out his heart in his compositions. He grows lyrical over the round of cups of tea he drinks. Puffs of cigarettes which season his palate with the peculiar flavour and stimulate his thinking punctuate the drinking of tea. His tea drinking with the help of metaphors drawn from goblets, intoxication, fire etc., creates a strong impression on our minds. He talks about the whole thing with a relish that makes us feel that he is not merely drinking tea but having a taste of the choicest of Rhenish wines.

In his letters Azad also raises some serious philosophical questions. He asks fundamental questions like : What is the purpose and meaning of life? What is the place of religion in human existence? Where does reality exist, in mind or in matter? It seems that like an artist Azad is aware of the unseen world and his experiences can be shared by those who seek goodness and truth.[15] Of all his works, *Ghubar-e-Khatir* is the only one where Azad tells us frankly how he rebelled against his parental authority and charted his own independent line of thinking. He longs for heights which no man has trod. He shares with us his experience of denial of God and tells us about the recovery of his faith in Him.[16] The passages in *Ghubar-e-Khatir* where Azad tells us about God are an echo of his *Tarjuman*.[17] We are made to realize that the mental anguish he expresses throughout these letters is not personal but universal and we share, if only in imagination, the meaning of sorrow, of solitude and of the gravity of human life.

Expression was a primary need for Azad like breathing. Each piece in *Ghubar-e-Khatir* has its own flavour of a specific mood. The sight of sparrows in his room inspired him to compose on them two brilliant letters which reveal his philosophic bent of mind as well as his narrative power.[18] He describes the frisky, chirpy and gay behaviour of these sparrows whom he begins to fondle. He sees in the elder sparrow whom he calls 'Qalindar' the attributes of tenacity, detachment and a will to touch the skies. Azad portrays the helplessness of a newly hatched baby sparrow which could not fly, but suddenly soared one day into the skies. He wrote :

> In this young one the capacity for flight had manifested itself. It had come out from its nest and was viewing the sky and the earth below. The feeling of self-realization had not yet been awakened. It was not yet fully aware of its own identity. The mother bird was beckoning it again and again. The breeze repeatedly brushed its wings. The tumult of life and movement was prodding it from every direction. But its own oven was so cold that no external pressure could warm it.[19]

Azad writes that as soon as the light of 'self-realization' dawned on the young one, it took forward a step and then only the sky was the limit. He draws a lesson from this story that it is the daring of a moment that decides the destiny of an individual. In other words, one step this way or that way alters the entire course of our life.[20]

In another letter Azad takes up the question of the role of 'ego' in literature, though the word 'bias' meaning personal opinion would perhaps be more appropriate to state what he intended to convey.[21] In this context he discusses Tolstoy, the venerated setter of goals and rare diagonostician of man and society. From the Indian side he brings in Babur and Jahangir who were active participants in big events inspired by a passion for glory and fame. He also tells us how his colleagues in jail were not a happy lot. He admires Nehru's passion for gardening.

He hears Nehru's snores at night from the next room and regards it as a sign of his excitable and emotional temperament. He shares with Asaf Ali the beauty of Urdu poetry. He mocks at Syed Mahmud's anxious concern for the crows who visit him as his guests to feed on bits of rice that he generously throws towards them. The combined melody of their cawing reverberates through the fort. And the last letter in this collection exhibits his deep and abiding passion for music and he offers here a brief scholarly survey of the history of music.[22] It is the haunting melody of Arabic music that stirs in him the deepest feelings.

Azad's account of his wife's death produces a profoundly moving effect on the minds of readers.[23] He writes on this tragic episode with great restraint.[24] He had learnt of her illness earlier. The Government was willing to release him but he declined. Every day he was anxious for some news about her. At last the telegram arrived! She was no more. Azad shed no tears and made no other demonstration of the deep sorrow he felt within. He bore all this with stoic composure. He remembered how on leaving her before his arrest he saw that, 'her eyes were dry but her checks were shedding tears.' There was a grave of an unknown soul in the courtyard of Ahmednagar fort. He had passed by it several times. It never meant anything to him. But now after his wife's death, he became passionately attached to it. In the silence of nights, Azad would keep gazing at it for long hours.[25]

*Ghubar-e-Khatir* is not a work entirely devoted to the larger questions of life and death and the mystery of the universe. There are lighter moments which Azad captures at some places. Syed Mahmud's company of the crows and his own sallies with the jail superintendent, Major Sandak, whom he named Cheeta Khan after the name of Chand Bibi's Governor of the fort, are some obvious examples. There are also occasional sallies on miscellaneous matters. Azad tells us, for example, about Aurangzeb's keen interest in music in his early youth and of his passionate love affair with one Hira Bai.[26] He attacks Badauni for his narrow-minded dogmatism.[27]

It would be unjust to compare *Ghubar-e-Khatir* with *Al-Hilal, Al-Balagh* or *Tazkira* as it belongs to a different category of writing. *Ghubar-e-Khatir* lacks *Al-Hilal's* passionate power, *Al-Balagh's* elevated tone and *Tazkira's* weight of scholarship presented in grandiose diction. *Ghubar-e-Khatir* echoes the *Tarjuman* on religious themes and is akin to it in lucidity and simplicity of expression. Of all his works, *Ghubar-e-Khatir* is the only one which directly throws light on Azad's style of life and his point of view and opinions on small matters. It is also the agony of an intellectual battling with life, who has the toughness and strength not to lose his heart even when the odds become heavy. In this work we find Azad representing the finest and richest values of Mughal culture. We cannot regard *Ghubar-e-Khatir* as a product of Azad's declining powers of old age as has been suggested by some scholars.[28] In this work Azad presents his philosophic vision which enabled him to see life steadily and see it whole. The keynote of this work is what Shelley had sung in pain, 'Our sweetest songs are those that tell of saddest thought'. Azad too says that in his life he always chose thorns and not flowers which he left for others to pick. It is the path of sorrow that he regards as the real mode of his life. 'Only those who know how to lose can find', he wrote.

Azad did not wish *Ghubar-e-Khatir* to be translated into any language as he thought that it would not be possible to render its true spirit in translation.[29] But he believed that this work would be a most appropriate specimen from the point of view of style for readers interested in studying his literary works. He knew that his other writings limited the circle of his readers, but *Ghubar-e-Khatir* could attract a wider audience.

The *Karwane-Kheyal* is another collection of letters exchanged between Azad and Habibur Rahman Sherwani which was published towards the end of 1946. It covers the period from 23 February, 1942 to 1 November 1946. It contains Azad's seventeen letters and Sherwani's ten. They are real and not imaginary letters exchanged between two old intimate friends, which exude a deep concern for human values and reveal a fine literary taste. No heavy stuff or verbiage–everything is natural and to the point. Azad nostalgically shares memories of the past that is no more. He laments the passing away of those men whose prime interests in life were the creation and enjoyment of aesthetic experience and pursuit of knowledge; the age that produced a galaxy of such men is sadly gone for ever. In a beautiful passage Azad confesses his debt to Shibli who helped him shape his life.[30] Theses letters are lit up with old memories and the two friends talk of tea, flowers, beauties of nature and poetry. But the overall impact of these letters is one of sweet melancholy which turns one's eye inward.

In both these works, *Ghubar-e-Khatir* and *Karwan-e-Kheyal*, Azad emerges as a great literary artist gifted with an acute power of observation and a refined sensibility. It seems that the extensive use of verses from poets in *Ghubar-e-Khatir*–alone they number seven hundred -

tends to hamper the flow of his narrative and deprives us of his deeper reflections on man and the world. It is inconceivable that Azad could have remembered so many verses correctly, though he had a prodigious memory like Macaulay. The final manuscript of *Ghubar-e-Khatir* was revised by Ghulam Rasul Mihr and Ajmal Khan and it is possible that they have added some verses. It is also possible that a particular verse first fluttered in Azad's mind at a point of time which inspired him to venture on a theme connected with it. Possibly to mark the end of his narrative Azad put the verse as a full stop. Ghalib figures the most in *Ghubar-e-Khatir*, and his influence on Azad is most marked in the style of letter writing. On the whole, *Ghubar-e-Khatir* remains a great literary piece. Its doleful note wrings a tear from every reader's eye. In these letters Azad wraps himself in contemplation and communes with beauty, love and truth that make life worth living.

Let us try to sum up Azad as a scholar. Like Bacon he took all knowledge to be his province. He had devoted himself to learning with the assiduity of a Petrarch and a Goethe. He was a sort of bibliophile who spent endless hours in early youth with books, exploring the frontiers of knowledge. By his mastery of the Quran he found his style. He often indulged in that idle curiosity, or 'vagabondage of brooding' which is necessary for a creative artist. He was an independent thinker who would not spare even a scholar like Shibli from his criticism.[31]

Azad possessed a remarkable gift for creating metaphors and similes which enriched the quality of his prose. But behind everything he wrote there lay what Nehru called a 'luminous intellect' and the force of a strong personality. Abdul Majid Daryabadi, Niaz Fatehpuri and Ghulam Rasul Mihr were influenced by his writings. But his style was beyond the control of anyone else. His style of writing varied in accordance with the theme he chose. He could not complete any work, nor could anyone imitate him. He remained a class by himself in literary domain and set a high standard difficult for others to follow. Despite his vast and critical scholarship, his literary output falls short of his extraordinary potential. His entanglement in politics prevented him from discharging his responsibility as a creative artist. Gifted as he was with profound scholarship, critical acumen and powerful command of language, he would have been equal to any Ibn Taimiya, Bacon or Hegel if he had devoted himself entirely to the pursuit of knowledge. But that was not be because the call of the times pulled him to other fields.

Before we conclude this section on Azad's contribution to scholarly pursuits we must refer to two of Azad's short pieces which are usually ignored but which are remarkable for their erudition and historical insights. One of these is his 'Foreword' to *Eighteen Fifty-Seven* by Surendra Nath Sen published on the occasion of the first centenary of the Revolt of 1857 in 1957, and the other his Introduction to *History of Philosophy, Eastern and Western* edited by Dr. S. Radhakrishnan.

As Education Minister Azad commissioned Sen to write the history of 1857 revolt. Sen was given complete freedom to express his views independently on this sensitive theme. Usually 'Forewords' are rituals performed mechanically by celebrities to gratify the ego of the authors. But Azad took even this task seriously. He maintained in this Foreword that the leaders of the 1857 revolt were not inspired by patriotic motives and had no clear notion of what they were doing. On the contrary, they were jealous of each other and were involved in petty intrigues. He wrote, "As I read about the events of 1857 I am forced to the sad conclusion that the Indian National character had sunk so low.'[32] He severely condemns Nana Sahib for the brutal atrocity of murdering helpless Englishwomen.[33] He expresses no sympathy for Emperor Bahadur Shah who, he thought, was lacking in qualities of leadership. Azad wrote sarcastically that the only qualification that Bahadur Shah possessed was that 'he was a descendant of Akbar and Shahjahan.'[34]

It would be clear from Azad's assessment of the Revolt of 1857 that he was not overwhelmed by nationalist fervour, a common malady of our historians. We have seen Azad's deep interest in the study of historical problems since his *Al-Hilal* days. Despite the fact that he was not a technical historian trained in the rigorous historical discipline, Azad could often go to the heart of a historical problem and grasp its essentials. This is also evident, I believe, from his candid and unconventional assessment of some of the personalities associated with the 1857 Revolt.

In the Radhakrishnan volume on *History of Philosophy*, Azad opens his Introduction with the following Persian couplet :

*Ma Zi Aghaz o zi Anjam-i-Jahan Bi Khabbar-Am*
*AWWL-o-I-Akhir-IN Khuna Kitab Uftad Ast*

In these verses a Persian poet has compared the universe to an old manuscript of which the first and the last pages have been lost. It is no longer possible to say how the book began, nor do we know how it is likely to end.

According to Azad, the object of philosophy is to recover these lost pages but despite all efforts philosophers have not recovered them. Azad raises the question of the origin of philosophy and wants it to be settled. He attacks the general notion that philosophy began with the Greeks and asserts through historical evidence that the Indian philosophical system had begun much earlier than the Greek and that Indian philosophy had established its position independent of religion.[35] Azad discusses the Buddhist philosophy not in isolation but in the context of earlier philosophical developments in India from which Buddha derived his inspiration. Emphasizing that the *Upanishads* existed prior to Buddha, he states that 'it is plausible to argue that the beginning of Indian philosophy can be traced back to a thousand years before Christ.'[36]

Azad complains that due to the Western bias Indian philosophy has been relegated to an inferior position and this distortion should end. The history of philosophy should begin with Indian philosophy. He maintains that it was Indian philosophy which influenced Western thought first but later the Greek thought too was assimilated in Indian thought. Azad strongly urges the study of Western and Indian philosophies through a comparative evaluation. In this Introduction Azad also makes some pertinent observations on the purpose and meaning of philosophy. He affirms that mere antiquity of a philosophical system does not necessarily establish its superiority over other philosophical schools of thought in the world.

Azad comes out in this Introduction as a man of universal outlook, a scholar of comparative civilization and a philosopher well-versed in the subtleties of interaction between philosophy and religion. He regarded philosophy as the real foundation of all knowledge. Through Arabic he had assimilated the Western philosophical system. Of course, he greatly appreciated the heritage of Indian philosophy. From *Al-Hilal* to this Introduction, he has travelled a long way. Here there is a broadening of his vision which sees man and his past in totality and does not keep him confined to just one segment of the world civilization.

Perhaps no book connected with India's struggle for freedom has provoked so much controversy among historians, journalists and public men as *India Wins Freedom* commonly known as Azad's autobiography. Generally speaking, the version of events presented in this work has been severely criticized in India as partial, one-sided, distorted and even motivated. Recently a full-scale study has appeared to show how untrustworthy Azad was in his assessment of the events leading to the partition of India.[37] Even so *India Wins Freedom* is now regarded an important source-material for the study of our national movement and partition of India. The thirty pages of *India Wins Freedom* which had been sealed earlier by Humayun Kabir and released now contain hardly anything new except a little information about Syed Mahmud and Rajendra Prasad.[38] The main argument of the original edition remains intact in the new volume.

The questions which agitate us in regard to *India Wins Freedom* are: Should the book be regarded primarily as Azad's individual work or an interpretation given by Humayun Kabir to views expressed by Azad before him or is it that Kabir thrust his own views and opinions here in Azad's name? *Tazkira* and *Ghubar-i-Khatir* were unquestionably Azad's individual products but *India Wins Freedom* was a different matter; he never wrote it, and both in its style and arguments it does not possess the characteristic ring of Azad's writing. The book bears the sub-title not 'Autobiography' but 'An Autobiographical Narrative.' The title of the book 'India Wins Freedom' was Nehru's formulation according to Louis Fischer.[39] The focus of the book is not on India's struggle towards freedom but on the transfer of power and the partition of the country. So the book's title does not fit in with the inside contents.

Kabir tells us in his Preface to *India Wins Freedom* that when he approached Azad to write his autobiography he was reluctant to do so and agreed only on the assurance that he would be relieved of the actual burden of writing. Kabir gives us an idea of how the book came to be written.[40] He spent on an average an hour or so every evening with Azad when they were in town. Azad recollected his experiences and described them in Urdu while Kabir took notes, sought clarifications on certain points, and prepared each chapter after collecting sufficient material. Kabir then gave the draft of each chapter to Azad who went through it, made some changes and finalised it after mutual discussions. Azad read each chapter himself and then both Azad and Kabir went over it, made changes, amendments and omissions. Thus *India Wins Freedom* did not flow from Azad's pen but is a collaborative work of both Azad and Kabir, Azad doing the talking and Kabir taking notes and preparing the text.

Kabir gave the first draft of the completed book to Azad in September, 1957. According to Kabir, Azad decided that "some thirty pages of the text dealing with incidents and reflections of a personal character should not be published for the present."[41] He directed that a copy of each of the completed text be deposited under cover in the National Library, Calcutta and National Archives of India, New Delhi. In compliance with Azad's instructions, Kabir expurgated from the text for publication these thirty pages and gave a revised and abridged version of the book to Azad towards the end of 1957. The text met with Azad's approval. Azad wanted this book to appear in November, 1958 synchronizing with his seventieth birthday. But alas! that was not to be! The Ms. is dated 26th January, 1958. Azad died on 22 February, 1958. Kabir's Preface dates 15 March, 1958. The book was published in January 1959 and sold out on the day it hit the market.

According to Kabir, *India Wins Freedom* is Azad's experiences narrated by him in Urdu and recorded by Kabir in English. Azad and Kabir were closely attached to each other. Both were intellectuals and shared many common beliefs and ideals on the freedom of India and Indian politics. Kabir, a Westernized intellectual trained in philosophy at Oxford with a restless and inquiring mind and a staunch protagonist of the composite culture of India acted as Azad's political adviser and interpreter during his discussions with Lord Wavell at the Simla Conference in 1945 and with the Cabinet Mission in 1946. He also worked in various capacities with Azad as Education Minister and represented him at national and international conferences. It is natural therefore that Kabir should enjoy Azad's special trust, and natural also that as an intellectual he should persuade Azad to write his autobiography for posterity. In Kabir's words, "a version in English under his (Azad's) direction would be better than no record at all."[42] Azad succumbed to this temptation in weaker moments and the upshot was *India Wins Freedom*.

The question is how far *India Wins Freedom* represents Maulana's views. Translation from one language to another is a trickly task, particularly when the languages involved are as varied in structure and tone as Urdu and English belonging to entirely different linguistic stocks. Azad was a great master of Urdu language with a discerning feeling for literature and his diction was known for its lush metaphors and metallic resonance. His conversation was of high literary flavour interlaced with Persian and Arabic constructions which eluded the grasp of even those who had a fairly intimate knowledge of Urdu. Azad did not speak English, and barely understood it. When he talked even informally to Louis Fischer at Wardha in 1941 it was Jawaharlal Nehru who acted at his interpreter. On the other hand, Kabir did not know Urdu. He could neither read nor write it. This writer translated for Kabir Urdu correspondence into English when he was Minister in the Ministry of Scientific Research and Cultural Affairs. Kabir did not know the meaning of such common words as *mijaz, haqiqat, nivazash* etc. In view of these linguistic difficulties one wonders how Azad, a literary giant of Urdu language, and Kabir unacquainted with Urdu communed and communicated with each other on high policy matters concerning the transfer of power to India with all their intricate complexities.

Azad's works except *India Wins Freedom* are saturated with religious fervour and are highly suasive. But *India Wins Freedom* belongs to a different category. Its scope is political. As it is written in English, so the tone and structure of its narrative is bound to be different from Azad's Urdu compositions. Despite the difference in languages employed in two distinct types of writings, one sadly misses in *India Wins Freedom* the stamp of Maulana's personality. Usually Azad's style was ornamental heavily loaded with Arabic and Persian diction enriched by a wealth of metaphors and similes. Azad's prose was stately like horses that gallop and trot but in *India Wins Freedom*, the narrative is pedestrian and matter of fact without frills and embellishments. From Azad to Kabir, it is like brocade to plain cloth. It is a strange irony that in *India Wins Freedom* there is wanting that temperate and solemn thinking of Azad which exacted respect from his peers and for which he was universally admired.

In fact it is Kabir's writings on Muslim politics which would provide a key to the understanding of *India Wins Freedom*. Kabir published in 1943 a series of articles on *Muslim Politics, 1906-1942*. These were followed in December 1948 by another detailed piece on *Muslim Politics, 1942-47* which formed later a chapter in C.H. Philips and M. Waniwright (ed.), *The Partition of India : Politics and Perspectives, 1937-1947*, London, 1970. Kabir's articles appeared in book form as *Muslim Politics and other Essays*, Calcutta, 1969. Parts of *India Wins Freedom* bear close resemblance to this book. A comparison of *India Wins Freedom* with Kabir's essays would show a startling similarity in analysis and assessment of political issues and personalities. The crucial issues raised in both the works are similar, the perspective identical, and the atmosphere almost the same.

About Jawaharlal Nehru's statement on the Cabinet Mission Plan at the Press Conference in Bombay on 10 July 1946 when he declared that the Congress had the right to modify and change the Plan, Kabir wrote that Nehru 'made a most unfortunate statement' (Muslim Politics, p. 16). In *India Wins Freedom* we find the following : 'Now happened one of the most unfortunate events' (p. 181). Kabir held Nehru responsible for Jinnah's rejection of the Cabinet Mission Plan and ten years later *India Wins Freedom* asserts the same view. About Jinnah's reaction to Nehru's statement, Kabir wrote :

> He (Jinnah) further declared that if the Congress could go back on its word even while the British were in India, what guarantee would there be that its assurances would be honoured after the British had left.[43]

Similarly in *India Wins Freedom* :

> (He) Jinnah argued that if the Congress could change so many times while the British were still in the country and power had not come to its hands, what assurance could the minorities have that, once the British left, Congress would not change and go back to the position taken up in Jawaharlal's statement.[44]

To Kabir, Gandhi's meetings with Jinnah in September, 1944 were a 'great political blunder' (p. 59) and in *India Wins Freedom* a similar view is expressed : "It was another instance of the many Himalayan blunders he (Gandhi) had made" (p. 109). These talks bolstered up Jinnah's image among the Muslims who regarded him as the only leader with whom the Congress was anxious to come to terms. On the Congress refusal to form coalitions with the Muslim League after the 1937 election there are identical views in Kabir's essays and *India Wins Freedom* (Kabir, *Muslim Politics*, p. 27; *India Wins Freedom*, pp. 188-89) though there is a more detailed account in the latter. On the Liaqat-Bhulabhai Desai formula in 1944 for cooperation between the Congress and League based on coalition at the Centre, there is similar assessment in Kabir's formulation and in *India Wins Freedom* (Kabir, *Muslim Politics*, p. 66; *India Wins Freedom*, pp. 158-59). On Liaqat Ali Khan's budget for 1947-48, which irked the Congress leaders, the reactions in Kabir's essays and *India Wins Freedom* are alike (Kabir, *Muslim Politics*, p. 70; *India Wins Freedom*, pp. 205-06). On direct Action Day declared by Jinnah on 16 August, 1946, and followed by the brutal Calcutta killings, the accounts in both the works coincide. Kabir calls 16 August 1946 as 'one of the darkest days', whereas *India*

*Wins Freedom* describes it 'a black day in the history of India' (Kabir, *Muslim Politics*, p. 67; *India Wins Freedom*, p. 186).

Several pieces in *India Wins Freedom* relating to events from Azad's arrest at Bhulabhai Desai's residence in Bombay to his arrival in Ahmednagar jail are translated from *Ghubar-i-Khatir* (*India Wins Freedom*, pp. 97-103; *Ghubar-i-Khatir* published in 1946, Sahitya Akademy edition, 1983, pp. 19-32). The moving account of his wife's illness, her death and its impact on his mind is entirely drawn from *Ghubar-i-Khatir* in *India Wins Freedom* (*Ghubar-i-Khatir*, pp. 20-29; *India Wins Freedom*, pp. 107-08). Portions on traditional learning, its baneful effect on Azad and his protest against it are also compiled from *Ghubar-i-Khatir* (*Ghubar-i-Khatir*, pp. 95-106). From the various sources it is clear that *India Wins Freedom* was not a straight autobiography composed from Azad's pen. When Jawaharlal Nehru was asked at a Press Conference on February 7, 1959 whether the reflections on the book represented Azad's views, he remarked "How can I be sure that these are as the Maulana would have liked. You must not take the book as verbally correct. Obviously it is not."[45] *India Wins Freedom*, in my view, is a sort of miscellany, a farrago, slipshod in execution, punctuated with sweeping generalisations and struck off at heat. Assuming that the Maulana shared his experiences with Kabir, much would have been lost in translation. Even as a compiler and interpreter Kabir could not be self-effacing. Stylistically *India Wins Freedom* is akin to Kabir's essays and his work, *The Indian Heritage*. There is far more of Kabir in *India Wins Freedom* than of Azad, and it is indeed difficult to say which is Azad's and which is Kabir's!

During 1956-57 when Azad is supposed to have prepared *India Wins Freedom* he was shattered in health, just a shadow of his former self. Those who knew him found him a recluse and tight-lipped. It was his cultural sophistication that he would not hit even those who condemned and vilified him. *India Wins Freedom* shifted the blame on Nehru and Patel for the Partition of India and did not even spare Gandhi. Azad seldom thought in individual terms. His thinking was complex, inimical to rash conclusions. He was known for his scrupulous disdain for criticizing others. We have seen in our study that being shy and reserved by nature, he avoided talking about himself. *India Wins Freedom* shows that if there was any individual who stood out boldly for fighting partition it was Azad. If *India Wins Freedom* was Azad's own work, then surely no bigger a glorifier of himself than Azad could scarcely be found. Knowing Azad as we do through his writings, speeches and also by the opinions of those closely known to him, the entire conception and spirit of *India Wins Freedom* is antagonistic to Azad's mode of thinking and style of writing. Dr. Rajendra Prasad too doubted whether Azad had decided about the publication of the book and 'the matter was ready for the press before he died.'[46]

Stylistically, *India Wins Freedom* does not echo Azad's voice. It is too drab and bumptious, lacking Azad's detachment, sparkling wit and spontaneous rhetoric. It is laid out like a long official note written with a sort of artificial felicity. He never said anything unkindly of anyone. Even when provoked he remained quiet or just smiled. On the contrary, Kabir gave an exaggerated importance to individuals which is evident in his essays, particularly on Sir Sikandar Hayat Khan and Allah Bux whose death, he thought, altered the political destiny of Punjab. Such facile generalisations Azad would not make.

Ghulam Rasool Mihr, one of Pakistan's foremost Urdu writers was Azad's disciple and trusted friend. A great authority on Azad's literary work, Mihr reflects in his own prose the influence of Azad's animated style. Intellectually, probably no one since 1947 was closer to Azad than Mihr. Mihr enjoyed Azad's full confidence and stayed with him on a number of occasions at his residence, 4 King Edward Road, New Delhi. Mihr's published work is a standing monument to his close association with Azad and his great understanding of Azad's mind and literature. In his letter to his friend, Riazul Rehman Sherwani dated 20 July 1963 (which has recently been published), after analysing *India Wins Freedom* Mihr says categorically that it is absolutely wrong to regard *India Wins Freedom* as Maulana's book[47] (*is kitab ko Maulana Ki Kitab qurar dena sarasar ghalat hei*).

A number of letters written by Mihr to Sherwani emphasize that Humayun Kabir did not understand Azad's mind and depending on his own intelligence attributed to him things which he could never have said.[48] In this connection, Mihr mentions a passage in *India Wins Freedom* which refers to Islam's failure to unify Muslim countries on the basis of religious affinity alone.[49] This passage begins : "It is one of the greatest frauds on the people to suggest that religious affinity can unite areas which are geographically, economically, linguistically and culturally different." Mihr does not accept it as Azad's statement.[50] Mihr accuses Kabir of having imposed his own views on the text attributed to Azad and sees in it very little of Azad's mode of thinking with which he was familiar.[51]

How can we disregard Mihr's contention? Those who knew Azad and have read his writings find *India Wins Freedom* absolutely alien to Azad's thinking and spirit. *India Wins Freedom* contains elements which are Kabir's inventions and where it presents Azad's views it subjects them to grave distortion and misrepresentation. It would be an exercise in futility to treat it as a reliable source on contemporary politics.

*References*


1. Douglas translated *Ghubar-e-Khatir* as 'Dust of Controversy' which is incorrect, see Douglas, *op. cit.*, p. 226.
2. *GK*, Introduction by Malik Ram, p. 8.
3. Montesquieu, *Persian Letters* (ed. C.J. Pretts), Penguin Classics, 1985.
4. Douglas, *op. cit.*, p. 228.
5. *GK*, Letter No. 7, p. 53.
6. Interviews with Acharya Narendra Deva who was a fellow-prisoner in Ahmednagar jail.
7. Bikhampur was the Nawab's ancestral estate which is now located in Habib Gunj in Aligarh.
8. *Karwan-e-Kheyal* (ed. Muhammad Abdus Shahid Sherwani) p. 62. For Azad's association with Sherwani, see, Riza ul-Rehman Sherwami, 'Abul Kalam Azad Aur Sadur Yar Jung Key Taulakat' in *Aiyana Abul Kalam Azad*, (ed.) Attiq Siddiqui, pp. 107-22.
9. Douglas, *op. cit.*, p. 227, No. 84.
10. *Karwan-e-Kheyal*, *op. cit.*, p. 61.
11. *Ibid.*, pp. 61-64.
12. *Ibid.*, pp. 61-64.
13. *GK*, p. 8.
14. *Ibid.*, pp. 28-30.
15. *Ibid.*, Letter No. 12, pp. 105-18.
16. *Ibid.*, Letter No. 13.
17. *Ibid.*
18. *Ibid.*, Letters 19-20.
19. *Ibid.*, pp. 231-32.
20. *Ibid.*, pp. 217-19.
21. *Ibid.*, Letter Nos. 12 & 13.
22. *Ibid.*, Letter No. 24.
23. *GK*, Letter No. 21.
24. *Ibid.*, p. 241.
25. *Ibid.*
26. *Ibid.*, Letter No. 24, p. 275.
27. *Ibid.*, p. 186.
28. Attiq Saddiqi, *Aiyana-e-Abul Kalam Azad*, p. 26.
29. Azad to Qasim Ali in *Ifadat-e-Azad*, p. 142.

30. Abul Kalam Azad, *Karwan-e-Kheyal*, pp. 92-95.
31. Syed Masih ul-Hasan, *Hawashi Abul Kalam Azad*, pp. 269-90.
32. Surendra Nath Sen, *Eighteen Fifteen Seven*, p. XV.
33. *Ibid.*, XVII.
34. *Ibid.*, XIX.
35. Sarvapalli Radhakrishnan, ed, *History of Philosophy, Eastern and Western*, p. 23.
36. *Ibid.*, p. 19.
37. Rajmohan Gandhi, *India Wins Errors*, New Delhi.
38. *IWF*, ed. 1988, pp. 18, 100-01 & 234.
39. *IWF*, p. XXII.
40. *Ibid.*, pp. VII to IX.
41. *Ibid.*, p. VIII.
42. *Ibid.*, p. VII.
43. Humayun Kabir, *Muslim Politics*, p. 66.
44. *IWF*, p. 184.
45. Rajmohan Gandhi, *India Wins Errors*. See Estimates after, p. X.
46. *Portrait of a President* : Letters of Dr. Rajendra Prasad to Mrs. Gyanwati Darbar, Vol. II, p. 53.
47. *Jamia*, Vol. VIII, Fed., 1988; No. 20, p. 44; see also Mihr to Mohd Qasim in Abdul Majid Daryabadi (ed.), *Urdu ka Adib Azad*, p. 453.
48. *Ibid.* See pp. 52-54.
49. *IWF*, p. 266.
50. *Jamia*, *op. cit.*, pp. 52-53.
51. *Ibid.*

# 8

# SUMMING UP

Very few individuals show the daring and courage to fathom their own minds and do self-scrutiny in their life, and with death it is all over. Azad, however, fought a continuous battle with himself to understand the inner turmoil and contradictions of his own personality. In spite of the fact that he had to play an active role in public life during a crucial phase of our national life and remain incessantly busy in organising programmes and conferences, he was by temperament a very shy and withdrawing person who would find introspection and philosophical speculation more congenial to him than making speeches or doing administrative and organisational work.

Being a man of highly sensitive intellect, the riddle and mystery of life haunted his mind and troubled his sleep. He indulged in constant self-introspection and was never satisfied with the kind of life he lived. He sought peace but found anguish. He concealed his sufferings from the gaze of the harsh, unsympathetic world. He wrote in *Ghubar-e-Khatir* that he chose thorns for himself but left flowers to be picked up by others. He thought that he did not belong to the age he lived in but was dragged into it. The anguish of this contradiction between what he was called upon to do and what he would have preferred to do stayed with him all the time. Often he would recite Sadra Shirazi's verse :

*Kam lazzat am wa kimtam afzoon shumar ast*
*Goyi Samar paishter az bag-e-wajoodam*[1]

Tr. My taste may be less but my worth is beyond calculation
Well, I am a fruit grown in the garden before the season

Azad greatly prized solitude like the sages of old. He would say with Gibbon, 'I am never less alone than by myself.' He always loved to hear the voices from the past. Azad's was too lofty a mind to be bound by any rigid system. He stood alone and he had no master. He rebelled against his father who had imposed on him a system of education in which he found no good. He did things which his father did not want him to do. He was too much of an individualist that imposed authority from outside. He differed with Gandhi on crucial matters. Gandhi wrote to him that they could not work together any more and the Congress Working Committee threatened to resign because of serious differences with him. He smoked freely in Gandhi's presence knowing well that he disliked such indulgences. In religion, literature and politics he disdained convention and followed new ways. He wrote:

> If people open a stall in the market one looks for a shop where good many possible buyers are expected to pass. If I should open a stall, I should look for a spot where merely a few customers were to pass.[2]
>
> Again :
>
> People set things for the market and bring such commodities which attract good sale, when I set my shop, I put wares that have no customers.[3]

Here Azad strikes a doleful note which is characteristic of his abiding mood in his old age. He could not have written like this in his *Al-Hilal* days. By early forties he had started feeling that the country was threatened by the rise of communal forces and he saw no remedy for it. He saw also that his influence among the Muslims was diminishing because of their growing support for the creation of a separate homeland for themselves through the creation of Pakistan. Azad was convinced that the Pakistan demand was absurd and would be a disaster for the Muslims as well as for India as a whole and he stuck to these views up to the end. In a memorable speech on the partition, he said while addressing the Muslim community in Jama Masjid, Delhi in October 1947 :

> Today when I see your ashen faces and desolation in your hearts, my mind goes back to the past. Do you remember I called for you but you pulled out my tongue. I took up the pen but you severed my hands. I wanted to walk but you cut off my legs. I wished to turn on my side but you broke it. I had warned you how the forces of poisonous politics unleashed by sinister designs would lead to the

tragedy of Partition but you refused to listen to me. You relied on your ignorance and today you feel as though you are threatened by new dangers.

Azad felt a sense of defeat although he stood for reason. Who would listen to the cold voice of reason when passions are fanned by hot winds raging in the country. Walpole has said : "No great country was ever served by good men, because good men will not go to the lengths that may be necessary." Bacon who possessed a rare understanding of human nature wrote, "It is the solecism of power to think to command the end and yet not to endure the means." Azad was fully conscious of the failure of his mission to save the unity of the country. It was not only his personal failure but the failure of Congress policy and ideology. Azad watched history in the making. His calculation was that the country could implement the Cabinet Mission proposals and then wait for sometime to see how things went. But the leadership of Congress and the League hastened the process of splitting the country.

This study has discussed some of the pivotal situations in our history when there were real possibilities of resolving the communal problem. Historians should discuss more closely than they have done so far the question whether these opportunities were missed by the Congress in their handling of the communal issue. This question is not restricted to stopping Jinnah or the Ali brothers from leaving the Congress but has larger dimensions. Opportunities were missed in the late twenties and thirties for negotiating the communal question through constitutional means by conceding some of the minority demands on which the Congress took a rigid and unimaginative stand. Had Azad's viewpoint prevailed, things might have been different.

When we reflect on Azad's role in Indian politics we find that his life was a failure. He was not able to do what he had deliberately set out to do. Who would have thought that the son of a *Pir* would turn into a front-rank nationalist leader dedicated to the cause of India's freedom. In *Al-Hilal* he had championed the cause of India's freedom from foreign rule. He was already a well-established non-cooperator about nine years before the Congress launched the non-cooperation movement. The Khilafat issue threw him into Indian politics and he found in Gandhi his leader. Thereafter there was no turning back. But the contradiction between the man's personality and the situation in which he was forced to play a public role remained.

The cause of Hindu-Muslim unit for which he worked passionately all his life foundered on the rock of communalism. His vision of a united India was shattered. The partition of India was his great failure but it was a part of a general failure. His life conforms to the pattern of a great tragedy. To use Carl Becker's expression he was a 'broken arch.' He had missed out his destiny and probably did not realize that he had missed it until it was too late. And if he knew it earlier, he concealed it and was too proud to share it with others. There was no denying the fact that he was the champion of lost causes. His life exemplifies the defeat of fine aspirations and laudable ambitions.

Failure is endemic in the life of a great hero. Napoleon's life was a grand failure. Gandhi too failed in his mission because he could not see a united India, Hindu-Muslim unity and abolition of untouchability. William Pitt, Prime Minister of England, died a sad man because he saw the failure of his mission. Pitt wanted to abolish slave trade but failed to do so. He also failed to resolve the Irish problem. His famous India Act increased rather than diminished political corruption. He recognised the necessity of introducing reforms but he had to compromise with the forces of resistance. Professor S. Gopal in his biography of Nehru says that in Nehru's lifetime innumerable lamps were lit but great parts of it were submerged in darkness.

The picture we have painted with regard to Azad's achievements in politics is perhaps too sombre. But this is the abiding impression it leaves on our mind. Through the pages of *Al-Hilal* Azad had taken up the mission of creating an awakening in the Muslim community, inspiring them to say goodbye to the policy of 'mendicancy' sedulously followed by the Aligarh school. The Muslim community stood shoulder to shoulder with the other sections of our society in the non-cooperation movement. But in the later twenties the Hindu-Muslim entente began to break. Jinnah, a staunch supporter of Lucknow pact of 1916, left the Congress and so did the Ali brothers after the Nehru Report. Ajmal Khan and M.A. Ansari died. Kitchlew took up the *Tablig* and *Tanzim* cause which tarnished his image as a nationalist. Khaliquzzaman, Nehru's favourite, changed over to the Muslim League. Mian Iftikharuddin resigned as President of the Punjab Congress Committee in September, 1945 and joined the League. Maulana Daood Ghazni who had taken over as President of the Congress after him also joined the League. The trooping out of such prominent leaders from the Congress seriously affected its character as a national organisation in the eyes of the Muslims.

The Muslim leadership in the Congress was a shambles. But Azad refused to flinch from his principles and stuck to the Congress to the very end of his life. How would have the Congress looked if he had not been the Congress President from 1940 - 1946! He too could have joined the League, but did not entertain any such thoughts. During his *Al-Hilal* and *Al-Balagh* period, he used a highly religious gospel to unite the Muslim community against the British rule. During the Khilafat agitation he enlisted the support of the Ulama to inspire the Muslims for anti-British struggle. During the 1937 election in U.P., Azad won over the Jamiat ul-Ulama-e-Hind to lend their support to the Congress. It is a bitter irony that the Ulama used the same religious gospel to fan the fires of communalism to defeat the Congress in 1945-46 elections. Formerly the fight had been waged against the British but now the target was the 'Hindu Congress.' The circle was complete. Azad saw this changing scenario as a sad man.

As a political leader Azad had enormous courage, perseverance and tenacity of purpose. He always held on to a cause to the bitter end. But he could not be a leader of the masses. Gandhi was a man of the people, an agitator who could create an environment of action. Nehru also had a charisma which endeared him to the people. The personality of Subhas Chandra Bose caught the imagination of the youth. Azad came into the limelight as the editor of *Al-Hilal*, during the Khilafat movement and again when he became the Congress President from 1940-1946. Even during the Khilafat, the Ali brothers dominated the political scene and Azad remained in the background.

J.B. Kripalani asked Gandhi how it was that he always preferred the Ali brothers with their 'loud tone and exuberant spirit' to the 'intellect and culture of Azad'. He replied that although he had tried to induce Azad to come to the front, he resisted it and preferred to sit in the back. With his shy and reserved temperament, Azad was too much of a scholar to come close to the masses. Mujeeb has aptly summed up the traits of Azad's personality on account of which he could not win a warm response from the people. He tells us :

> He was too aloof to concern himself with persons, too intellectual to relish political small talk, too proud to think in terms of alliances, affiliations or opposition, a statesman who would not accept the normal functions of a politician, and he was so engrossed in principles that he could not become an administrator. He had to be taken for what he was and with no other credibility than his personality.[6]

A successful politician is one who selects a policy that can immediately work with the people and fertilize the public mind. Azad would not come down from the standards of public conduct and morality he cherished or use any crude methods to capture the public attention. It is not merely that society did not ardently accept him but he too did not accept society on its terms. He ran away from the crowds. He never signed an autograph nor did he allow anybody to dedicate a book to him. He wrote only to the chosen few; his secretaries wrote on his behalf. The letters he wrote were as precise and to the point as entries in a telephone directory. He received few visitors at his residence. Rafi Ahmad Kidwai's residence was thronged by Muslim refugees during the 1946-47 communal disturbances, but in Azad's residence which was next to Kidwai's no body dared to intrude. Those who unknowingly went to Azad's place were directed to go to the right place. It is not that he had no feelings for them, but his style of doing things was entirely different and it did not include bending before the immediate needs of visitors not known to him.

Azad sought no fortunes. He built no house and always lived in a rented house. Hakim Ajmal Khan had asked Malihabadi in early twenties about Azad's sources of income as there seemed no obvious support from any quarters. In *Al-Hilal* days Azad sought some financial help from his father's disciples, but he mostly lived in financial straits. He had no Birla, Bajaj or Lala Sri Ram to support him nor did he inherit any patrimony. When he became the Minister of Education, he asked for an advance of Rs. 15,000 from the Ministry of Finance for the purchase of a car to be paid in five instalments. Under the rules he was allowed Rs. 12,000. Nehru had to intervene and the entire amount was to be paid by Azad in sixty instalments in five years.[7] There is no reason to believe that he ever showed undue favour to anyone. When his nephew Noor-ud-Din who was serving in Indian Council of Cultural Relations asked for payment of arrears to him which as Minister Azad found unjustified, his services were terminated.

Azad seldom said a word to an opponent. His sophistication did not let him hit others. When he supported the Congress policy he was condemned by a large segment of Muslim society as a traitor to their cause. When he pleaded for the protection of the right of the Muslim community he was branded a Muslim communalist. Reviled and disowned by the Muslim community for being a puppet in the hands of the Congress, his *bona fides* as a Congress nationalist were also questioned by the Hindus. But he bore these unfair slights and slanders with perfect composure. When Jinnah insulted him by calling him a Congress show-boy and refused to shakes hands with him, Azad just ignored it. He defended himself from others' criticism by a nod, a smile or a shrug of his shoulders or just through silence. When India became free he was allotted the Education portfolio in the Ministry which may not have been thought important for him. He was not made Deputy Prime Minister after Patel's death nor was he offered the office of the President of India. He bore no grudge to anyone for things like this and his attitude could be summed up in Shakespeare's words from Hamlet, 'Readiness is all.'

It seems that Gandhi was not in favour of his appointment as Education Minister. During his tenure as Education Minister the University Grants Commission and National Laboratories were set up, plans for the National Museum and National Library were prepared and the activities of the National Archives and Department of Archaeology expanded. The three Akademies of Arts, Literature and Music were established during that period. The Indian Council of Cultural Relations also started functioning effectively for the promotion of cultural relations with foreign countries, particularly with the Middle East. The Adult Education programme received special impetus in those years. No exhaustive list of the institutions established during his tenure is required to stress the point that much thought and planning had gone into the building of foundations in those days for the future development of education in India.

Two points need special mention. First, Azad brought into the Ministry of Education some outstanding educationists like Dr. Tara Chand, K.G. Saiydain and Humayun Kabir to undertake comprehensive planning in education. He was convinced that the right course for him was to put education into the hands of eminent educationists rather than bureaucrats. Secondly, he was convinced that it was necessary to give large funds for educational development.[8] About the language problem he took the liberal view that love for one's language should not mean hostility towards other languages. In a powerful speech delivered in the Lok Sabha in reply to Purshottamdas Tandon's attack on him for giving financial aid to the Shibli Academy, Azamgarh, Azad said that a narrow approach on the language issue would create further problems for the country. He reminded the Lok Sabha that it was such a narrow-minded approach and the Muslim League's fanaticism that had created Pakistan.[9] He also suggested that the words 'Muslim' from Aligarh Muslim University and 'Hindu' from Banaras Hindu University should be dropped.[10] In his famous Jama Masjid speech already referred to, he suggested that all communal bodies including the Muslim League should be banned as there was no place for such organisations in free India.

Both Azad and Iqbal owed their inspiration to the Quran. They often spoke on the same wavelength. Although in politics they completely differed from each other, their idiom was religious. Their admiration for *Mumin* and *Sufi* and contempt for obsolete ritualism was common. In their passion for restoration of the true spirit of Islam they were one. In the preface to *Tazkira*, Fazluddin wrote that Iqbal's *Asrar-i-Bekhudi* and *Rumuz-i-Bekhudi* were the echoes of *al-Hital* Iqbal complained to Sulaiman Nadwi that the implication of the statement was that before *Al-Hilal*, he was not a true Muslim. When Azad learnt about this he thought that Iqbal's reaction was justified. At that time Azad, however, said that while Iqbal was absorbed earlier in Sufi mysticism, there had lately been a distinct change in his attitude.[11] Later when Iqbal was asked how it was that Azad did not quote his verses, he replied that Azad had already said what he was trying to say in his poetry.

It is rather curious that Azad and Iqbal hardly met each other and perhaps never exchanged letters. Iqbal had subscribed to *Al-Hilal*. In his works Azad quoted only one poem and two verses from Iqbal's poetry. On Iqbal's death Azad expressed his anguish in a private letter in a single sentence. I think that the Azad-Iqbal relationship needs further examination from the literary angle to see how far Azad's writings had influenced Iqbal's thinking and poetry.

Whatever writer or text Azad chanced to lay his hands upon, he always chose the best portions for comment or reference. Among the poets whom he admired most were Naziri, Baidel and Ghalib. Of the theologians his most favourite was Ibn Taimiya whom he made a hero in *Tazkira*. He acknowledged his debt to Sayyid Ahmad Khan for his religious and intellectual development. He had great reverence for Gandhi because he stood for truth. He held C.R. Das in high esteem for his political sagacity and candour. Nehru, of course, he trusted always as a friend.

Nehru and Azad came altogether from different social and religious backgrounds – one, a westernized intellectual educated at Harrow and Cambridge, and the other a product of religious orthodoxy. However, they shared common values. They believed that human knowledge is the common heritage of all mankind. There was nothing narrow in their outlook. They fought for the same ideals: freedom of India, Hindu-Muslim unity, secularism, democracy and peace in the world. If we were to choose two personalities to represent us in an international conference of world statesmen, we may like to be represented by Nehru and Azad, Nehru first and Azad second.

If there is one word that could aptly describe Azad's personality, it is 'Qalindar' meaning a person completely indifferent to the mundane affairs of the world, and to whom nothing mattered except the passionate contemplation of the beautiful and the good. He was bad at keeping accounts. He spent most of his time in his bedroom which was stocked with books and loose scattered papers. He received his visitors in an unostentatious sitting room. There was no photograph hung on any wall. Except his bedroom and the sitting room he did not bother about the rest of the house. That is why he fell down twice without realizing that there were steps for him to get down.

The art of living was a life-long preoccupation with Azad. He set upon the most difficult task, the quest of the self and search for meaning in various forms of life. He would look at the stars at night, commune with the minarets of the Taj and see a 'shiver' in its white dome. How wide was the gap between such sensitivity and intellectual curiosity and the topsy-turvy world of politics in which he was entangled. All humanists are individualists and there was a divergence between Azad's individualism and his commitment to serve the Indian people. That explains his dilemma as an intellectual in politics.

When Nehru, the Prime Minister, inaugurated the All India Urdu Conference in the Jama Masjid parade grounds of Delhi on 15 February, 1958, Azad urged the Government to implement the Constitutional provision which had recognized Urdu as a national language. Nobody could imagine that the cruel hand of death would snatch him away so soon after that. A strong physical health had never been Azad's forte. He had been complaining of his poor health since 1891. Nehru always felt proud of his 'unmedicated body' but Azad's case was different. Early death of his mother when he was just four had left a permanent vacuum in his life. The suffering and sense of neglect from which he had suffered seriously impaired his physical and mental growth. A long spell of prison-life when he was cut off from his family and friends and heavy pressure of political work combined with continuous financial strains led to the ruination of his health. This happened with some other nationalist leaders too. Most of them continued to suffer from ailments. Only a few managed to cross their seventies.

Tilak died at sixty-four, M.A. Ansari at fifty-six and Ram Manohar Lohia could not cross fifty-seven. Dr. Syed Mahmud, Acharya Narendra Deva, 'J.P.' and a host of others had serious health problems. When India became free in 1947 our leaders were tired men who did not possess enough strength to organise a movement against the Partition to save the unity of the country. Patel, the iron-man, too had also lost his elan.

Azad's health had been delicate throughout. He smoked and enjoyed his tea but his addiction to tea was not obsessive like that of Krishna Menon who would consume seventy cups of tea a day. Azad was also fond of drinking, though he did it alone. Gandhi said to Nehru, 'I hear that Maulana drinks.' In his characteristic fashion Nehru said, 'What of that. I too drink.'[12] Azad was never interested in games. Nor did he ever take to swimming like his father. Yoga or gardening did not interest him as they did Nehru. He could not ride a horse. He never went for long brisk walks like the Mahatma. He was too private a person to indulge in sun-bath as the Mahatma did as he was being massaged by his devotees. Both in and outside the prison, Azad remained always a scholar of the library, sitting and poring over books uninterruptedly for long hours. Introvert men tend to forget the needs of their body. Marcus Brutus was mostly seen in his study with a book but he was quite negligent about physical exercises.

After partition Azad was a shattered man. He said that all that he had stood for had collapsed. He was now a shadow of his former self. He was lonely and desolate at heart. Professor A.A. Saroor says that during his visits to Azad he seldom saw him laugh.[13] He entertained few visitors. In his last days he had difficulty in lifting himself up from his sitting posture. Long sittings and lack of physical mobility had stiffened his legs, which made it a little difficult for him to walk. Often he would stagger. Once or twice he fell down as he was unable to balance himself.[14] On 19 February, 1958, he stumbled in his bathroom, broke his hip and fell unconscious. Thereafter he never recovered. Dr. Abdul Latif, who had translated Azad's *Tarjuman* and was now staying with him said later that just a few hours before his death, the doctors attending on him wanted to give him injections but he declined and said, "Leave me alone, leave everything to God.[15] Professor S. Gopal told this writer that Dr. B.C. Roy flew from Calcutta to examine Azad who was lying unconscious. Very briefly he regained consciousness when Nehru came to enquire about him. On seeing him, Azad said 'Jawahar, *Khuda Hafiz* (May God protect you).[16] These were his last words. On

22 February, 1958 at about 2.00 a.m. Azad died. The rest is silence! 'Now cracks a noble heart'.

Thus we take leave of a truly great patriot, a staunch nationalist, an apostle of Hindu-Muslim unity, a *Mir-i-Karwan*, a man of iron nerves who never flinched from his principles even though he suffered from calumnies. He was an admired leader who was seldom loved, and who failed to create a large following. He was a scholar *par-excellence* who could not create a monumental work, a humanist like Erasmus, a tower of moral strength who devoted all his energies to the cause of our freedom movement and one of the greatest Indians of all time. We will not see the like of him again! In the manner of Edmund Burke as a practical politician, he may have been a failure but for political wisdom he is for posterity!

*References*

1. *GK*, p. 90.
2. *Ibid.*, p. 92.
3. *Ibid.*, p. 84.
4. *Khutbat-e-Azad*, p. 337.
5. J.B. Kripalani, 'Voice of Reason' in Humayun Kabir (ed.), *Maulana Abul Kalam Azad*, p. 39.
6. M. Mujeeb, *Indian Muslims*, p. 442.
7. B.B. Misra, *Government and Bureaucracy in India*, p. 81.
8. *Constituent Assembly Debates*, 15 March to 31st March 1948, see 11 March, 1948, pp. 1942, 1948.
9. *Parliamentary Debates*, (Lok Sabha) 20 March to 15 April, 1954. See Azad's speech on 29 March, 1954, pp. 3416-19. See also Abul Kalam Azad, *National Tehrik* (unpublished manuscript), p. 2. He had suggested the use of Urdu script in the Central Provinces in 1937.
10. *Constituent Assembly Debates*, 11 March, 1948, p. 1945.
11. *Tazkira*, pp. 13-14.
12. Conversations with S. Gopal,
13. From an unpublished paper by Professor Saroor presented at the Sahitya Akademi Seminar on 19 August, 1988.
14. *Zikr*, p. 458.
15. Extracts from *Sidq* by Abul Majid Daryabadi on 'Maulana Azad key Akhri Lamhat' in *Aiwan-e-Urdu*, Nov., 1988, p. 86.
16. Sabri also accepts the view. See Maulana Amdad Sabri, *Imam ul Hind Maulana Azad*, p. 24. But this is also confirmed by Mr. Ansar Harwani, a former, M.P., and closely associated with Azad, see, *Times of India*, 22 Feb., 1989. Malihabadi writes that Azad never recovered from his paralytic attack. See Dr. Riaz ur Rahman Khan Qureshi, *Mir-e-Karwan, Abul Kalam Azad*, p. 101.

# GLOSSARY

| | | |
|---|---|---|
| *Alah-o-Akbar* | : | Literary meaning, God is great; a mode of greeting among the followers of Din-i-Illahi. |
| *Alim* | : | A learned man, scholar of Islamic literature, a Muslim theologian. |
| *Amir-i-hind* | : | The leader of India, a title of high order among the Muslim community. |
| *Anna* | : | A coin equal to 1/16 of a rupee. |
| *Azad* | : | Meaning free from all restraint. |
| *Dastar-Bandi* | : | The ceremony of tying a sash around the tur-banon an auspicious occasion. |
| *Dars-e-Nizami* | : | Syllabus of Muslim education prepared by Mulla Nizamuddin Sihalvi; a contemporary of Emperor Aurangzeb. |
| *Diwan Khana* | : | Main audience chamber in Muslim household. |
| *Fatwa* | : | Religious injunction, legal opinions or legal decrees. |
| *Fiqa* | : | The science of Muslim jurisprudence. |
| *Hadith* | : | Traditions attributed to the sayings of Prophet Mohammad. |
| *Harem* | : | The apartments for females. |
| *Haram Sharif* | : | The sacred mosque in Mecca, containing the Ka aba. |
| *Hartal* | : | Cessation of work; strike. |
| *Hidayat* | : | Divine grace. |
| *Hijrat* | : | Departure from one's country and friends; preparation of lovers and friends in particular, the flight of the Prophet Mohammad from Mecca to Madina. |
| *ID* | : | Feast festival, the Muslim festival. |
| *Ijtihad* | : | To exert with a view to forming an independent judgement on legal questions, to establish the ruling of a Sharia upon a given point. |
| *Imam* | : | Leader of the congregational prayers of Muslims, the spiritual leaders of the Islamic community as successors to the Prophet. |
| *Jazia* | : | A tax charged in an Islamic State from the non-believers. |
| *Jihad* | : | War waged in the name of Islam. |

| | | |
|---|---|---|
| *Ka aba* | : | The shrine of the sacred black stone in Meccaf |
| *Kafir* | : | Non-believers of the true faith, i.e., Islam, Infidel. |
| *Khaddar* | : | A hand-woven coarse cloth. |
| *Khilafat* | : | A Successor to the Prophet, the Movement launched to preserve it. |
| *Koarnish* | : | Salutation by placing the right hand on the forehead and bending down to head. |
| *Kotwal* | : | Officer in charge of police duties in a town. |
| *Kufr* | : | Unbelief, infidelity. |
| *Maqulat* | : | Rational scenes. |
| *Masjid* | : | A mosque. |
| *Maulvi* | : | Derived from Maula, a lord or master, a term generally used for Islamic scholar. |
| *Mujtahid-e-mutaq* | : | The absolute interpreter. |
| *Mijatahid fil mazhab* | : | Interpreter of a juristic school. |
| *Millat* | : | A community of religion (Islamic community). |
| *Mould Shareef* | : | The Prophet's birthday. |
| *Muazain* | : | One who gives a call for prayer in a mosque. |
| *Mukhamat* | : | By which man is invested with power to grasp the truth. |
| *Mullah* | : | Persian version of the Arabic Maulvi, i.e., a learned man. |
| *Mutashabha* | : | By which human efforts fail to apprehend reality. |
| *Mutazilites* | : | Rationalists, those who believe in the doctrine of free will. |
| *Nakis* | : | Worthless. |
| *Panchayat* | : | Court of arbitration. |
| *Pir* | : | Spiritual teacher, specially in Sufi orders. |
| *Qasida* | : | Panegyric, a poem in praise of some one. |
| *Qurat* | : | The science of reading and chanting the Quran. |
| *Roza* | : | Fasting in the month of Ramazan. |
| *Sharih* | : | A technical term for the rules guiding the life of a Muslim in law and ethics. It means a clear path to be followed. |
| *Satyagraha* | : | Truth force, soul force. |
| *Shaid* | : | Honey. |
| *Sufis* | : | Mystics saints of Islam. |
| *Tabligh* | : | Conversion. |
| *Tafsir* | : | The science of Quranic Exegesis, explanation of scripture. |
| *Taqiya* | : | Dissimulation or a concealment permitted according to Shia doctrine. |
| *Taqlid* | : | Strict obedience to religious authority. |

| | | |
|---|---|---|
| *Tarke-mavalat* | : | Cessation of work. |
| *Ulama* | : | The plural of alim, popularity known as Muslim theologians and legal scholars. |
| *Wahabis* | : | Followers of the eighteenth century Arab reformer, Abdul Wahhad (d. 1791) who fought an anti-Sufi Hanbali Islam; also the term used by their opponents to describe nineteenth century Indian reformists. |
| *Zikat* | : | To contribute two and a half per cent of the income. |

# BIBLIOGRAPHY

## 1. Works by Abul Kalam Azad

### a. Books

*Azad Ki Kahani Khud Azad Ki Zabani*, As dictated to Abdur Razzaq Malihabadi, Calcutta, 1959, reprint, Delhi, 1965.

*Baqiyat-e-Tarjuman al-Quran*, Gulam Rasul Mihr, ed., Delhi 1965.

*Al-Biruni aur Jughrafiya-e-Alam*, Ziya ul-Hasan Faruqi, ed., New Delhi, 1980.

*Ghubar-e-Khatir*, Malik Ram, ed., New Delhi, 1983.

*Hayat-e-Sarmad Shahid*, Jahangir Book Depot, n.d.

*India Wins Freedom: An Autobiographical Narrative*, Humayun Kabir, ed., Bombay, 1959 and also the complete version, Hyderabad, 1989.

*Jami' al Shawhid fi Dukhul Ghair al-Muslim fi' l Masijid*, Delhi, 1960.

*Karwan-e-Kheyal, Ya' ni: Majuh' a Khutat Maulana Abul Kalam Azad wa Maulana Habibur Rahman Khan Sherwani*, Reprint, Lahore, n.d.

*Khutbat-e-Azad*, Malik Ram, ed., New Delhi, 1981.

*Makatib-e-Abul Kalam Azad*, Abu Salman Shahjahanpuri, ed., Karachi, 1968.

*Malfuzat-e-Azad*,, Muhammad Ajmal Khan ed., Delhi, 1959.

*Mas' ale-e-Khilafat wa Jazirat-al-Arab*,, Reprint, Delhi, 1959.

*Mazamin-e-Lisan al-Sidq*, Abdul Qawi Dasnawi ed., Lucknow, 1967.

*National Tahrik*, unpublished, mss., written in 1939.

*Naqsh-e-Azad*, Ghulam Rasul Mihr, ed., Lahore, 1959.

Preface in S. Radhakrishnan ed., *History of Philosophy, Eastern and Western*, Vol. I, London, 1953.

*Qaul-e-Faisal*, Calcutta, 1922, Chaman Book Depot, Delhi.

*Tabarrukat-e-Azad*, Ghulam Rasul Mihr, ed., Hyderabad, 1959, Delhi, 1963.

*Tarjuman al-Qur'an*, Dr. Syed Abul Latif ed., Vols. I and 2, Bombay,

1965 and 1967.
*Tarjuman-al-Qur'an*, Malik Ram, ed., 4 Vols., New Delhi, 1964-76.
*Taswwurat-e-Qur'an az Maulana Abul Kalam Azad*, Syed Abdul Latif, ed., Delhi, n.d.
*Tazkira, Fazluddin Ahmed*, ed., Calcutta, 1919, Rev. ed., Malik Ram, New Delhi, 1968.

**b. Journals edited or co-edited by Abul Kalam Azad**

*Al-Balagh* (Calcutta)
*Al-Hilal* (Calcutta)
*Al-Jamia* (Calcutta)
*Al-Nadwa* (Lucknow)
*Lisan al-Sidq* (Calcutta)
*Paigham* (Calcutta)

**2. Government of India, Records and Documents**

**a. Unpublished**

*Home, Political Department, 1914-1922 (NAI)*
*Foreign and Political Department, 1914-1922 (NAI)*

**b. Published**

*Constituent Assembly Debates*, 1948.
*Parliamentary Debates* (Lok Sabha), 1954.
*Report on Indian Constitutional Reforms*, 1918.

**3. Private Papers**

*B.R. Ambedkar Papers* (NAI)
*C. Rajagopalachari Papers* (NAI)
*Govind Ballabh Pant Papers* (NAI)
*Malik Ram Collection* (Private)
*Rajendra Prasad Papers* (NAI)
*Dr. Syed Mahmud Papers* (NMML)
*Zulekha Ki Diary* 1908, (Azad Bhawan Library, New Delhi)
Malik Ram's collection of Azad's Correspondence.

### 4. Other Journals and Newspapers

*Aiwan-e-Urdu*
*Ajkal*
*Amrita Bazar Patrika*
*Hindustan Times*
*Indian Quarterly Register*
*Times of India*

### 5. Other Works Relating to this Study

Ahmed Manzur, *Maulana Abul Kalam Azad: Fiqr-o-Fun*, Lucknow, 1969, Reprint, 1978.

———, *Maulana Abul Kalam Azad al-Hilal Ki A'ine men*, Lucknow, 1972.

Badauni, Al, *Muntakhab-ut-Twarikh*, Vol. II, Delhi, 1973.

Beg, Aziz, *Jinnah and His Times, A Biography*, Islamabad, 1986.

Brecher, Michael, *Jawaharlal Nehru: A Political Biography*, London, 1959.

Brown, Judith M., *Gandhi's Rise to Power, 1915-1922*, Cambridge, 1972.

Chagla, M.C., *Roses in December*, Bombay, 1973.

Chopra, P.N. (ed.), *Justice Wickenden's Reports: Historic Judgement on Quit India*, 1989.

Churchill, Winston S., *A History of the English Speaking Peoples*, London, 1957.

*Collected Works of Mahatma Gandhi*, Vol. 32, (Government of India Publication), 1966.

Collins, Larry and Dominique Lapiere, *Mountbatten and the Partition of India*, Vol. I, New Delhi, 1982.

Coupland, R. *The Constitutional Problem in India*, Pt. II, Oxford, 1944.

Darbar, Gyanwati, *Portrait of a President, Letters of Dr. Rajendra Prasad*, Vol. II, Delhi, 1974.

Daryabadi, Maulana and Abdul Majid, *Maktubat-e-Sulaimani*, 2 Vols, Lucknow, 1963-67.

———, (ed.) *Khatut-e-Majidi*, Karachi, 1986.

———, *Urdu ka Adib Azad*, Karachi, 1988.

Dasnawi, Syed Shahabuddin, *Shibli*, Delhi, 1970.

Datta, V.N., *Madan Lal Dhingra and the Revolutionary Movement*,

New Delhi, 1978.
Datta, V.N., and B. Cleghorn, *A Nationalist Muslim and Indian Politics*, Delhi, 1974.
Datta, V.N., and S.C. Mittal, *Sources of National Movement, 1919-1920*, New Delhi, 1985.
Desai, Mahadev, *Maulana Abul Kalam Azad: A Biographical Memoir*, 2nd ed., Agra, 1946.
Douglas, Ian Henderson, *Abul Kalam Azad: An Intellectual and Religious Biography*, Delhi, 1988.
Gandhi, Rajmohan, *India Wins Errors*, New Delhi, 1989.
Ghaffar, Qazi Mohammad Abdul, *Asar-e-Abul Kalam*, Delhi, 1958.
Ghosh, Sudhir, *Gandhi's Emissary*, Calcutta, 1967.
Gopal, S., *Selected Works of Jawaharlal Nehru*, Vol. VII, Delhi, 1975.
Gordon, R.A., *Locality, Province and Nation, Essays on Indian Politics (1870-1940)*, Cambridge, 1957.
Grunebaum, G.E., *Islam*, London, 1961.
Halevy, Elie, *A History of the English Peoples in the Nineteenth Century England, in 1815*, London, 1949.
Haq, Mushirul, *Muslim Politics in Modern India, 1857-1947*, Meerut, 1970.
Hasan, Muhammad, *Khutbat-e-Azad*, Karachi, n.d.
Hasan, Mushirul (ed.), *Communal and Pan-Islamic Trends in Colonial India*, 2nd ed., New Delhi, 1985.
———, *Muslims and the Congress*, Delhi, 1979.
Hodson, H.W., *The Great Divide*, London, 1969.
Iyer, R. Subramania (ed.), *The Role of Maulana Abul Kalam Azad in Indian Politics*, Hyderabad, 1968.
Jalal, Ayesha, *The Sole Spokesman: Jinnah, The Muslim League and the Demand for Pakistan*, Cambridge, 1985.
Kabir, Humayun (ed.), *Maulana Abul Kalam Azad: A Memorial Volume*, Bombay, 1859.
——— *Muslim Politics, 1906-47*, Calcutta, 1969.
Ker, James Campbell, *Political Trouble in India, 1907-1917*, Calcutta, 1917.
Khaliquzzam, Chaudhry, *Pathway to Pakistan*, Lahore, 1961.
Khan, Abdul Ghaffar Khan, *Thrown to the Wolves*, Calcutta, 1961.
Khawaja, Jamal, *Quest for Islam*, New Delhi, 1977.
Malihabadi, Abdur Razzaq, *Zikr-e-Azad Maulana Abul Kalam Azad Ki Rifaqat men Artis Sal*, Calcutta, 1960.
Mansergh, Nicholas, Lumby, E.W.R. and Moon E.P. (eds.), *The Trans-*

*fer of Power, 1942-47*, 12 Vols., London, 1970.
Mihr, Ghulam Rasul (ed.), *Naqsh-e-Asad*, Delhi, 1980.
Mill, J.S., *Autobiography*, World Classics.
Minault Gail, *The Khilafat Movement: Religious Symbolism and Political Mobilization in India*, Delhi, 1982.
Misra, B.B., *Government and Bureaucracy in India*, Delhi, 1986.
Montesguieu, Charles Louis, *Persian Letter* (ed.) C.J. Pratts, Pengiun, 1985.
Moon, Penderal (ed.), *Wavell: The Viceroy's Journal*, London, 1973.
Moore, R.J., *Escape from Empire, the Attlee Government and the Indian Politics*, London, 1983.
Muir, Sir William, *The Life of Muhammad*, London 1858-61.
Mujahid, Sharif Al, *Quaid-i-Azam Jinnah, Studies in Interpretation*, Karachi, 1981.
Mujeeb, M., *The Indian Muslims*, London, 1967.
Muzzammil, Safia, *Abul Kalam Azad, Islam and Humanity*, Hyderabad, 1988.
Naim, C.M., (ed.), *Iqbal, Jinnah and Pakistan: Vision and Reality*, New York, 1979.
Nadwi, Sayyid Sulaiman, *Hayat-e-Shibli*, Azamgarh, 1943.
Natarajan, J., *History of Indian Journalism*, New Delhi, 1953.
Nehru, Jawaharlal, *An Autobiography*, London, 1955.
——— *A Bunch of Old Letters*, Bombay, 1958.
Noorani, A.G., *Indian Political Trials*, New Delhi, 1976.
Page, David, *Prelude to Partition, The Indian Muslims and the Imperial System of Control, 1920-1932*, Delhi, 1982.
Qureshi, S.Y. (ed.), *Hali (1837-1914)*, Chandigarh, 1972.
Ram, Malik, *Hali*, New Delhi, 1982.
——— *Kuch Abul Kalam Azad Kay Barey Main*, Delhi, 1989.
——— (ed.), *Tazkira-i-Mu'asirin*, 4 Vols., New Delhi, 1972-78.
Robinson, Francis, *Separatism among Indian Muslims: The Politics of United Provinces Muslims 1860-1924*, Cambridge, 1975.
Sabri, Maulana Imdad, *Imam-ul-Hind Azad*, Karachi, 1986.
Sadiq, Muhammad, *A History of Urdu Literature*, Delhi, 1984.
Saiyidain, K.G., *Maulana Azad's Contribution to Education*, Baroda, 1961.
Sarkar, Sumit, *The Swadeshi Movement in Bengal (1903-1908)*, New Delhi, 1973.
Sen, Surendra Nath, *Eighteen Fifty Seven*, Delhi, 1957.
Shahjahanpuri, Abu Salman, *Urdu Ki Taraqqi main Maulana Azad Ka*

*Hissa*, Delhi, 1988.

——— (ed.) *Ifadat-e-Azad*, Karachi, 1984.

——— (ed.), *Maulana Abul Kalam ki Sirat aur Ilmi Karnamey*, Karachi, 1986.

Siddique Attiq (ed.), *Aiyana Abul Kalam Azad*, Delhi, 1976.

Sisson, Richard & Stanley Walport (ed.), *Congress and Indian Nationalism*, Berkeley, 1988.

Sitaramayya, Pattabhi, *History of the Indian National Congress*, Vol. II, Delhi, 1955.

Smith, W.C., *Modern Islam in India*, London, 1916.

Spear, Percival, *Oxford History of India*, Vol. III, Oxford, 1958.

Sufi, G.M.D., *Al-Mihaj: Being the evolution of communalism in the Muslim education*, London, 1941, Reprint, Delhi, 1977.

Symonds, Richard, *The Making of Pakistan*, London, 1950.

Trevelyan, Sir George Otto, *The Life and Letters of Lord Macaulay*, London, 1889.

Troll, Christian, W., *Sayyid Ahmad Khan: A Reinterpretation of Muslim Theology*, New Delhi, 1978.

Zeine, N. Zeine, *The Emergence of Arab Nationalism*, Beirut, 1966.

# INDEX